ABOUT THE AUTHOR

ANNE O'CONNOR is a freelance journalist who worked for the *Minneapolis Star Tribune* from 1994 to 2000, covering education and crime beats. She has been a full-time stepmother for eight years. O'Connor and her family live in Wisconsin.

The Truth
About Stepfamilies

THE TRUTH ABOUT STEPFAMILIES

Real American Stepfamilies

Speak Out about What Works

and What Doesn't

When It Comes to

Creating a Life Together

❧

Anne O'Connor

MARLOWE & COMPANY
NEW YORK

THE TRUTH ABOUT STEPFAMILIES:
*Real American Stepfamilies Speak Out about What Works
and What Doesn't When It Comes to Creating a Family*

Copyright © Anne O'Connor 2003

Published by
Marlowe & Company
An Imprint of Avalon Publishing Group Incorporated
245 West 17th Street, 11th Floor
New York, NY 10011-5300

The names of people in these stepfamily stories
have been changed to protect their privacy.

Library of Congress Cataloging-in-Publication Data
O'Connor, Anne, 1968–
The truth about stepfamilies : real American stepfamilies speak out about what works and what doesn't when it comes to creating a family / Anne O'Connor.
p. cm.
Includes bibliographical references and index.
ISBN 1-56924-494-4 (pbk.)
1. Stepfamilies—United States. 2. Stepfamilies—United States—Case studies.
I. Title.
HQ759.92.O24 2003
306.874—dc21   2003044483

ISBN 1-56924-494-4

9 8 7 6 5 4 3 2

Designed by Pauline Neuwirth, Neuwirth and Associates, Inc.
Printed in the United States of America
Distributed by Publishers Group West

To my stepson, Nate, my entrée into this world.

Contents

✥

INTRODUCTION

As a STEPMOTHER, I belong to a secret society. We don't usually wear funny hats or have complicated handshakes, but we have something better—an immediate understanding of each other's lives. When I meet a stepmother, I'd be pretty safe in betting that she's argued with her husband about how much time he spends talking to his ex-wife, that there are dark moments when she wants her stepchild to go to his mother's house and never return, and that if she got a card on Mother's Day she was at once overjoyed at the acknowledgment and guilt-stricken for that nasty thought about disappearing.

Men, women, and children in stepfamilies are in a unique situation among families. Stepfamilies are always second families. That is, one parent and the child have a relationship outside of the husband and wife. The parent and child have a history, an established set of habits, customs, and ideas that come from their life together before the stepparent ever entered the scene. And the other members of their first family are always a part of their lives, whether or not the child even sees the other members again.

As divorce and remarriage rates soar in our country, the number of stepfamilies formed is growing rapidly. A day will quickly come when stepfamilies are the "normal" families. As more and more people enter these arrangements, it helps to know that there are predictable patterns, similar struggles, and ultimately, helpful ways to navigate these sometimes rocky waters. It helps to know that most people in stepfamilies have been overwhelmed at one point or another and that many people have made it through to a family that works.

I have been a stepmother for nearly a decade—most of that time as a full-time custodial parent. I wish I could tell you that I wrote this book because I'm so good at this stepfamily thing. It would be nice to say that I have always done the right thing, that I have never been mean or small-minded or bitter about my stepfamily situation. That I figured out all these difficult dynamics between the households and within my own household and managed them gracefully. And that I listened sincerely to everyone and soothed over the difficult feelings so we could all live peacefully together and raise my stepson in love and harmony.

But then I'd have to change this book to fiction.

The real truth about stepfamilies

WHEN I FIRST began researching this book two years ago, I had been raising my stepson for years. I'd talked to scores of people about their experiences in stepfamilies and I felt reasonably comfortable that I knew a few things about stepfamilies. And I did know a few things. But I could never have guessed how much I'd learn as I researched and wrote this book.

I read a mountain of books about stepfamily dynamics, I talked to sociologists and psychologists, lawyers and mediators, to people who work every day trying to make things better for stepfamilies.

And then I did the most important thing. I went around the country and into the homes of men, women, and children in stepfamilies. We talked over meals, during car rides to pick up kids and run errands, on walks around their neighborhoods, or as we drew pictures together. These families invited me into their homes for Sunday dinners, and to celebrate birthdays and graduations. They took me to their places of worship, their favorite restaurants, their theater rehearsals, and their back stoops and living rooms where we sat late into the night talking about how we got to where we are today in our stepfamilies.

When I first thought about writing this book, I had the idea that I would talk to all the men, women, and children in the stepfamily and sort out some kind of objective reality based on everyone's input. But after a short time, I realized that there wasn't going to be any sorting out of the "facts" of each family. Every person in a stepfamily sees things from his perspective. Each person has his own perception of how things are run in the family. I soon learned that it is normal in stepfamilies to hear completely conflicting stories about the same situation.

I really don't believe anybody is lying. At any given moment, there are many different realities in the same family. In Mesa, Arizona, a stepdad feels frustrated and left out of his own family; he thinks his wife is too lenient with the children and that she doesn't support him in helping to run the household. The mother sees her children struggle with their stepfather and feels like her husband is too harsh and has unrealistic expectations of the kids. One of the kids is happy to have a strong stepfather to stand up to his mother, the other wishes the stepdad would just leave her alone.

They're all living in the same house, they all have the same experiences, but each person sees things differently. We all have to make our lives make sense to us.

Every situation can have multiple perspectives: A mom thinks she's being friendly and comfortable sitting at her ex-husband's table and chatting when she drops the kids off, but the new wife finds her presence an invasion and wonders why she won't just leave.

A dad and stepmom can't figure out why their child's mom doesn't come to her soccer games, while the mom feels left out and unwelcome at the games.

A mom feels that she's a strict disciplinarian, while her husband marvels at what his stepchildren get away with.

A dad talks to his child honestly about everything, feeling that it's best to be open, but his ex-wife thinks that their child has to hear too many adult problems.

Many things can be true at the same time. There are examples in this book that are harder to reconcile. Either the dad paid full child support on time or he underpaid it for years. Maybe both things were true for some time. Maybe someone is completely wrong. There is no reconciling it and I haven't tried to.

The real truth about stepfamilies is this: *It depends on who you ask.*

With that in mind, I have tried to give each person the space to tell what it's like to live in his or her stepfamily. In the following stories, you get to eavesdrop on kids talking about what they like and dislike about the way their mother or father parents with their new partner. You will hear the ex talk about what it's like to raise her child with her ex-husband and his new wife; a dad talk about feeling like he has to choose his wife or his child; and a stepdad share what it feels like to live as an outsider in his own home.

HOW DID A NICE GIRL LIKE YOU . . .

ANYONE WHO COMPLAINS in a stepfamily has surely heard: "Well, you knew what you were getting yourself into." It is true that you choose to be in a stepfamily. Nobody forces you to remarry. Nobody forces you to marry someone with children. But these are the kinds of issues that most of us could never have anticipated when we signed up for a stepfamily.

As you read these stories, it might be tempting to think, *I'd* never get myself in that kind of situation. It's always easier to look at someone else's life and think that we would know better, we would do better. But the families who have shared their stories here aren't intolerably dysfunctional. They are, for the most part, incredibly nice people. They're artists and architects, financial planners and firemen. They're Web site designers and schoolteachers. They're office managers and deejays; they're television photographers and city-hall workers. They're just people, just like you and me.

Men, women, and children in stepfamilies often feel that the work of creating a well-functioning stepfamily is the hardest thing they have ever done. It's common to hear people amazed at their own survival. It's common for people to become clinically depressed and to require antidepressants. Sure, you may have understood that you were marrying someone who has children or that you were bringing another adult into your child's life. But it's usually impossible to grasp what the ramifications for creating a second family are until they start knocking at your door.

The reason is that people fall in love. Even rational, list-making, goal-setting, thoughtful people fall in love. And people in love don't always have a clear idea of what hardships they're facing. And even if they do, they feel empowered by their love—they CAN do this.

Often, the children aren't even around for much of the courting relationship. People hang out and get to know each other while the children are at the other house. Or the parent waits until the children are in bed and then talks for hours on the phone to his newfound love. This is when love is fresh and powerful and heady and you know that this person is THE ONE. There are lots of ways men, women, and children in stepfamilies approach the new family:

"The kid and I get along great. This is going to be great."

"Finally, a decent father for my children."

"Well, how hard could it be? They're only here every other weekend."

"Well, they're teenagers, they have their own lives, and they'll be leaving soon."

"Oh good, I'll have a real family again."

"Dad, can we just live alone again?"

The fact of a marriage with existing children doesn't technically escape people. It's the reality of what that means for them that they can't grasp. That takes longer to sink in. In the early stages of a relationship, children often get along well with their parent's boyfriend or girlfriend. Adults, too, are willing to overlook things in the beginning that will become festering sores as the relationships progress. And for a child, new stepparents are more likely to be friendly and forgiving in the beginning, which is a lot more fun than another parental figure telling the child what to do.

Add to this the fact that the general public remains woefully uninformed about how stepfamilies differ from first families and it's easy to see how the future difficulties are unclear at the beginning of a new relationship.

To be fair, there are plenty of parents and stepparents who have thought long and hard about how they will raise children together and with another household. But even the smartest people usually end up sometime down the road saying something like, "I never thought it would be this hard." When people start to realize what the commitment means to their lives, the path to anger, frustration, and loneliness is all too clear. Sometimes it just seems too damn hard.

ISN'T THERE AN EASIER WAY?

IT WOULD REALLY be helpful to understand, in some way, what it is like to live in a stepfamily before you find yourself in one. Or, once there, it would be comforting to hear that other people have lived through many of the same difficult circumstances to have even stronger families. What if people who were contemplating divorce knew what to expect?

The one thing that I found pretty consistently in the stepfamilies that I've spoken to is that a bit of perspective, some practical ideas, and a little support goes a long, long way in accomplishing the monumental task of living together peacefully and happily.

If you are in a stepfamily, you have probably heard the grim statistics. At least 60 percent of all second marriages fail. This number might be low because it only counts the actual marriages. In my mind, if two people move in to the same place and try raising children together, they're doing the stepfamily thing. And if it doesn't work out, most people involved, including the children, don't care much that there wasn't an official piece of paper stating that the couple was married. It hurts and it is hard just the same.

And with numbers like that, it's pretty clear that most people could use some kind of help figuring out what they are doing. In this way, the world is becoming a better place for stepfamilies. As they become the norm, everyone from the schools to the courts is going to have to change the way they address stepfamilies. Ten years ago, there were very few places for families to turn to find guidance or support. Today, there is some great help out there. There are dozens of books that you can read to figure out how to ease some of the challenges you are likely to face in a stepfamily.

But there is still not a lot out there that allows the people in the families tell what they think it's like to be a stepmom, to be a stepchild, to be a mom who sends her children away every other weekend, to be a stepdad who gets a house full of someone else's children every other weekend.

That is where this book comes in.

VOICES OF STEPFAMILIES

MY IDEA WAS this: Let people tell what it is like from their perspective and help other people to hear those perspectives. My favorite part of any book I have read about stepfamilies is the anecdotes, the times when real people are interacting or talking about their lives.

It is good to hear about the struggles and hardships because they help you know that you are normal, and sometimes hearing about them also helps you figure out how to avoid them. You also need to hear about the things that work in stepfamilies, about the perks that first families don't get. Living in a stepfamily has its rewards and privileges. You will hear in this book about parents who cherish their weekends without the children, and about children who recognize how having additional family members has opened up new worlds to them.

What's more, there is a lot to be said for creating deliberate bonds between human beings. And that is what people do in stepfamilies. People in stepfamilies don't have that built-in tolerance or unconditional love that exists between biological parents and children, or between siblings. There is no parallel for stepfamily relationships. Stepsisters aren't quite sisters, but they're certainly more than friends. Stepdads aren't dads, but they are definitely more than, say, uncles. Any warm relationship here comes out of dedication, hard work, and an understanding of the different dynamics and expectations. And when it works, deep, meaningful relationships can form. A working stepfamily can be incredibly satisfying.

It's the "working" part that can be problematic.

It helps to know what to expect. It helps to hear that there are definite stages most stepfamilies go through. And it helps to hear from people who have made it through some of the toughest points along the way. They not only made it, but they can laugh about some of the things that used to enrage them.

In addition to the family members' stories, I've included some discussions about several key topics that stepfamilies deal with. Some are more concrete issues, such as the ways families deal with money or discipline. Other chapters examine the overall framework in which stepfamilies operate. You will see these issues come alive when you read the families' stories in each chapter. Each story sheds light on the intricacies of dealing with these topics within a stepfamily system.

In chapter 1, I explore why stepfamilies are different from first families, debunking the common assumption that the hardships in stepfamilies are the same as in first families.

Chapter 3 talks about creating boundaries of respect and comfort both between homes and in your own home. This chapter reminds divorced couples of some of the realities of raising a child in separate homes—your relationship has changed, and you have to establish new ways to interact and communicate. And in your own home, figuring out who will do what in terms of caring for the children and dealing with the other household can go a long way toward creating a peaceful environment.

Some of most difficult aspects of stepfamilies arise simply from people having very different ways of doing things—both with the newly formed stepfamily and in between homes. Chapter 5 gives you some ideas about what is worth fighting about and how to learn to let the small things go.

Money can cause plenty of bad feelings in stepfamilies and chapter 7 discusses some common pitfalls to avoid.

Chapter 9 gives an outline of the predictable stages that stepfamilies go through so that you can look to see where your family might be on that path.

Disciplining the children in a stepfamily can get very complicated. In chapter 11 you will learn that this is one area where a lot of research has shown that there are clearly helpful and unhelpful ways to approach this issue.

When living in a stepfamily—as a stepparent, as a parent raising your child with a new partner, as a parent in the other household, or as a child— it helps to understand some of the common problems that each of these roles encounter. Chapter 13 discusses the predictable roles usually created in stepfamilies and how these roles heavily influence family members' interactions. When interactions are difficult, it can help to ponder the effect of the roles and gain a new perspective on both your own and others' feelings.

Children often bear the brunt of feuding adults in separate households, or even in the same household, and chapter 15 offers some practical strategies for helping children adjust in these difficult circumstances.

You will see how these families have handled a lot of these issues in their stories. Some wish they had handled them differently; some are proud of their work. All of the families have a lot to teach us. The biggest reason most of them bravely laid out the most intimate details of their lives for this book is so that no one else will have to suffer the way they have. They deserve respect for this act of generosity.

As I went across the country, listening to the people in these families, watching them interact, looking at their photo albums and family memorabilia, I found that every one of them has struggled to do the right thing. But the right thing is not always clear. Although there have been low moments when some have fallen far short of the mark, I believe overall that all the people I spoke to have the same aspiration: to create a loving home for the children and themselves and to have a manageable and respectful relationship with the child's other home.

After talking to hundreds of people about their lives in stepfamilies, I learned some important things that have helped my household come ever closer to achieving that goal. I have always felt like I was a pretty decent stepmom. But I looked back on some of the ways I'd treated people and cringed. Listening to all these people tell their stories about living in stepfamilies began to change my expectations of my stepson. It changed the way I saw my own situation and helped me understand what *I* could do differently, instead of blaming other people for the mess. I began to understand my husband in a brand new way. I learned to be more lenient, to let my husband do more for his son—even if I don't always like how he does it. I am even working on a new relationship with my stepson's mother, with whom I have really struggled over the years.

That is why I'm writing this book. My hope is that in reading about other peoples' lives, their struggles and successes, you, too, will be inspired. I hope that you will see why those other people in your life are acting the way they are. That you will cut them, and yourself, some slack. Families are never easy. Stepfamilies are even harder. When the heat gets too intense, you need to remember to step back, take several deep breaths, and count to ten—some of us need to count to a thousand—and try again.

I am still an imperfect stepmother. But I know I keep getting better at it. I figure that by the time my stepson is heading off for college, I'll about have it down.

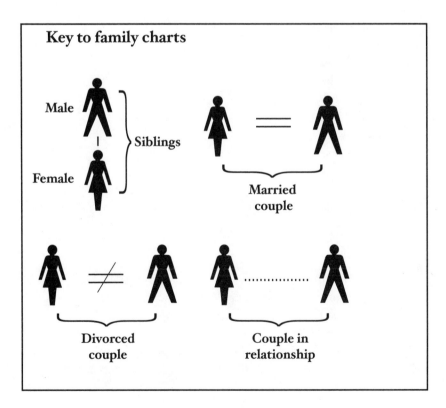

[9]

1

*W*HY STEPFAMILIES AND FIRST FAMILIES ARE DIFFERENT

❦

*T*ODD MADSEN SWEPT Helen off her feet. Growing up in a small town in western Minnesota, Helen had been raised a Christian and hadn't dated much. When Todd came into her life, it was easy to talk to him for hours at a time. Their relationship was comfortable and fun. His daughter, Jamie, was a cute cuddly one-and-a-half-year-old who joined them at the zoo, or for dinner out. Things moved quickly, and soon Todd and Helen married.

Helen had grown up knowing that she wanted a family; she wanted to stay home and be a mom. Jamie wasn't with them all the time, but Helen felt warmly toward the girl and felt ready to set up their home together as a family.

It wasn't long before Helen began to realize that her ideas about what a family should be weren't matching up with what she was living. When Jamie was four years old, a simple haircut became a major turning point in how Helen thought about her marriage and family.

At the time, it seemed like a good idea. Jamie would come over and the bedtime routine was always exasperating. Jamie screamed miserably every time Todd washed the girl's long hair and tried to comb it out. To Helen, the logical thing to do was to eliminate the struggle. Get rid of the hair, get rid of the problem.

Jamie's mother, Wendy, walked into their home to pick Jamie up, took one look at the new haircut, and hit the roof. She was outraged that Helen would cut Jamie's hair. At first, she was so livid she considered court action. Although the whole incident blew over, it's still a pointed reminder to Helen of a time when she tried to simply live as a regular family—a first family.

Now, years later with her own children, Helen understands why cutting Jamie's hair without talking to Wendy about it created such problems. She would be livid, too, in the same situation. But back then, she was doing what she thought she should.

Stepfamilies are different from first families. The process of accepting this fact can be long. The differences can strengthen you and fortify your families or they can slowly drain your family of its energy for survival. The more you act as if you're part of a first family, the more painful the reminders will be that you are not in one and the more impossible the task of forming a successful stepfamily will become.

LIKE USING DIESEL IN A GAS ENGINE

MEN, WOMEN, AND children in stepfamilies are bound to have hardships; every family has them. Every family has to deal with personality conflicts, child-development headaches, struggles over money, discipline, and the running of a household. In this way, stepfamilies are no different.

But stepfamilies are created from a particular set of circumstances that differ radically from those of first families. These circumstances lead to issues that stepfamilies have to confront beyond issues of first families. Left unattended or ignored, these issues will continue to influence the family, usually in some not-so-pretty ways.

Helen wanted to treat Jamie like her own daughter, but the haircut showed her that the relationship was going to be a lot more complicated. She soon recognized that it was not her place to cut her stepdaughter's hair without permission from the girl's mother.

It is not always easy to recognize the differences in stepfamilies, especially in the beginning. Sometimes, things are just hard and no one can figure out why.

A car that is all tuned up, its battery juiced, with the fan belts all in place, will still not run if it is filled with diesel fuel. Furthermore, that fuel will do serious damage to the car.

Men, women, and children in stepfamilies can be full of love and completely committed to the challenge, but their family won't run well if they are using strategies based on their idea of what a family—a first family—should be.

They often end up feeling like they are doing something wrong, that they are not any good at making a family work, that no matter what they do it doesn't end up being the right thing. They are pointing to their full tank of fuel and the brand new battery and wondering why the car is standing still. Their families feel chaotic, difficult, and sometimes, not worth the effort. It can be a demoralizing, frustrating experience.

Understanding the ways stepfamilies are different can often clarify a lot of the reasons people in the family do what they do. The way these differences can fortify your family is by acknowledging them, planning for them, and working your butt off to make sure they keep you and your family strong rather than pulling you apart.

THE OUTER CIRCLE

THERE ARE TWO general ways that stepfamilies are different and the two are inextricably interconnected. The first, the "outer circle," may seem the most obvious, although a lot of people don't really understand its power when they enter a stepfamily. The outer circle is the realm of the first family. It includes the ex-spouse, and everyone in the ex's household. It also includes any other family members on the ex-spouse's side, as well as the grandparents, the aunts, uncles, neighbors, and family friends that make up a child's life in another home. The outer circle also includes those powerful intangibles—the pain, the guilt, the sense of failure, and the distrust—that may have come from the first family experience.

First families don't have this kind of an outer circle. There are grandmas and aunts and uncles, but all of them are related to you or your partner. There is only one set of family friends, neighbors, and work colleagues. Whatever intangible forces each partner brings to bear on a first marriage, they aren't usually as powerful until children are involved.

Having an outer circle can be a wonderful thing in a stepfamily; it can mean extra adults to help raise a child, many avenues for a child to explore, and more resources and love at a child's fingertips. But the outer circle is not without potentially enormous issues.

A family formed from loss

The existence of an outer circle means that every stepfamily is formed out of pain and loss. The loss may have been the death of a parent or, more commonly, the divorce or separation of the parents. The loss is felt by each family member in a stepfamily. The child may long for her original family, for time spent with both parents, for the same house and school she had before her family moved. She may resent having to share her parent with a stepparent. A parent may grieve over the death of a partner, the failure of the first marriage, the burden of divorce and remarriage on her children. A stepparent may feel a loss of not having a family where familial love stops at the front door, where decisions are made between only two parents and where both parents are equally connected to all children. The emotional weight of these issues can wreak havoc on practical day-to-day living.

The other household

Dealing with the other household is one of those practical things in the outer circle that is often the most difficult. You may have to negotiate visitation, child support, school, and a hundred other things. You have to raise your child with her other parent, who is now your ex-spouse. The adults may have clashing ideas about how to raise a child, how to live a life. Add in an ex's new partner to the mix and things can get really interesting. Often communication between homes is strained and difficult— so much so that fantasizing about exes dropping off the face of the planet is a common pastime in stepfamilies. But then, most adults realize, the child would have to deal with that loss, so it's really not even a very good fantasy.

Dealing with the other household becomes even more challenging when the other parent doesn't understand the reality that both parents are important to the child. Whether the child sees that other parent once a year or 50 percent of the time, she has roots and ties to the other parent and the other parent's life.

Money issues

In first families, whether you are rich or poor, the family is in it together. In stepfamilies, money often pits one household against another. There can be extreme inequities, such as the case of two half-brothers in Texas. The parents they lived with were mom and dad to one brother, but mom and stepdad to the other. The father of one of the boys lived in another house, was wealthy, and lavished gifts on his son—the latest electronic games, fashionable clothes, trips around the world, summer camps, and a new car on his sixteenth birthday. The rest of the family lived rather modestly and the other son didn't get any of these privileges. The situation caused major friction between the households.

This is an extreme example, but the truth is that money issues can cause friction in any family. When Helen and Todd sit down to pay their bills, one of the checks they write is the child support payment to Jamie's mother. The money, gratefully, is not a problem or a hardship for them, as it is for so many families. But it is one more reminder that their family isn't just their household. In most stepfamilies, you are either paying the support and (often) being told you are not paying enough, or having to ask for it and being frustrated by refusals. Neither position is an enviable one. Running two households is simply more expensive and often there isn't enough to go around.

Juggling schedules

Scheduling children's lives is a tricky outer-circle issue. The biggest difference between first and stepfamilies is that the child in a stepfamily is moving between two homes—an issue that first families don't have to deal with at all. But even the things that first families do have to schedule become a lot more complicated when there are two homes involved in the planning. There are school events, extracurricular activities, and basics such as doctor and dentist appointments. Children who live in more than one home sometimes have four sets of grandparents to try to fit in on holidays, birthdays, or other family events. There are often four extended families to visit on summer vacations. Todd and Helen can't simply decide to pack up the kids and take off to the Grand Canyon. It has to be cleared with Jamie's mom. Jamie's mom can't decide to enroll Jamie in an intensive weekend piano class that takes place on her dad's weekend time unless Todd and Helen agree and are willing to get Jamie there on their time.

This outer circle complication isn't all bad. Sure, there are a lot of added layers of organizing to attend to, but having more than one household often means that children are exposed to opportunities they wouldn't have otherwise. Many children in stepfamilies told me that their world was vastly broadened because of their stepfamily connections.

THE INNER CIRCLE

EVEN IF EVERYONE from the other households dropped off the face of the planet, most people would still have plenty of stepfamily issues to figure out in their own homes. And the issues in your own home may seem as menacing as the issues with the other household.

The "inner circle" includes the people who live in your immediate household. There are all kinds of combinations: mom, stepdad, kid; dad, stepmom, children; dad and children, mom and children.

It is in looking at the inner circle that we can most clearly see how the outer circle and the inner circles of stepfamily lives are inextricably linked. Every issue that begins in the outer circle plays out in some way in the inner circle as well.

The parent and child's relationship predates the marriage

In a first family, everyone is related and the family has a single history. A woman and a man marry and they usually have time to adjust to each other's ways of living before a child comes along. And when the child does come, she's an infant, helpless and needing her parents. The parents may argue over ways to raise the child, but she's their child and they both have a chance to grow into the role of a parent. In a first family, the mom and dad are basically a single unit to their children. Children don't think of their parents, at least until they are older, as two separate human beings. Their parents are just parents. (It takes a long time, if it ever happens at all, for the children in stepfamilies to start thinking of the adults as the parents again instead of Dad, his kids, and his wife.)

Still, stepparents themselves sometimes expect to, and are expected to, take on the responsibilities of parenting. It is an unrealistic expectation that can generate an endless amount of grief.

In a stepfamily, there is no gradual learning curve for the stepparent. Adjusting to another family's life can feel like being thrust upon a stage in the middle of a play in which everybody's got the script except you. People know their lines, what role they're playing. Alliances are already in place. Habits are formed. Trying to figure out how things work and how to fit into the mix can be a full-time job.

Single parent no more

And the stepparent isn't the only one doing major adjusting. Single parents have been parenting their children for a time, sometimes a long time, before the stepparent arrives. Suddenly, there is another adult in her home, watching, having opinions and making demands about how the parent should behave and how the child should behave. The conflict is often immediate and severe as adults who are used to doing things their way suddenly have to accommodate a completely new set of expectations from the stepparent. Parents looking forward to some help from their new partner may be sorely disappointed to discover that their family dynamics become more difficult before they become easier.

"Dad, can we go back to just you and me?"

Children often have the biggest struggles adjusting to stepfamily life. A child is accustomed to her parents, to her home's routines and familiar comforts. Things may change drastically for her. In addition, she has to figure out how to interact with a new adult in her life and, possibly, to new stepsiblings as well. One of the most difficult adjustments comes for children who enter stepfamilies after living with their single parent for a time. These children are used to having their parent to themselves when suddenly they have to share their parent's time, attention, and love with a new adult.

INTERACTIONS BETWEEN THE INNER AND OUTER CIRCLES

THERE IS A lot of crossover in conflicts between the inner circle and the outer circle. Todd used to occasionally have dinner with his ex-wife when they met to exchange their daughter Jamie. The three of them would sit and have a quick meal, a friendly chat, and say good-bye until the next weekend. This was an outer-circle issue, but the dinners drove Helen crazy. She just didn't want her husband being so cozy and intimate with his ex-wife. So what seemed ordinary and acceptable in the outer circle caused an inner circle struggle.

It's not really important how you classify these struggles, but having a framework gives you an understanding of how you got where you are in your family. You can start to see how what you say and do fits into the bigger picture of the family.

With that bigger picture in mind, it is easier to understand why it may be important to speak tolerantly of the other household. Not because you love them or because you want to be pals (although if you do, great). But because children in stepfamilies are part of the inner circle in both homes. Even if the contact with one of the households is strained, sporadic, or nonexistent. When one household is dealing with or talking about the other household, the child feels the effects of those interactions profoundly, whether they are nasty and inflexible, or kind and generous. Over and over again, the evidence shows the same results: children who live with conflict between households don't adjust well to their new life.

Another thing to consider when thinking about the differences between first families and stepfamilies is how you get the help you need to make it work. You need good support to understand your role, to accommodate the complicated history of your family and sometimes just to vent your frustrations and anxieties.

First families have a lot of places to go for support. Moms and dads talk to other parents about child development, and about problems with spouses and with in-laws. They go to counselors, to clergy, and to teachers looking for guidance. They scan Web sites and read books about family development.

But stepfamily members always have to be conscious of using the right kind of fuel to make their engine go. If you talk to people about the struggles of stepfamilies and the people trying to help don't understand the specific dynamics of these arrangements, they may try to advise you as if you were a first family.

When venting, it is important to find a safe place to talk about your frustrations. Many stepparents, stepmothers especially, try to explain to a friend the challenges of raising stepchildren. Especially if that friend is not a stepparent, he or she may have a difficult time with the intensity of your emotions about, after all, just a child. You need to be sure that the person you're asking to support you understands how to do that.

Check your expectations

Sometimes, it helps to readjust your expectations of yourself, your stepchild, your partners, and your ex. These are complicated situations and everyone is usually trying to do what they think is best. People in the same family often have different ideas about what's best, but it helps to get some perspective, from books, support groups, or friends on what you can realistically expect from each other.

If you expect your partner to listen to rants about how her children drive you nuts, you are asking too much. If you expect your partner to love your children and treat them as her own, especially in the beginning, you are asking too much. If you expect your children to be pleased with all the changes that you have foisted on them, you are asking too much.

In stepfamilies, more than anywhere else, you constantly have to examine your expectations and see if they come close to reality.

When you find that right mix of expectation and reality, when you find the right support, you are on your way to becoming a solid family. Never a first family, but a strong, united, and resourceful family, a stepfamily.

2

THE MADSEN/SHORT FAMILY SYSTEM OF MINNESOTA

⊰✠⊱

CHILD/STEPCHILD: Jamie Madsen, thirteen years old, daughter of Todd and Wendy, stays three weekends a month and long blocks in the summer at her dad and stepmom's house, and the rest of the time with her mother. Dad and Mom divorced when she was a baby.

DAD: Todd Madsen is a band teacher in a junior high school and plays the trombone in a community band.

MOM: Wendy Short has worked for twenty years at a chiropractic clinic, where she runs the front desk. She volunteers extensively at Jamie's school.

STEPMOM: Helen Madsen, a special education teacher, has been married to Todd since Jamie was three years old.

(EX-) STEPDAD-LIKE GUY: Keith Larson lived with Wendy and Jamie since Jamie was a baby. He left when Jamie was thirteen years old.

STEPSIBLINGS: Adrienne Madsen, eight years old, and Christy Madsen, six years old, are the daughters of Todd and Helen.

In this family system, the stepmom has felt disregarded and that she and her family have not been her husband's first priority in light of her husband's good relationship with his ex-wife. She has begun to demand changes and the entire family system is feeling the repercussions.

*W*HEN TODD MADSEN was married to Wendy Short, they bought a house that wasn't perfect for either of them. Wendy wanted a big, old farmhouse in the middle of nowhere, Todd wanted a more modern house in town. They compromised and settled on a semi-modern house on the edge of a small city in central Minnesota.

Wendy and Todd's relationship was built on compromise. Even when she found out he was cheating on her, and he thought she was cheating on him, even when their marriage was falling apart, the two were amicable enough to still live in the same household for almost a year while they considered themselves officially separated. Todd lived downstairs; Wendy and their daughter, Jamie, lived upstairs. It worked.

They didn't go to court for their divorce, they used a mediator. They consciously made a decision always to try and arrange their lives so that Jamie would never feel like she had to choose between her mother and father. After Todd moved out, the two parents continued to work well together to raise their daughter. They both know how important it is for Jamie to have unfettered access to both of them.

After a couple years of casual dating, Todd met Helen and started seeing a lot of her. She was heavily involved in the local Lutheran church. Todd had been involved in the church when he was younger but didn't have much to do with it when he and Wendy were together. After the troubles in his marriage and his divorce, he felt that it was high time he return to spiritual guidance. In Helen, Todd saw a solid woman with a good, moral base. He was hopeful that with their shared faith in God, he and Helen could create the kind of family he could be proud of. He quit partying, quit playing music at bars, and started taking Jamie to church. As a band teacher and a trombone player, Todd kept playing music, but now he turned to church concerts and other venues, staying away from the fast-paced nightlife of a blues and rock musician.

Todd and Helen married when Jamie was three years old. Todd knew that a second marriage with child would present some challenges, but he felt confident that he could manage things pretty smoothly, given the fact that he and Wendy had worked so hard to maintain friendly relations. He couldn't have known that the very thing that he saw as an advantage would be one of the most difficult things for his new wife to accept.

Over the years, the two families continued to raise Jamie between the households, with her mother's house as her primary home, but with lots of time at her dad and stepmom's house. Jamie is a talented pianist and Helen and Todd went to her recitals and often sat with Wendy and Keith, Wendy's long-time live-in partner. At school events, and at plays that Jamie was in, the two families sat in the same row and mingled together afterwards.

The stepmom speaks up

Helen had struggled from the beginning to try to figure out what her relationship with Jamie would be. At first, she thought that she and the girl would be close. Helen, a special education teacher, loves children and thought that Jamie was an adorable, sweet girl. She figured that now that she was married to Jamie's father, her role was going to be like that of a mother. She wanted to take the girl out and do things with her. She wanted to be close to her and she wanted Jamie to like her.

But it wasn't as easy as she thought it would be. As a newlywed, Helen was startled the first time that adorable girl climbed into their bed with them. She didn't know how to respond. She didn't want the girl to feel shut out, but Helen was disappointed that she didn't have her husband to herself. She didn't say much about it.

Helen got pregnant a short time after she and Todd married and their first child, Adrienne, was born when Jamie was almost five years old. Jamie was delighted at the arrival of the baby; she was a big sister at her dad's house. About two years later, her younger sister, Christy, was born.

Jamie loves having sisters, but she also feels that when Adrienne was born, Helen started to pull away from her.

Helen sees it as having been a self-protection move. She had tried to spend time alone with Jamie, but Jamie wanted only to be with her dad. It seemed petty to feel so rejected by a small child, but the repeated rejections made Helen finally stop trying. When she cut Jamie's hair without consulting Wendy, she felt so badly about Wendy's reaction; she knew right away that she had screwed up. Helen felt like she had fuddled the whole stepmothering situation so badly that she had better just bow out. She was still friendly to Jamie, but she didn't go out of her way to make the relationship work. She decided that she would concentrate on her own girls and not try to force a relationship with Jamie.

During all these years, Jamie grew up with weekend exchanges. Sometimes, Wendy would bring her over for the drop-off and sit at Helen's kitchen table and chat for a while before heading out. Wendy, who is comfortable in a crowd, remembers these as good visits, friendly and easy. Helen is more reticent in groups and in this particular group, she wanted to shrivel up and fly away.

Todd, Wendy, and Jamie were sitting, talking, having a great time, just like a family. For Helen, the situation was almost intolerable. She felt completely left out. She sat there, in her own kitchen, and wondered why she was there. For a while, she tried to get along like everybody else, tried to act as if having her husband's ex-wife sitting in her kitchen, talking about people she didn't know, a life she hadn't been a part of, was just fine with her. It was important for Jamie's parents be able to parent well together. So why did she feel so undermined? She wondered over and over again, *Why can't I just get over this? What is wrong with me?*

After eight years of struggling to figure out what to do, Helen decided she had to make some changes. Now she's working on being more honest with herself and with the other players in her family. She's started asking her husband to create clear lines around his relationship with his ex-wife. And she has started taking steps to build a relationship with her stepdaughter.

These changes have been hard for Helen, and they have been hard for everyone else, too. The more Helen has pushed and stood up for what she's believed was right, the more tense and conflicted relations between the two households have become.

A MOTHER'S DILEMMA

WENDY TRIES TO understand Helen's struggles, but there are times when she wants to say, "Could you just deal with it?"

After all this time, after raising Jamie between two households for almost a decade, Wendy has a hard time believing that Helen is working all that hard to overcome the problems with Jamie.

Wendy has tried to promote good relations between the households, and there are times when she has had to bite her tongue, too—like when Helen bought polka-dotted outfits for everyone in the family for a professional family photo. Everyone except Jamie. Every time Wendy sees that picture, with Jamie in a red shirt, she shakes her head.

Wendy knows that Helen dislikes her and the hardest part about that is the impact on the children. For one thing, Helen's two daughters really like Wendy. Helen has made it clear that she resents that fact. But Wendy likes the girls, too. Wendy doesn't want the children to feel badly, but she doesn't want to step on Helen's toes, either, so she feels she's been put in a tough spot deciding what to do about it.

More recently, she's begun to worry about Jamie feeling badly. When Helen does things like sit separately at family functions, Wendy worries that Jamie is put in the position of having to choose between her families. And Wendy is starting to wonder about what life is like for Jamie at her dad and Helen's house. She's starting to wonder what Helen is doing to Jamie.

As far as her relationship with Jamie's dad, Wendy doesn't make any apologies. She said that even though they couldn't make their marriage work, she still likes him and enjoys talking to him. She is sorry that bothers Helen, but she's not going to change the way she interacts with Todd to make Helen more comfortable. Wendy says that if something needs to change, it needs to come from Todd.

DAD'S DIVIDED LOYALTIES

TODD PRIDES HIMSELF on his relationship with his ex. In a country where it is assumed, in books, in TV shows, in movies, and in comic strips, that divorced couples hate each other, Todd and Wendy have been able to build an amicable, workable relationship. They are friends and Todd sees this as only a good thing.

When the issue of their relationship came up over and over again with Helen, Todd got frustrated. He felt like she was making an issue over nothing.

At some point, though, he had to deal with the fact that his relationship with Wendy was doing damage to his marriage. He felt trapped between bad choices. He saw the working relationship with Wendy as a major benefit in Jamie's life and he didn't want to give that up. Besides, he likes Wendy; they have a child together. Why not be friendly?

But he also saw that Helen was growing more resentful of the situation and as time went on, it threatened the peace in their marriage and his and Helen's ability to nurture and trust each other.

Todd started struggling with depression and began to see a counselor to try to sort out these issues. He's beginning to better understand how sensitive Helen is about trying to create their own separate family. He's beginning to understand that it is, at least to some degree, something that he has to help deal with.

WHERE TO GO FROM HERE

THIS FAMILY SEEMS to be on the brink of some major changes. Helen is pushing for them and everyone else is deciding if they want to do something about it or not. About a year ago, Helen and Todd moved about two hours away from Wendy's home. With the distance between the two homes, Helen doesn't really have much contact with Wendy anymore. Helen found the logistics of going to Jamie's piano recitals and making sure her two smaller children got enough sleep were too demanding. She still tries to support Jamie's piano work and enjoys listening to Jamie and Todd play together, but she doesn't often make the trip for recitals or exchanges anymore.

Helen wants to make things easier; she knows that she has to deal with her feelings about Wendy. She doesn't want Jamie to feel torn between the households and she doesn't want her marriage to constantly have to deal with this issue. Wendy wants peace between the homes, but mostly she wants Jamie to feel good about the people in her life.

Jamie does feel torn sometimes. She likes her dad and she likes her stepmom. But she's not convinced that Helen really likes her. Jamie knows that her mom and Helen have a hard time. She'd just like to be accepted and comfortable in both of her homes.

HELEN MADSEN

HELEN CALLS HERSELF a "failure-to-thrive" stepmom—using the medical term for newborns who aren't getting enough nourishment and stop growing at a normal rate. She uses the term wryly, but it's clear that after nine years as stepmother, she feels like her growth in the role is stunted.

When she first met Jamie, she tried hard to do the right thing. She played with the little girl and cared for her. But as Jamie got older, it became clear that something wasn't clicking between the two of them. Helen felt that no matter what she did, it wasn't right. She would offer to take her out to the store, but Jamie wanted to stay with her dad. She would buy Jamie clothes, but Jamie left them hanging in the closet and would only wear the ones from her mom's house. It felt like the more she tried to encourage her to be a part of the household, the more Jamie backed off. After a while, Helen just quit trying.

Helen wishes things were different. She's spent a lot of time over the years mentally lashing herself for feeling resentful about Todd's former life, for wishing that his ex would drop off the face of the planet, for not loving Jamie the same way she loves her own two daughters.

But she can't just wish away these strong feelings. Todd was the first and only boyfriend that Helen ever had. The idea of multiple partners is foreign to her, and the idea that she has to share her life with Todd's past is a heavy weight. After nine years, she is still grieving the loss of not having the kind of family she dreamed of. But she also feels that if Todd were able to accept that grief, that sense of loss she has, she might be able to get over it a lot faster. His insistence that it's simply not that important has made it all the more important for her.

Helen is starting to realize that a lot of her frustration with the other household is really about how she and Todd interact about it. She feels that her husband is still uncertain of his loyalties, as if she's still sharing her husband with his first wife.

It's not just that Todd and Wendy used to eat dinner together when they met for Jamie's drop-off, or that Helen's mother-in-law implores her to get along with Wendy, or that her own family urges her to forget about it and smile through it, although those things sting. It is more that she knows her husband is platonically intimate with this person that he used to share his life with. Instead of standing with her, his wife, Helen sometimes feels as if Todd is embarrassed to set limits with Wendy, saying things like, "Well, Helen doesn't like it that. . . ." It's a betrayal of their marriage.

Helen is beginning to make it clear to Todd that she needs to feel that he is her husband first, that his loyalties need to be firmly in place with her. She is not asking him to lessen his responsibilities to his daughter, but she is asking him to change his relationship with his ex.

In the beginning, Helen didn't say very much about it. Growing up in a home with four sisters, she had learned that sometimes the easiest way to get along was to just keep quiet. She felt like she needed to be a good, supportive wife to her new husband. She tried just keeping quiet for years. But when she felt like she would burst, she knew she needed some help.

Setting a boundary

About a year ago, Helen started going to talk to a counselor, trying to sort out what to do about these issues that weigh so heavily on her, her marriage, and her relationship with her stepdaughter. She heard that many stepmothers experience the same frustration and resentment. She knew she had to figure out a better way; she felt that if things didn't change, her marriage wasn't going to make it.

It wasn't that Helen never said anything to Todd about her discomfort. But she was waiting for him to understand what she needed and make it right. And when she complained about having to share him with his ex, Todd became defensive and dismissed her feelings about the situation. Basically, he told her that he couldn't possibly understand what there was to be upset about and that if there was a problem, it was her problem. He wasn't planning on changing anything about his situation with Wendy, so Helen had better figure out how to deal with it.

After some time in counseling, Helen started to get specific about what she wanted. She asked Todd to try to empathize with her disappointment about being a second family. She asked Todd to stop having dinner with his ex-wife. Helen told Todd that she wasn't going to sit with Wendy anymore at functions such as piano recitals. And she began to take small steps toward an independent relationship with Jamie.

One event that caused a lot of friction was when Todd invited Wendy to a concert he was playing at a church with his community concert band. Helen had been looking forward to the concert as a time for her and the girls to go see their dad. But at the last minute, she found out that Wendy would be there too. The plan, set up between Todd and Wendy, was that Wendy would just take Jamie after the concert and head home, saving Todd the trip up to meet her halfway.

Helen was furious. What was Todd doing inviting his ex-wife to his concert when he knows how Helen feels about it? Why didn't it matter to him? And why couldn't they ever just have their family be their family? And what was Wendy doing? Why did she want to come to her ex-husband's concert anyway? Didn't she have something better to do?

Helen made a scene. She told Todd that she didn't want to sit next to Wendy, that this was an event for their family, and that Wendy wasn't invited to sit with Helen and the girls. Todd called Wendy and explained the situation, a brand-new arrangement after eight years of sitting together.

Helen said that when they arrived at the concert, she told Jamie that she was welcome to sit with her mother, but that she and the girls would be sitting elsewhere. Jamie went and sat with her mother.

After the event, Helen said that she felt relieved that Todd had stood up for her. Helen wasn't interested in being one big, happy family and she wanted Wendy to understand that.

"Finally, she knows it has not been comfortable for me," Helen said. "I don't want to be an add-on to the first family. That's what I felt like for the last eight years.

"It's one of those situations where it just needed to be said. Unfortunately, Jamie got caught in the crossfire, but I just can't continue to feel like an extension of the first family. I just can't keep living that way. This is our family and that's Wendy's family. We're separate families now."

Making things happen

The next time Jamie came to their house Helen said that she felt like the concert incident opened the door for her to say things to Jamie that she'd been unable to before.

"I told her that this had absolutely nothing to do with her," Helen said. "I told her that sometimes there are weird things between stepmoms and biological moms, but it really isn't her fault. I said I was trying to get more comfortable with the situation. I told her how I think she's a great kid, a talented kid, and that she's fun to have around. I told her that I'm not her mom, and that her mother is a good mother to her. And I told her that I love her and gave her a hug."

It was an unburdening for Helen. She had spent so much time being guarded around Jamie; it felt so good to really tell her what was going on. Helen said that since her conversation with Jamie, she feels as if things are starting to get better. Their relationship had already begun to improve a few months earlier, as they worked together to decorate Jamie's bedroom in their new house in the colors the teenager picked out. It was a good feeling for Helen and she thinks it was for Jamie, too. It's not that she and Jamie are best buddies, but Helen thinks they're doing OK, and getting better. She hopes that she can keep this relationship growing and improving, now that she has a better idea of what to expect from it.

Helen's hopeful about her relationship with Todd, too. She's started to see what she can do for herself, and she sees that Todd is starting to understand. There are still times that he says or does something that send her reeling, but she knows he's finally listening to her.

The situation with Wendy is a whole different thing. At this point, Wendy is kind of the boogie monster of Helen's life. Helen doesn't really have any contact with Wendy, she doesn't really know her. But Helen has spent a lot of time being really annoyed that Wendy simply exists. If Helen thinks about it long enough, she'll admit that her resentment toward Wendy isn't really personal. It's just that Helen hasn't ever felt like she can have the family she thought she would have. She keeps trying, though, and Wendy is the most obvious and safest place for that disappointment and resentment to settle on. Helen is on high alert for things that reveal too much intimacy between Todd and Wendy for her comfort level. Like the way Wendy still calls him "Maddy" instead of Todd. Helen feels that when you get divorced, you lose your right to call each other nicknames.

And Helen and Wendy are very different people. Helen's suburban, upper-class home is meticulously maintained, the yard is landscaped, and the radio plays the Christian station. If she's upset, going to the Mall of America is a refuge for her. Her hair is permed into soft curls and neatly trimmed over her ears. She is polite and proper, in a kind way. But her world is very different from Wendy's and she often feels intimidated by Wendy's world because it's so foreign to her.

Helen knows she needs to deal with Wendy, but the thought scares her. She's not sure what she'll do, what she'll say. Every time she gets around Wendy, she feels about two inches high. It's not the best place to start a productive conversation.

But Helen has started down this path of reconciliation and change-making in her life. She has started to realize that her hardships with Todd are really the issues she has to deal with. Once she feels stronger on that front, she knows that the path will eventually lead to some kind of reckoning with Wendy. So Helen is gearing up.

WENDY SHORT

WENDY ALWAYS THOUGHT she had one of those great stepfamilies in which the divorced couple actually worked well together. She had known over the years that Helen wasn't always comfortable around Jamie, and certainly not around her. But overall, relations between the two households have been good. She's happy that Jamie has had the opportunity to experience two really different ways of living. She feels that her daughter has been able to see the world more clearly because of her many experiences in different situations.

Wendy recognizes that her household is very different from Jamie's dad and stepmom's. Wendy's front yard is open and is across the street from a cornfield. Her home is a comfortable conglomeration of the dozens of pictures of Jamie, the huge woodstove that heats her home, the beanbag and Papasan rattan chair, the big gray couch. Wendy cans and stores fruits and veggies cooperatively with her family. She doesn't like shopping and the Mall of America seems like punishment to her. She considers herself a spiritual person and works hard to do the right thing in the world, but she's not a churchgoer. Her hair is black, long, and wild. She doesn't wear makeup and she's not likely to go to a salon for a manicure. She is, physically and otherwise, a complete contrast to Helen.

When Helen and Todd were dating, Wendy was happy to have Helen around; she seemed to enjoy Jamie and Todd seemed happy. Wendy thought they were all getting along well until Todd mentioned that Helen was uncomfortable around her and that they should start doing the Jamie exchange elsewhere.

"Maddy and I decided that we would meet at a restaurant and have a meal together," Wendy said. "Once a week, or at least once a month, when we did the exchange, we would sit down together and have a meal, the three of us. We want Jamie to know that we do not have animosity. She grew up with us doing that on a regular basis.

"And when we meet at Nana's [grandma's], we sit and yak for sometimes an hour or even longer and you know, spend time together, and talk about what's going on."

Relations strain

But recently, the stances that Helen has been making have set Wendy wondering whether the environment at Todd and Helen's house is a good one for Jamie. As Helen becomes more vocal about what she wants, Wendy sees Jamie getting stuck in the middle of her struggle. It seems unfair to Wendy and she gets annoyed that Helen can't just lighten up and let things go. There have been several incidents that have made Wendy wonder what she ever did to make Helen feel so threatened.

Helen's girls, Adrienne and Christy, really like Wendy and they run into her arms and greet her with a hug whenever they see her. It drives Helen crazy. Once, when Jamie was in a play, both households were there, and

Wendy was working backstage. Helen's daughters came back to see her and Wendy was going to give them a little tour. At that moment, another parent who was videotaping the scene had the video camera focused on the two girls, and there's a clear picture of Helen grabbing both of the girls by the shirt and yanking them away from Wendy.

"Like I have the plague," Wendy said.

Wendy can handle the rejection herself, but she hates to see it fall on Jamie, the way it did at the concert Jamie's dad played.

Wendy was talking to Todd about the schedule and he mentioned that he was playing in a concert. Wendy said that she'd love to hear him play. He had always loved playing music and she was glad he was playing again. So they arranged a time for her to come see the concert. At the last minute, Todd called and said that Helen didn't want to sit with Wendy.

"Maddy calls me on the phone and says 'I just want to talk to you about the concert today. Helen didn't know you were coming, she's kind of upset. She thought it was going to be a family thing and you're not in our family.' And I said, 'So you're asking me not to go, not to come and see your band play?' He said, 'No, but I just want to make sure you don't go and sit with them or anything.' It didn't really bother me, although it kind of peeved me a little bit because he knows that I have always been very conscientious about not putting myself in their faces. We've gone to many things together and we've often sat together, but I always respect their space unless they come and talk to me in which case I become really animated and we interact and we get along really great."

So when Wendy arrived, and Jamie came to sit with her, Wendy said she could just feel the icy breeze from across the room coming from the rest of Jamie's family. The entire situation was painful for Jamie and Wendy just thought it was so unnecessary.

"I'm not really angry about it, I understand it's a struggle," Wendy said. "But at one point Maddy told me that Helen's going to counseling and she's trying to figure out what her role is in Jamie's life, and I did become a little angry and wanted to say, 'It's not like Jamie just showed up.'"

So lately she and Jamie have been talking about the relationships between the two households. Wendy is open and honest about how she feels when she talks to Jamie about the situation.

"The hard thing for me is that I don't hate Helen, I don't even dislike her. I actually thought that we got along well. You know, I mean I didn't want to push interaction with her because Maddy has told me a couple times that she's uncomfortable with me. He's made it clear that she's uncomfortable with the fact that we have an amicable relationship," Wendy said. "She's of the mind that when you get divorced, you should just dislike each other and my feeling is that it's not that I can't dislike him, I don't dislike him. I love the man and he's Jamie's dad. I don't want to live with him, I don't want to be married to him, I don't have delusions of us reuniting. But the part that's frustrating for me is that it's obvious that she feels like I am some sort of negative influence. It wouldn't be honest to say that it doesn't affect me — I don't like feeling like I have the plague. I think it's very small-minded. I don't think that I'm way, way above that or that I'm better than her. But I think it's very small-minded to assume that people can't get along. That's one of the faith issues that I would argue her into the ground over. Good thing you spend that hour at church every Sunday, darling."

Wendy gets angry when she feels that Helen isn't being straight about dealing with Jamie. Wendy said that when Jamie talks about being over at her dad's, she says she has to bring everything she needs for the weekend, that it's not really like her own home. And then there are other powerful incidents, like the family picture in which Helen makes sure everyone is matching except Jamie.

"That's a bigger statement without words than all the words she's ever said to the girl," Wendy said. "So she can say to Jamie 'I wish you were here every day,' but her actions when she's there tell Jamie otherwise. Helen says the right words and presents the right picture, but when Jamie goes home from the photographer, everyone knows what's going on."

For years Wendy just let things go, just thought, well, we're two different households, and it's a struggle sometimes. She's never talked to Helen directly about any of these issues. She said that Todd has discouraged it, and she doesn't really feel like Helen would open up to her. So she just left it alone.

After years of feeling like things have been OK, Wendy is beginning to wonder if she needs to do something about the situation between Jamie and her other household. In better times, she was able to give Helen the benefit of the doubt, even when Helen was trying to "protect" her children from Wendy. But now Wendy is wondering if she has her own protecting to do.

"The issue for me is not whether I should be concerned about what I'm doing to her children, it's whether I need to be concerned about what she's doing to mine," Wendy said. "And how valuable is it for Jamie to spend time with that? How valuable is it for Jamie to hear them saying

'We've been trying real hard for the last twelve years to welcome you into the family?'"

JAMIE MADSEN

JAMIE FEELS LIKE there are probably more advantages to her life in a stepfamily than disadvantages. She spends three weekends a month with her dad and Helen and the rest of the time at her mom's house. She said it's sometimes hard to miss things on the weekends at her mom's house, but that she loves going to church with her other family.

"Sundays are a highlight of the weekend, learning about God and Jesus," she said. "And it's nice, too, to have so many different kinds of people in your family."

"It's like having separate lives, but not separate," she said. "You'll always be loved no matter what by lots of people. That's my happy thought. If I feel down I think about all the people who love me. It makes me feel better."

Like her sister, Christy.

"When she laughs, she really laughs," Jamie said. "You tickle that one nerve and she just goes."

Jamie said that she has the perspective of an only child at her mom's and of a sister at her dad and Helen's. She loves having little sisters.

"I play with them, especially Adrienne," she said. "When they're crying and sad, I just give them a hug and comfort them."

She remembers one time when Adrienne lost some special tubes for her ears at the park.

"She came home and she was crying and sad and she felt really, really bad. She ran to her room," Jamie said. "I went down there and comforted her and I told her a story about how I had lost my mom's keys. We went back to the park to look for the plugs. As we were leaving, I saw these green and blue things. 'Are these them?' 'Yeah!' Adrienne is still thanking me today. She got all glowing, she was all happy. She said, 'You're the bestest sister ever. She still calls me 'Eagle-eye woman.'"

It goes both ways. Jamie said she doesn't like cleaning her room. One time, Adrienne heard her complaining about it and went down to Jamie's room.

"I came down and she had folded everything up nice and neat and put everything away for me," Jamie said. "I was like, 'Thank you, thank you, thank you.'"

Jamie feels like she has a pretty good relationship with her dad. ("He's really funny, so he's like, my kind of guy. I like funny.") The three girls wrestle with him, they watch movies together, and Jamie and her dad play music together.

Jamie shares a lot with her mother, as well. Jamie says she tells her mother everything and that her mom helps her sort things out.

"I'm pretty much exactly like her," she said. "She has glasses, I have glasses. We even have moles in the same place. It's kind of scary sometimes. Once, I was over at my dad's house and I got my pinkie jammed in a door. When I got back to her house, she'd done the same thing. I'm very close to my mom. She's very nice."

When Jamie was a little girl, she used to think that she wanted a smaller family, that maybe it would be good for her parents to get back together.

"But now that I think about it, I wouldn't have Adrienne, I wouldn't have Christy, I wouldn't have Helen and all the relatives on Helen's side, I wouldn't have Keith or Keith's relatives. I wouldn't have met Emily (a friend from her dad's neighborhood).

"I like it because it's just interesting to get different perspectives. It's like you get around more. I've got four loving parents."

A painful loss

Things haven't felt that loving to Jamie lately, though. Jamie has had some difficult things to face over the past year with both of her stepparents.

Her mother broke up with Keith, who had lived with them since Jamie was a baby. Keith still lived in the house with Jamie and Wendy for a while after their breakup, but things started to unravel and he moved out.

Jamie is quick to point out that Keith wasn't ever actually married to her mother, but that he counted as a stepparent. She doesn't remember her life without Keith in it.

But now, Jamie hasn't seen Keith since he moved out months ago. Jamie knows that he was going through some hard times. Before he moved out, he seemed to be "kind of messed up." When he left, he told Jamie to let him know when her concerts were, that he wanted to come to them. But she hasn't called him. At the end, Keith was getting weird and she hasn't felt like contacting him.

"He comes home drunk and he's talking to himself, he's talking to imaginary fish in the fish tank," Jamie said. "One time he got really drunk and yelled at my mom a lot. I didn't feel very good about sleeping with him in the next room. I got scared, so I went down and slept with my mom. He's OK when he's sober."

She doesn't miss him, she said.

Uncertainty about stepmom

Things with Helen have been rocky lately as well.

Jamie doesn't really remember, but her sense of her relationship with Helen is that it's gone through good times and bad times. She digs through her closet and pulls out a photo album with pictures of her as a toddler at the zoo with Helen.

"When I was younger, we were really close," she said. "But then Christy and Adrienne were born and attention eased off me and went on to them a little more. And now, we're getting closer again. So it's kind of like: Close. Not so close. Close."

"We didn't talk that much the last few years, then my room came and we're working together and shopping and stuff. We went shopping for my bedspread. Helen's really fun. She's fun to be around."

Other times, though, Jamie sees Helen in a completely different light. There are things that Helen does that really hurt Jamie. Sometimes, Jamie wonders if Helen likes her at all.

"She makes it very clear, like when I'm with Adrienne and Christy and somebody says, 'Are these all yours?' She points right to me: 'She's not. These two are.' And that kind of feels, it feels like crap.

"Dad says she's trying really, really hard but I don't think she really is because nothing has changed," Jamie said. "When I was younger, I see pictures of us going to the zoo and she seems all happy, but then, that's not how she acts. It's like an act."

And then there was the concert Jamie's dad was in. She didn't know that she would have to choose between sitting with her mom or sitting with Helen, the girls, her grandparents, and cousins. When she picked her mom, she felt shut out.

"I was shunned," Jamie said. "I walked in with everybody and went with my mom and everybody just walked away. And they didn't say a word to me the whole rest of the night. I went to them and said 'Hi,' and they said, 'Hi.' But I was completely ignored. Except for Daddy, he asked me to help him put on his tux.

"After the concert, nobody said good-bye to me, nobody at all. I told Adrienne and Christy I would be right back, I was going to the bathroom and I would come back to say good-bye. When I came back they were gone. I was pretty heartbroken."

Jamie knows that her mom and her stepmom struggle with each other. She wishes it were easier. Sometimes, she feels that if she loves Helen, it seems like her mom might wonder why. But she does love Helen, even though it's not anything like the love she has for her mother.

Two houses, two homes

Both of her homes, she said, hold a lot of love for her. And both homes have some conflict for her as well, although there's probably more conflict at her dad and stepmom's house.

"When I'm here (at my dad's) this is like my home, but when I'm there (at my mom's) it feels like home," Jamie said. "But it would feel more like Mom's is home because I'm there more often. I go to school there, I do everything there. I go on bike rides with my other friends, I go shopping."

There are some big differences in the way the two families live. For one thing, she's an only child at her mom's, and a sister at her dad and stepmom's. That's a huge difference. Jamie sees other, more philosophical differences as well. Like in attitude about how children should behave (more strict at dad's, more loose at mom's) and about religion (more focused on trying to do the right thing with the help of the church at her dad's, more focused on trying to do the right thing through everyday living and relationships at her mom's).

But Jamie, as most children in her situation, really notices the practical, everyday differences between her two homes. At her dad's, if she doesn't make her bed, it's a problem; at her mom's, her room is her room and she can do what she wants in it. (Incidentally, both of her bedrooms are neat.) At her dad's house, she has to watch her language carefully. At her mom's, if she drops a glass of milk and says, "Oh, shit," she's not going to get in trouble. At her dad and stepmom's, everyone wears just a little bit more formal clothing — the khaki and collared shirt look — but her mom's is pretty much a jeans and sweater or sweatshirt kind of place. The food is different, too. At her mom's they make a lot of their own food along with her mom's family. They have jars of salsa, veggies, and jams that last them through the winter. At her dad's, the veggies and fruits mostly come from the grocery store. Her dad and stepmom don't appreciate some of her taste in music (like Eminem); her mom just lets it go or talks to her about it, but doesn't forbid it.

Jamie doesn't feel that the differences in the two homes have been a huge burden for her to navigate. She said that she likes having all these different kinds of perspectives, although there are times when her dad and stepmom's rules grate on her.

Lately, as the tension builds between the adults in her life, Jamie just wants some kind of peace. She loves everyone, she wants everyone to love her, she just wants to feel like she's part of the family—both families—wherever she is.

TODD MADSEN

TODD FEELS AS if reaching peace is so close. Not only in his own home, but between the two households where Jamie lives. If there were a way he could just make it happen, he'd be willing to try. But he feels he's been trying so hard to make it right and things just keep getting harder.

There's a big part of him that would like to go back to Helen and say, "I was married before, I have this life from before. Deal with it."

But he's tried that with some pretty meager results. It simply doesn't work. It's taken him a while to recognize that he does play a role in his wife's anguish about the other household. The past year has been one of screaming matches between him and Helen and phone calls to his ex to try to explain some of the changes that he's making. It's been a really difficult time, but Todd tries to be hopeful.

"Change is good, it makes you take stock of what's going on and see how you're weathering it," Todd said. "By struggling a little bit you start to find out what's really important to you. Over this last year, as many struggles as we've had, there's been a lot of blessings, too. It's opened our eyes to what we both really feel is important. That's our relationship and our family."

Todd has been relieved to see Helen interacting with Jamie more, working on spending time with her, talking to her, working toward building their relationship. In the past, Todd has felt that he has had to mediate Helen and Jamie's relationship. He's also felt that he's had to mediate Helen's relationship with his ex-wife.

"This feeling of being in the middle is the feeling that I've had a lot over the past few years," Todd said. "The hardest part of this whole thing has been Helen trying to figure out what is her role. And I know from reading stepfamily stuff that that is the hardest role."

Todd is referring to the research that shows that stepmothers usually have the most difficult time adjusting to life in stepfamilies.

"It's frustrating, because I really can't do anything about it," he said. "They're not my feelings. I really don't have too much trouble with seeing my ex-wife when I have to pick Jamie up. So from talking and working things out, we get to the point where Helen's telling me that those are real sensitive issues to her. So we don't sit together as one big happy family. That bugs her to death. Instead we sit over here with our family and my ex-wife and her family are over there and that's fine."

"I'm trying to be there to support Jamie, trying to show her that, 'Yeah, we're supporting what you do' and Helen, when she's thinking rationally, she wants to support Jamie, too."

It's been painful for Todd when Helen is annoyed with Jamie or when they're just not interacting very much. A lot of the time, it's been the two of them just existing in the same household, not really communicating, not really connecting. Jamie has come to him and asked him why Helen doesn't hug her or treat her like she treats the other two girls. Todd does his best to explain that Helen's struggling with the situation, and that it's not a personal thing about who Jamie is.

Circumstances have thrown Helen and Jamie together more over the past year. Todd has been struggling with depression and there are days when he just can't get out of bed. Those times, Helen is in charge of all the parenting—including Jamie's. Todd has been happy to see that Helen is feeling closer to and better about Jamie. He can see that the more he supports Helen, the easier it is for Helen to feel warm and loving toward Jamie.

Todd would like Helen to work on things with Wendy as well. Todd wants Helen to carry her own water—deal with her own issues. It's not that he doesn't want to support her, or that he doesn't want her to be happy. But he's not the one who has issues with his ex-wife, Helen is. Todd has spent a lot of time trying to explain Helen's position to Wendy over the years, and he wants out of the middle. He'd like Helen to take up the issue directly with Wendy.

Todd is confident that his family life will continue to get easier as time goes on. He is proud that his daughter seems to be taking all these difficult challenges in her life in stride. She's doing well in school, she's smart, friendly, and creative. Todd figures they all must be doing something right.

KEITH LARSON

KEITH WAS THERE when Jamie started walking. He was there when she started playing the piano, when she started school, when she learned to ride a bike, when she got her braces. He was there to put her to bed at night and to greet her in the morning. After school, he was there to care for her until Wendy got home.

Keith never expected to feel like a dad—he knew that Jamie had her dad and he didn't have any ideas about taking on that role. But he grew close to the girl and he feels as though she's a part of his family. He wishes that he had worked a bit harder on their relationship. He couldn't imagine his life without Jamie in it. Now he doesn't have to imagine, he's living it.

"Looking back now, I wish we were closer emotionally. It might be easier for us to have stayed in touch," Keith said. After living with Wendy and Jamie for eleven years, Keith moved out several months ago. He hasn't seen Jamie since.

Keith has been on a downward spiral since he broke up with Wendy. Since then, Keith has been struggling just to do everyday tasks. He's had serious, deep depression and has been suicidal on several occasions. He got fired from his job, he lost his company car, he doesn't want to see his friends, and doesn't have a lot of energy for reaching out to people.

But there's even more to it when it comes to reconnecting with Jamie. When he was still living in the house, he was really struggling with depression, and Jamie became scared of him. Wendy asked him to leave and Keith's not at all sure he's welcome to call or see Jamie. He needs to ask Wendy, but he's afraid that she will say it is a bad idea. Right now, he said, he's in too fragile a place to find out. If he's rejected, he doesn't feel he can deal with that right now.

Keith has never lived alone before and there are times when his empty apartment is too lonely, too quiet. He misses Wendy, but not nearly as much as he misses Jamie. He thinks about what the teenager is up to. He knows that, for example, when Christmas comes, he'll be missing her concerts, her plays. She always had something going on, even if it was just the day-to-day routines. Keith remembers Jamie and Wendy wrestling in the living room, or sitting with Jamie after school and playing games.

"I miss her," Keith said. "I miss especially the piano. There were certain times she always played. Like she always played a little bit in the morning before school. It was almost a guarantee that once she got out of the shower she'd sit down and play for a little bit. Plus when she practiced."

Keith participated a lot in the everyday care of Jamie, helping her with her homework, driving her to and from day care, fixing dinner. But the parenting between Keith and Wendy was clear. Keith did practical things and had a good relationship with Jamie, but Wendy made the major decisions and handled any problems. Ultimately, Keith didn't stay with the family, but he hopes that his relationship with Jamie doesn't have to be a permanent casualty of the break-up. He doesn't have an ounce of resentment about the girl.

"Jamie wasn't a burden for me ever," Keith said. "Jamie was a joy for me to be around. I was always very proud of Jamie."

Keith knows that Jamie is an incredibly resilient girl and he's hoping that will work in his favor. He knows that he scared her when he left and he hopes that he can mend that. He's working on getting stronger and when he's ready, he's going to try to reconnect with the girl.

"I would just take her out for dinner or a movie or something," Keith said. "I'm not looking for anything huge."

3

ℰSTABLISHING RESPECTFUL BOUNDARIES

∽✷∾

*T*HERE ARE SO many things to sort out in a stepfamily that first families can take for granted. In a stepfamily, someone will always be ready to scrutinize and criticize what you do—or don't do—with your biological kids and your stepchildren, with your spouse or ex-spouse, with your life. But there are ways to minimize the scrutiny, or at least the criticism and its effects in your life.

Pamela Kertz thought it was sweet that her six-year-old stepdaughter wanted her to be the one to give her a bath. She had been doing a lot of mothering for the girl, so giving Fern a bath seemed like a perfectly natural thing to do. And Matt Jorvig, Pamela's future husband, thought it was great; it was one more sign that his daughter and his soon-to-be wife were getting along and making their way together.

But when Fern was at her mother's house, she mentioned something about Pamela giving her a bath, and that didn't sit well. Her mother thought, "Now, what is this woman doing bathing my child? Where is her father?"

If your husband is spending an hour on the phone with his ex and it is driving you crazy, or if your husband's new wife starts taking over responsibilities where you feel she has no place, or if your ex-wife won't allow your new wife to participate in your child's life, then it is time to think about where your boundaries need to be drawn.

YOUR OWN HOME

THERE ARE A number of common trouble spots within inner-circle stepfamily homes that you can try to avoid or change. But first you have to recognize that they are causing trouble. Sometimes, stepfamily members don't even realize what the trouble is until they have hurt each other for a while and finally understand that something isn't working.

One of the difficulties in stepfamilies is that the stepparent and the child do not have the same bond as the parent and the child do. The stepparent will be watching the parent, thinking, if not commenting loudly, about things that seem off to him. The parent will be watching the stepparent, thinking, if not commenting loudly, about the ways that the stepparent is interacting with the child. And of course, the child will be watching both parent and stepparent, looking for a parent's assurance of love, sensitive to a stepparent's discomfort. The scrutiny, when handled well, can produce some rich, helpful feedback, but it can also be a heavy weight.

It will help everyone in the household if the stepparent and the parent can sit down and clearly sort out who is going to do what when it comes to the child and the other household. Whatever the plan is, it helps to make it explicit.

Ideally, the best time to do this is when you are setting up your household together. When everyone is starting fresh and knows the plan, there is less room for resentment and misunderstanding to grow.

However, most people don't live in an ideal world. Often, it is not possible to even realize what needs to be sorted out until the issues start causing resentment and misunderstanding.

Each family has its own tension areas, but stepfamilies have some common ones, so you can at least try to plan for the things that can cause hard feelings.

Let parents parent

Stepparents often have the most difficult position in a stepfamily, trying to figure out what their relationship should be to this child and to their partner, not to mention the ex-spouse and the other household. Are they another father? A friend? An uncle? None of these roles is the right model for a stepparent.

When stepparents and parents form a new family, it is very easy for men and women to fall into traditional roles. Although things are changing, the day-in and day-out work of parenting—making doctor appointments, buying school supplies, getting haircuts, arranging extracurricular activities—is still mostly done by women.

Between a mother and a stepfather, these traditional role assignments generally work out well. The stepfather may be asked to take on some parenting work, but generally, mothers still do the lion's share of the nitty-gritty work.

But when the situation is a father and a stepmother, the traditional roles don't work very well. A common scenario is this: A stepmother throws herself into the role, doing what she can to really make it work. She is encouraged to do so by friends, family, and often, more importantly, her husband. But at some point, she realizes she's doing more for her stepchild than the child's dad. Often, not only is she not thanked for her well-intentioned efforts, but she's questioned and resented by the child, the dad, and the mom. Stepmothers who curb their instinct to mother, to change their husband's ways of doing things, to take on a child's scheduling and disciplining, are usually happier stepmothers with happier stepchildren and happier husbands.

Stepdads who attempt to become the disciplinarian of the house find a similar frosty reception from their wives and their stepchild. They simply don't have the authority to run the show. The best a stepparent can do is enforce the house (the parent's) rules. In time, the stepparent may gain more authority, but initially, this kind of jumping in just doesn't work.

Stepparents will have an easier time if they let the parent be the parent, taking the lead in discipline, planning, and guidance. Fathers will have a better relationship with their children, their wives, even their exes if they get used to planning their children's birthday parties, taking them to the dentist, and buying them new underwear. Involved parents know details about their children, like their shoe sizes.

Mothers, too, will adjust to their stepfamily more easily and not set themselves up for major disappointments if they don't expect their new husbands to be the father they always wanted for their children. Parents need to continue to be the main providers of love and parental grunt work for their kids.

Let children set the pace

In addition to expecting too much from a stepparent, it is unrealistic to expect too much from a child. Children aren't going to immediately love their stepparents. They may not even like them very much. Try to just accept it with the hope that maybe it will change with help and time. That doesn't mean you should allow nasty behavior. The parent needs to set the tone and expectations for respect in the house, but you cannot force a child to like someone, let alone love someone. Especially in the beginning, stepparents should stick to building the relationship with the child. This is important for children of all ages, but particularly with older children. Adolescents are busy trying to distance themselves from the parents they already have. They simply aren't ready to take on another parent; try not to force them. Take an interest in what they do, try to engage them, and let them know you want to have a relationship with them.

This is not to say that stepparents don't sometimes become very much parental figures to their stepchildren—many do. But expecting this to happen quickly is a sure path to frustration.

One-on-one priorities

Successful stepfamilies pay careful attention to all the relationships in the home.

Each relationship needs nurturing and one-on-one time to grow. Only by assuring that each relationship is given the commitment of time and energy it needs will a family hold together as a solid unit.

Parenting is always tough and stepfamilies can strain the strongest couple's commitment. A strong marriage is a solid base for a family—the adults in a family need to spend time alone together and show the children that their relationship is important and deserving of that time. In trying to create a strong marriage, some people go too far and leave the kids out. Kids can feel excluded by the solidity of a marriage; to them it's like a new club was formed and they weren't invited.

Having a strong marriage obviously doesn't mean that you'll never disagree with your partner. And it's not necessarily a bad thing for your children to see you disagree and resolve your differences constructively.

But especially early on in the formation of a stepfamily, it is important that the adults don't contradict each other in front of the children. If you disagree about how something should be handled, sort it out later when the children aren't around. Parents can acknowledge that the house is changing with a new stepparent and that there will be some things the kids have to adjust to and some things the stepparent will have to adjust to.

Kids need security in their new situation and parents can foster this feeling by spending time alone with their kids, without the interference of the stepparent. Children need their parents to show them that they are still their top priority—that no matter how their family changes, there will always be time for the parent and the kid to be alone together.

The stepparent and the child will also benefit from time without the interference of the parent. The stepparent and the child can find their own common ground when they spend time alone together, playing a game, taking a walk, going to the park. As the stepparent and stepchild's relationship grow, the couple's marriage becomes stronger.

Find safe places to vent

One of the key things that men, women, and children in successful stepfamilies figure out is where and when to vent. Being in a stepfamily is often a very frustrating business. Most people in stepfamilies need to vent about it at some point. Some people need to vent about it at several points during a single day. But while your husband or wife is the logical person to share your frustrations with on most things, this simply doesn't hold true for some stepfamily issues, especially in the first few years.

One thing that stepparents would be wise to remember is that no matter how much your wives or husbands love you, they will almost always be fiercely loyal to their children. They should be. Chances are that it is one of the things that attracted you to them in the first place. But it is a lot easier to admire someone's parenting from afar. After living with your spouse and his or her children day in and day out, you may occasionally consider getting a separate apartment on the side.

It will not help you or anyone else if you tell your partner that his child is a spoiled brat who rules the house, even if you are convinced it is true and have plenty of evidence to support the assertion. But you can tell your (carefully selected, stepfamily-aware) friends that. I am absolutely not advocating that you don't talk to your partner about things that bother you. Please do. Talk, discuss, strategize, write notes if that works for you. Just don't vent. Venting is blowing off steam, complaining, whining, threatening, demanding change, name-calling, and criticizing. None of these things go very far in living together well. That's why you need some (carefully selected, stepfamily-aware) friends to whom you can talk about things that get under your skin and fester. And then, more clear-minded and calm, you can talk to your partner about what you are going to do and what you expect from a situation.

Realistically, there are going to be times when you need to vent to your spouse. Just try to keep it respectful. Criticism is always easier to hear when it is coupled with support and praise about what a parent does well. Stick to constructive and explicit suggestions: "I'd like to see you be firmer with Kate." Try to stay away from name calling: "You're a lousy parent." Use descriptive statements about specific behavior, such as "Kate didn't say hello to me when she walked into the room," not general labels, such as, "Your daughter is so rude."

Venting doesn't change the situation and it may make it worse. A stepmother may vent to a father about his children. The father may try to be understanding of his wife's dissatisfaction; he may be good at letting criticism of his child roll off his back. More likely, he feels stuck in the middle and disloyal to his children when he doesn't defend them. He may understand his wife's frustrations; he may even share them. But he is likely hurt by them as well and the resentment against his wife will begin to build.

Speak up

It is not fair to harbor resentments and expect that the person who is bothering you will eventually figure it out and make it better for you. If it bothers you to hear your partner bad-mouthing your children, or even your ex, then you need to ask him or her to stop. If you can't stand your partner letting his children run through the house with shoes on, you need to bring it up (away from the kids, thanks). If your stepchild is being hurtful, you need to tell your partner that.

Facing the issues head on doesn't always mean that the issues will be resolved to everyone's liking. But it sure beats waiting for the problem to go away. Stepfamilies live or die on communication. There is no way to overemphasize this point. If people in your family can't talk to each other about anything important without having a major fight and resolving nothing, it is time to recognize that you all might need some help.

It is hard to bring up things that may be painful or difficult. But not dealing with them does not make them go away. The longer you wait to talk to each other, the more ground there will be to cover. If you can really let something go, great, let it go. But try to keep your resentment file empty; don't hang on to issues that eat you alive. And if open communication seems impossible at this point, back up and start rebuilding the relationship.

Boundaries between homes

IF YOU WENT to most any neighbor's house and sat and watched how their family interacted over a long enough period of time, especially when they didn't know you were there, you would likely find yourself thinking, "Oh, my. I'd never do that with my children." If you picked a high stress time of day, say, the early-morning routine of a family that has to get out of the house by a certain time, you may be uncomfortable, even aghast, at some of the ways that the family interacts. If you had to think about sending your own children there every other weekend, the thought might make you panic. But you don't get to do that with your neighbors. It's what you do with stepfamilies.

OK, that might sound a little grim. There are plenty of you who are really good parents and almost never threaten to lock your children in the attic until they're eighteen. Still, most stepparents and parents have their share of challenges. People often divorce because they can't live together peacefully. Now, the parents are in two separate households, but the child is still being raised, in most situations, by those two parents. And although most people wouldn't dream of demanding an explanation from a neighbor about why their child hasn't had a bath in two days or why they were late to the parent-teacher conference, often ex-spouses don't hesitate.

Sometimes, parents forget what it means to be divorced and remarried. Divorce means that the ex doesn't answer to you anymore. Divorce means that the ex gets to raise his child the way he thinks is right, especially in his own home. Divorce means that you have to share your child with another household. And remarriage means that there are people intimately involved in your child's life whom you did not pick and may not particularly like. Remarriage also means that you have to accommodate, at least to some degree, your spouse's ex. This is the mother or father of your stepchild.

Sometimes, two households get along well enough to plan things for the child together, to be flexible enough to allow for each family's needs, to create two environments in a way that the child feels at home in either place. This is the best for the children. And really, it is the best for the adults as well.

Unfortunately, relations between the two homes can become one of the most divisive issues in many stepfamilies. Conflict between homes has dire consequences for children in stepfamilies. Children who have to deal with conflict between their homes do not adjust as well as children who live in a cooperative, respectful environment.

Given those facts, there are a lot of things to do to ease the sometimes bitter and unproductive interactions that happen between two homes. You have to raise this child with the other parent, so it is worth it to figure out some ways to get along and try to make that child's life, and your own, a workable one.

Don't fight in front of the children

This becomes harder to do the more necessary it is. When you are living in a high conflict situation, the tension builds on itself. It is as clear to the children as it is to the adults that the relations are strained. Sometimes, the best thing to do is just commit yourself to staying calm and respectful in front of the children, no matter how your ex-spouse behaves. You can't ever control what someone else is going to do, but you can strive to control your own actions and reactions to a situation. If there has to be an argument, pick a time and place when your children don't have to hear or see it.

Be all business

The thing to try to do with the ex in your life is to treat him like the dentist. I don't know what your relationship is with your dentist, but I'm always just a little sick that I have to go to him—but that doesn't stop me from being polite and respectful.

What would happen if you treated your dentist like you treat your ex? Would you be embarrassed?

"You know, my appointment was at 3 P.M. I've been standing around here waiting for half an hour. You are just a waste of my time. It's always the same thing. Last time I came in for an appointment you were late, too. You're so unreliable. And what do you think that does to my kids? To have them sitting out here, waiting for you? And for what? So that you can go digging around in my mouth with your sharp instruments? Wow, what kind of person must you be to pick this for a profession? Of course, you're probably making enough money from it. You know, if you don't stop these cavities from coming, I'm going to stop paying my bills!"

A little hard to imagine, isn't it?

But sometimes people end up treating their exes this badly or worse. If you can be respectful and clear, the relationship may begin to get easier over time. Of course, your ex is used to you being who you are—whether that is huffy and puffy or quiet and steamed. So you may get the same treatment for a while. But if you can change the way you act, eventually, your ex will, too. And your children will be so happy not to have to deal with the tension-filled air every time their parents are in the same room.

Stick to the point, don't attack, and be clear and respectful about what you want.

A more respectful way to talk to the dentist—or your ex—might be something like this:

"I see that you're running late. This has become rather inconvenient for me, as I plan my schedule around our appointment time. It's difficult for my kids to wait for me. How can we plan appointments that are closer to on time?"

Ultimately, I know, talking to your ex isn't like talking to your dentist. But the point is to find some way to be respectful in your interactions.

Pick your communication tool

One of the simplest things to do when tensions are very high is to decide how to communicate with the other household. Obviously, the telephone is the fastest and sometimes most convenient way to communicate, especially if things come up at the last minute. But that's not always the best way for feuding parents to communicate. Whatever you decide, define the parameters and stick to them. If scheduling visitation with the ex over the phone erodes into arguments, try e-mail or even snail mail instead. If you find that writing each other gets really nasty, consider working through a third party, either unofficially, as with a family member, or with the help of a professional.

When children, especially young children, are going back and forth between homes, some families use a simple notebook that the parents exchange with the child. You can write what you need to say and the other parent can respond in the notebook. You don't have to confront the person directly, which can be a good thing if you are not able to have a civil conversation with that person.

Deciding *how* to communicate is a good first step in figuring out how to communicate better. Whatever you decide, keep the communication clear, simple, and brief.

Don't ignore history

Every stepfamily grew from a first family. And the people in that first family had ways of interacting that, for good or bad, developed into habits.

Often, first families continue to operate under those same habits until someone decides that something needs to change. Often, the person pushing for change is the stepparent. They have seen the way that this divorced couple interacts and they don't like what they see.

But while the stepparent may have a fresh perspective on how a family operates, that perspective may not always be appreciated or welcomed. Parents may feel threatened and judged by a stepparent's criticisms or even constructive suggestions. Especially for the parent in the other household, a new stepparent can feel like an interloper.

Many parents, particularly mothers, feel like the relationship that they had with the other parent was a workable one, until the stepparent showed up. A mother may appreciate how she and her ex work together to raise their child, even if she does not particularly get along with him. Mothers often feel like the stepmother comes in and ruins the way that the divorced couple works together. One mother told me that she knows her ex-husband's new wife is the one writing all the e-mails she gets, even though they are signed from him. She said there is no way her ex-husband would make the kind of demands he is making on his own.

Stepparents, on the other hand, are sometimes amazed at how much control the ex has over their spouse's relationship with the children. Stepmothers often push their new husbands to take on more responsibilities with their children, and they are often the ones pushing for more equitable time. Stepparents are also the ones likely to be advocating clearer boundaries between the homes.

Sometimes stepparents deal with the ex themselves. If you live in a family system in which the stepparent and the ex-spouse are respectful and on good terms, this can work well. But if relations are edgy and tension-filled, it is best to let the divorced couple do the work of sorting out their child's life.

Stepparents may have some legitimate complaints about how their partner deals with the ex and the other household. But if there is tension between the households, the best place for a stepparent to apply the pressure for change is in his own home with his own wife. Stepparents who back off from negotiating time or making pick-ups and simply make respectful contact with the ex are sometimes amazed to find the ex suddenly more accepting of them and the entire situation.

Ask the adults the prying questions, or don't ask at all

Everyone is curious about what goes on in the other household. This is particularly true in high conflict situations, in which you may be concerned that there are unpleasant things happening for your children. But especially in these kinds of situations, it helps for the child not to feel that he has to explain the other household for you.

Even asking children seemingly polite questions about the other parents can feel like an intrusion to a child. You simply ask, "How's your mom's new job going?" But the child may hear, "So has that loser mother of yours been fired yet?"

If you sense your child is uncomfortable, it's better to ask less specific questions such as "How was your weekend?" Don't try to sniff around the edges with your kids, trying to find out some information about the other household. It is not fair to put them in a position in which they feel like they have to justify, explain, or defend their other household's decisions, activities, or habits.

If you have a problem with what is going on at the other household, or you are curious to know what is happening over there, you could ask the parent. Obviously, if the relationship is strained, that might not go over well. But if you are genuinely concerned or feel that there might be some insight you could gain that would help you be a better parent, it's worth a try.

You might say, "I've noticed that Karen is so nervous about going to school lately. Have you noticed that? I'm trying to think of what might be stressful for her right now and wondering if you have any ideas on your end of things?"

It might open the door to a good conversation. It might not. But unless you are gravely concerned about something at the other household, always keep in mind that being divorced and remarried means you do not get to be privy to all the inside information in your child's other life. Think hard about what issues are important enough to bring up with the other household.

Sometimes it takes years to establish the kinds of boundaries that make people comfortable in stepfamilies. Sometimes, you just sort it out as you go along, and finally get to a place that works for everyone. If relations in your household or between your households are really tough, establishing a basic set of ground rules for communication can be a great way to start a new chapter in these relationships.

4

THE DIAZ/JORVIG/KERTZ FAMILY SYSTEM OF DALLAS, TEXAS

❦

CHILD/STEPCHILD: Fern Jorvig, eight-year-old daughter of Matt and Valerie, stays a few days a week at both parents' home, with more time at her father and stepmother's home.

DAD: Matt Jorvig divorced Valerie when Fern was three, and married Pamela when Fern was seven years old.

MOM: Valerie Diaz divorced Matt when Fern was three, and married Tony when Fern was six years old.

STEPMOM: Pamela Kertz married Matt when Fern was seven years old.

STEPDAD: Tony Diaz married Valerie when Fern was six years old.

Both sides of this child/stepchild's family love her and have good things to offer her, but the adults are focusing on their problems with each other, not the good points, so they spend a lot of time sniping at each other—inadvertently putting the girl in a tough spot.

*I*F BEING DEDICATED to the child and loving the child made living in a stepfamily easy, this family system would have not a single worry. Fern, a bright-eyed eight-year-old, has the love and dedication of each of the four parents in her life.

But making a stepfamily function smoothly takes more than dedication and love. It takes cooperation and acceptance of the other household, and it is here that this family struggles.

Fern's mom and stepdad can't stand that Fern is learning the lyrics to racy songs at her dad and stepmom's house. When she comes home, singing a song, grabbing her crotch, and yelling, "Don't I look sexy?" her mom almost can't control her gag reflex.

Fern's dad and stepmom can't stand that every time Fern comes home from her mom and stepdad's house they have to spend the first day reining in her mouth, reminding her of their rules, and making sure that she gets a bath for the first time in three days.

There are plenty of obvious differences between these families. Dad and stepmom go to church, mom and stepdad don't. Mom and stepdad have their apartment decorated with Marilyn Manson posters and dozens of tall jar candles with religious figures on them. They were, for a time, into the Goth scene. Dad and stepmom's apartment is decorated with strings of white lights and purple stars and moons; it doesn't have dark edges. The stepmom is the kind of person who at one point went to have a highly stylized photo from Glamour Shots done. The mom is the kind of person who at one point would flash her breasts when she was getting her picture taken. These are the kinds of differences that grate on the two families.

Fortunately, both for Fern and for the adults in this family, they have all kinds of strengths to draw on. Their core values are more alike than different, their places in life are more alike than different. There have been enough changes lately that when the dust settles, chances are both families will be more tolerant of each other and see the things they have in common.

Fern's parents separated and divorced five years ago, but the past two years have been a time of great change for the entire family system. Both parents have remarried, throwing stepparents into the mix. Both families have moved into new homes. Fern started at a new school. And all of the adults have had to sort out just who does what when it comes to raising this child together.

The two families share many values and ways of being in the world. All the adults believe in being kind to strangers, in being not only respectful of people's differences, but understanding how race and class keep some people in disadvantaged positions in the world. They are all concerned about doing the right thing for Fern and they all have some pretty strong opinions about what the right thing is.

Some similarities are specific. When I walked into the Jorvig and Kertz home, I found their bright blue couch an unusual shade, a funky sort of couch that fit their personalities. So when I walked into the Diaz home and saw a couch almost the identical shade, I found it an interesting detail. There are other things. One afternoon, I arranged to first meet with Pamela and Matt and then, immediately following, with Valerie and Tony. They picked the spots and they both picked restaurants on the same street about a block apart. The part of town wasn't near either one of their homes, they both just liked that area. Fern's bedroom at both homes contains a bunk bed and scads of stuffed animals. Her room has more books at her mom's, more electronics at her dad's, but it is similar in both homes. She has her own bathroom in each home, as well. It is clear that Fern feels comfortable and at home at both houses.

These families share all kinds of habits and values. They have spent a lot of time focusing on the things that are different about their households and those differences can drive them crazy. If they could start to see the similarities, the shared values, they might be able to dissolve some of the tension between the two homes, some of the past resentments that people haven't been able to get over.

Fern's families form

MATT AND VALERIE married in 1993 while they were in college, struggling both financially and emotionally to make it in the world. They had Fern about a year later and separated in 1997.

Looking back on those days, Valerie regrets some of the ways things worked out. She said she dropped out of college to support Matt in finishing his degree and she never returned to school. Not having a college degree is something she feels that Matt now holds over her. Valerie said that Matt was very controlling during their marriage and after a while of trying to change for him, she figured out that there was no pleasing him. So she left, taking Fern with her.

There were attempts at reconciliation. One time, Valerie even moved back into Matt's apartment. She only lasted a few hours before realizing that their marriage was over.

In those early days after the divorce, Valerie said she wasn't as stable a parent as she is now. She was dating men who were abusive to her and she maybe wasn't paying as much attention to Fern as she should have.

Matt, too, was sorting out what his life looked like after his marriage fell apart. He decided pretty quickly that it was about Fern. Matt, who did not want the marriage to end, was doubly frustrated that Valerie wasn't taking on her responsibilities with Fern. Valerie quit her job at the bookstore where she worked, which meant that Fern was no longer covered for medical insurance under Valerie's plan. Matt felt like Valerie just wanted to go off and live the life of a single, carefree person, leaving the major responsibilities of raising Fern to Matt.

When Matt met Pamela, she seemed to be everything that Valerie wasn't—stable, responsible, completely excited about having a family and raising children. Their relationship moved very quickly. Within six months, they were living together. A year later, they married. Even though Valerie was still very much part of Fern's life, Matt and Pamela grew to believe that their home was the most stable place for Fern, the place where she felt most comfortable.

And then Valerie got remarried. Valerie had known Tony for some time when he was a student in college and she was working in Deep Ellum, a funky neighborhood of bars and shops in Dallas. He would come home on break and the two would hang out together. When he came home for good, he and Valerie became close. After a couple years, they married, in a very small ceremony before a justice of the peace.

After Valerie remarried, she became more focused on her relationship with Fern. She started seeing her more regularly, spending more time at her school, showing up at her soccer games.

Matt and Pamela had mixed feelings about her renewed commitment to Fern. A big part of them was happy about it; they wanted her to be there for Fern and they knew that Fern loved having her mother more fully in her life.

But another part of them felt wary, not sure if this new commitment was real or if Valerie would stick around for long. Besides, they had spent all their energy building a stable home for this girl; where had her mother been?

Matt and Pamela can get very annoyed with the other household, both because they are burdened by the inconsistencies they have to deal with and because they worry that Fern is hurt by her mother.

"MY MOM'S STILL A GOOD MOM"

WHEN I ASK Fern about her family, she talks about the things she likes and the things that are hard. She talks about the most obvious things to her—not having all of her parents in one household, having to go back and forth between two homes where she feels so connected.

But Fern says more than she knows about another struggle she can't even identify at eight years old. Fern doesn't talk explicitly about feeling torn between two homes, and she may not recognize that she does feel divided loyalties. But there are things that she says that show that she is terribly defensive about loving all of her parents—particularly her mother and stepmother.

Sometimes, parents in separate households don't realize that when they complain about each other, the child is put in an almost impossible position. Fern's two homes have different ways of dealing with their frustrations with the other household. At Valerie and Tony's house, everything is out on the table. It is their way to talk about everything. Valerie is very clear with Fern about how she feels about Pamela. She also is clear that she understands how important Pamela is to Fern and that she's OK with that.

At Matt and Pamela's house, they try never to say anything negative about the other household. They try, but it doesn't usually work out that way. They are both aware that it is hard for Fern to feel badly about her other household, about her mother in particular. And they certainly don't explicitly bad-mouth Valerie in front of Fern. But the way they feel about Valerie becomes pretty clear to Fern by how they deal with their frustrations with her mother.

When Valerie decides she will not allow Fern go to a friend's house after a soccer game, Matt and Pamela are clearly upset and tell Fern that they don't know why her mother wouldn't let her go. When Valerie doesn't come to pick up Fern at the scheduled time, Matt and Pamela are openly exasperated at her inconsideration of Fern. Fern feels the sadness of not seeing her mother, but the sadness and rejection is complicated by having to reassure herself, despite what her dad and Pamela say, that her mom really does love her.

This defensive stance is clear when Fern talks about her life. She says things like, "I didn't see my mom that much this summer, but my mom's still a good mom." And when Pamela asks her if she's had a bath at her mom's house in the past couple days, Fern hesitates, because she knows the answer will simply reinforce Pamela's already negative view of her mother. So she says, "No, but that doesn't mean my mom isn't a good mom."

Pamela and Matt are completely devoted to Fern. They get upset with Valerie because they believe that she does harmful things to Fern. But what they might not see is that their own anger or judgment about what Valerie does is at least as hard to take for Fern. Fern doesn't need them to get angry at her mom on her behalf. Some day, if Fern doesn't like the relationship she has with her mother, she'll get angry and do something about it herself.

For now, maybe things aren't perfect between Fern and Valerie. But Fern is pretty clear that her mother loves her—it is abundantly obvious when they're together. Pamela and Matt would help Fern more if they just trusted that love and trusted that Fern will sort out her own relationship with Valerie.

It works both ways, of course. Fern also knows that her mother doesn't like Pamela very much although Fern herself loves Pamela. But since her mother has basically said, "Yeah, you love her, that's fine. It doesn't mean I have to," Fern is much more comfortable with her love for Pamela.

When she talks about her stepmom, she says, "I get along with her very well, actually, believe it or not."

THE DUST IS STARTING TO SETTLE

AS TIME HAS gone on in this family, the two households are becoming more careful with each other. They're more polite and more likely to let things that bother them go without comment. At one point, Valerie wanted to pull out of this book project because she was afraid that some of the tough things that she had said would damage the new and fragile peace that the two families were building together. But she wasn't the only one who said tough things. Both she and Matt were wishing each other off the planet.

They all love Fern so much, they want to protect her from any pain, to love her, and help her through the world. They are all starting to realize that they each have a part to play in Fern's life.

Fern is an exceptionally bright child. She is kind and generous. She has that eight-year-old energy that is sometime difficult for her parents, all her parents, to tolerate. But if the adults in her life sort out their issues with each other, it is likely that Fern will only get stronger, will see more and more of the benefits and less and less of the difficulties of being in a stepfamily.

Matt Jorvig

Matt is at once kind, giving, cynical, and brusque. He has deeply held opinions about social justice and racism and he believes that people should be tolerant of each other. The only people he is intolerant of, he says, are intolerant people. He doesn't add his ex-wife in there, but he might.

Valerie left Matt and he was stunned. He tried to get her to come home, and bailed her out several times when she was left stranded by her crazy boyfriend.

These days, Matt is mostly annoyed and a little bitter that he has to deal with his ex-wife. He is clear that he would never wish Fern away—he loves her completely. But he wouldn't mind if Valerie just dropped off the planet. Just like that, he imagines, his life would vastly improve.

He envies the divorce without children. He would like to just get on with his life, but there is his past, always making his new life more difficult, always part of the plan with his new family.

It took him a while after the divorce to define what he wanted for his life. He dated for a while and hung out just having fun. But it didn't feel right while raising a little girl. The days of carefree dating and fast living were over for him and he decided that Fern came first. If there was going to be another woman in his life, she would have to understand that Fern was his priority.

Matt is a ruddy-faced, heavy-boned man with red freckles all over his pale skin. The Mohawk haircut of his college days is gone, but he still has the hole in his nose where he used to have a ring, and his daughter likes to point this out to people.

These days, Matt has a buzz cut, and wears button-down collared shirts and khakis to the architectural firm where he works. He helps design buildings like the Miller Park Stadium in Milwaukee and he loves his job. At home he wears Birkenstocks with socks when the Dallas air bites, and

T-shirts, shorts, and sandals when it's hot. But the spirit of the Mohawk, he says, is still with him.

He has strong opinions about doing the right thing in the world and he says it's important for him to raise his daughter with respect for all kinds of people, young and old, black and white, rich or poor. These beliefs are evident in his life. When they married, Matt and Pamela decided to ask their guests who planned on giving a gift to donate to the food shelf organized by their church instead. Their church has a 90 percent gay congregation and is a pretty lefty-liberal kind of place. Matt and Pamela are heavily involved in the outreach programs for children and the poor.

Matt wants to set a good example for Fern and teach her to be just, kind, and thoughtful in the world. When it comes to dealing with his ex, he's just not always sure what the right thing is.

A daughter in two homes

Matt knows that there have been times when he's put Fern in an uncomfortable position between her two homes. He gets so frustrated with some of Valerie's decisions and the way she justifies them to Fern. Like the time that Valerie scooped Fern up after her soccer game instead of letting her hang out for a while afterward with the other kids on the team.

"That made Fern feel very bad. She kind of hung her head down and threw her snack away," Matt said. "I felt horrible. I didn't want to make a big scene on the soccer field. But later that week we were talking about it and I told Fern 'I felt badly that you didn't get to spend more time with your new friends. Next time, we'll really try to stay longer.' She said, 'You know, Mom had a lot of stuff to do that day and she just doesn't have time. We have to run errands all day on Saturday.'"

"I said 'Fern, here's the deal. I've asked your mom to be involved with soccer. I've asked her to be involved because I know you like it when she's involved and you like her to come to games. Your mommy has more than enough time to take care of her personal business on the days that she doesn't have you. If she's saying that it's more important to go shopping than to take you to your soccer game, that's wrong. This is how Pamela and I do stuff, we do all our errands when you're at your mom's to make sure that our time with you is special. For your mom to say that she doesn't have enough time with you is wrong.'

"At that instant, I thought, 'Oh shit. I've overstepped my bounds. I've told her too much. It's beyond what she can comprehend for her maturity.' She's very defensive of her mom and I think she truly believes I'm going to take her away from her mom. She told me 'I don't want you to take me away from my mother.'"

Matt used to feel that he should try to go back to court and get Fern full-time. He knows that's what Pamela wants, she's pushed for it a lot. He said he doesn't really care what Valerie does for herself, but that for Fern's sake, he wishes Valerie would grow up and stop acting like she's still in college, or even high school. He also knows how much Fern loves her mom and he's worried that his daughter would be sad to see her less. He knows Valerie loves Fern, too, but Valerie's not exactly a pillar of reliability. Maybe it would be easier on Fern to have one big disappointment rather than being disappointed by her mother on a regular basis.

But he's starting to listen to his daughter. And things started to change with Valerie, in any case. After Valerie married Tony, she became a lot more involved in Fern's life. She took Matt up on his offer to be a part of the soccer scene, something she had not traditionally done.

Matt had mixed feelings about this new interest. Part of him felt really happy for Fern because her mother was now paying more attention and he knows she needs that. The other part of him felt like it might just be easier if Valerie went away all together and then he would have his family the way he wanted it.

He doesn't have any question about Pamela's commitment to Fern. He says frequently that Pamela would throw herself in front of a bus for the girl. And, bonus points, she's an educator—she spends her days with children, so she has a lot of experience.

Matt immensely respects Pamela's views on raising children. He feels that because she is an educator and has had some training in the area of child development that what she has to say carries some weight.

And Matt has high expectations for Fern, both in behavior and in academics. Fern brought home her first grade below an A ever this year (she got a B), and Matt set up teacher conferences right away to see what needed to be done to fix the problem.

He expects Fern to behave well at home, too. Usually, she does. There are times, though, when he comes home and he gets in the middle of a screaming match between Fern and Pamela. He sends child and stepmother their rooms to calm down and they start over. Mostly, the relationships work.

Screaming matches aren't that uncommon in Matt and Pamela's home. Matt has a hot temper. His words can sting and he can be a fairly dominant force in a conversation. When he deals with his ex-wife, he sometimes lays into her over the things that she does with Fern. Often, the argument carries over to Pamela and they end up arguing about how to deal with Valerie.

Matt and Pamela see themselves as mostly doing things right for Fern and Valerie as mostly doing things wrong. Matt and Pamela have united behind this idea and it has become a focal point for their relationship with the other house. They spend a lot of time talking about his ex-wife. Valerie is the third party in their marriage. Neither Matt nor Pamela is happy about this arrangement, but Valerie seems to be the subject on which a lot of their energy is spent.

Matt has seen some changes in the ways the two homes are dealing with each other. He'd like to feel hopeful, and sometimes he does. Just as often, though, he's got his guard up.

"Valerie has been strangely friendly lately," Matt said. "She's really trying to be a lot more communicative and talking to me about Fern and I'm just like, 'What's going on here? What's your motivation?' I hate thinking that way because I'd like to think she's grown up and she's serious about it.

"I would like to think that she's trying to get along, but my instincts and history and all those other things make me think there's something else going on, there's some other reason she's doing this. I hate thinking that way, I hate to prejudge people. You like to think that people grow and change."

FERN JORVIG

FERN SLEEPS ON a bunk bed at both of her houses. At her dad and stepmom's, she sleeps on the top bunk. At her mom and stepdad's, she sleeps on the bottom bunk. It's a good metaphor for her life between the two homes.

The people in her mom's house are more protective, more wanting to hold her close in a world that is sometimes scary. The people in her dad's house say "get up on the top bunk and check it out."

Fern doesn't "visit" either home. She really lives in both places. She may spend more time at her dad and stepmom's house, but both of her homes are comfortable for her, both feel like her place.

Fern has her own VCR and TV in her room at her dad's house. On the wall is a cutout silhouette of her with longer hair, before Pamela cut it (and Valerie flipped.) There's also her Great Grizzly Super Student Award. On her dresser are pictures of her soccer teams from previous seasons, which

Matt and Pamela coached. She still has her hat from two seasons ago. There are shelves full of games—Operation, Bingo, Sorry, Harry Potter, Trouble, Candyland—and a toy kitchen which is stacked with stuffed animals. There are more everywhere. A rope with clips on it hangs from the ceiling, dangling Kermit the Frog, Ernie and Bert, bears, monkeys, bunnies, and turtles. In the closet is another huge box filled with stuffed animals. On her door is a life-sized poster of Rusty from the Rangers. Fern has her own bathroom and it's filled with body lotions, soaps, hair detangler, and a little heart-shaped glass shaker with hearts instead of snow floating around when you shake it up. Pamela gave it to her for Valentine's Day.

At her mom's house, her own bathroom and her bedroom have a lot of the same stuff. There are more books here and there's no TV or VCR as there are at her dad's house, but both her rooms are fully Fern's place.

One of the best things about her family, Fern said, is that everyone is a really good person. She said that she feels they all love her and she loves all of them, so she feels lucky that she doesn't have many complaints.

Fern said that all her parents in both houses and between houses argue sometimes, but not too much. It bothers her when they do. Fern feels good about spending time at both of her homes. She just wishes it were more consistent and more equitable between the two homes.

"If there were ten days in a week, then I would want five days at my mom's house and five days at my dad's house," she said. "It's kind of hard because you don't get to see some people as much, and it changes. It's kind of hard, you're not in one house, you're not all together, you have to go back and forth."

In the end, Fern is loved and cared for by both households. She's curls up in her mom's lap at her mom's home, she snuggles with her stepmom at her other home. That's the reality for Fern. She has a real life with real love and real ties at both houses. The two houses are different in some ways, but nothing so important that Fern can't navigate the differences. Fern is feeling good about her two homes and it seems that all the adults are on their way to making their reality as cooperative as Fern imagines it.

VALERIE DIAZ

VALERIE SAYS THAT if she spent all her time trying to defend her life against the complaints of her ex-husband and his new wife, she'd get nothing else done.

They don't like her clothing or her tattoos, they don't like the music she listens to or the friends she hangs out with. They don't like her schedule, or her tendency to change the schedule at the last minute, they complain about her "lifestyle" and take every opportunity they can to let her know that they're not impressed with her role as a mother to Fern.

It could be exhausting, but instead she works to try to minimize the time she spends thinking about the whole situation. Still, it's annoying and insulting to have someone second-guessing her all the time. It can be just small things, but depending on her mood, she can feel them in big ways. Like the time that she was going to take Fern to the doctor and Matt asked if she remembered where the doctor's office was. Fern has had the same pediatrician since she was born eight years ago. The pediatrician that Valerie picked. Of course she remembered. To her, Matt's question was just one more way for him to say she's not a good mother.

The implication is offensive to Valerie, and she is hurt by it. She knows that she hasn't always been as stable as she might have been with her child. But ultimately, when her little girl, her "Bootie Poot," snuggles up next to her and asks her for another math problem to solve, when they build a birdhouse together, or even when that girl bellows out a complaint about something she has to do, Valerie knows that her girl is her girl. There's nothing that Matt can say to take that away from her.

"She's definitely my kid," Valerie said. "She'd talk to a hole in the ground. Personality-wise, she's a lot more like me, we're both hollerers. She didn't fall far from the tree."

Teaching Fern values

Valerie is outspoken and she has a precise and piercing sense of humor. Her hair is starting to grow out from when she shaved her head and bleached her hair almost white. Today, her hair is maroon, so dark you could mistake it for black. She has blue stars tattooed on each of her fingers and a large star tattooed on her chest. She has a bold circle on her upper right arm and a half-naked goddess spans across her back. Her mouth is wide with bright lipstick and her eyes are sharp.

Valerie knows that when people see her, they are sometimes intimidated by the way she looks. ("When I walk down the hall at Fern's school, all the mom's are holding their babies close to them.")

But if her look is tough, it doesn't really reflect who she is. Valerie believes in opening doors for old ladies, in being kind to store clerks and other people who have difficult jobs. She says that anyone who is rude to some poor child who has to work in a fast-food restaurant almost deserves to have his burger spit on. She won't buy her clothes at international chain stores, because she doesn't like how those companies treat their employees. It's important for her that her daughter understand that all people share common ground, no matter what their race, or background.

Valerie was born in a small Midwestern town. People all knew each other, they knew each other's children, they knew each other's business. People walked to get places. Living in Dallas is about as different from all that as you could get. And when Valerie first moved here with Matt, she didn't know how to handle it. So she stayed in the house and didn't go anywhere for a year.

She can still get freaked out by the expansive freeways and skyscrapers of her city, but she's come a long way in the past few years. She drives on the freeway every day to get to her job helping people figure out their worker's compensation. Part of that growth is figuring out a new relationship with Fern's dad.

Dealing with the other household

Overall, Valerie said she mostly tries to ignore the negative interactions between the two households and concentrate on her life with her husband, Tony, and their life as a family with Fern.

But especially earlier on, when Valerie and Matt were getting used to having new partners in their lives, new stepparents for Fern, things were pretty dicey. She said that she really blames Pamela for the demise of the parenting relationship that she used to have with Matt. She said that instead of working as the two primary parents in Fern's life, Matt has turned to Pamela for his discussions about what's best for Fern. Matt's even told Valerie that Pamela knows best because she's an educator.

"Pamela always has to have her nose in it. What pisses me off the most is that me and Matt worked so hard to stay friends and to work together and to never fight in front of Fern. We were model frickin' divorced people," Valerie said. "We had the same rules at our houses, we talked about school and everything. He meets Pamela and all of the sudden, Tony and I are low-class, dirty white people. Matt's really mean now. I try not to take it personally."

At one point, both she and Matt went to the hospital to be with Fern when she got her cast removed from her broken wrist. They were at the doctor's office for a couple hours and they sat, talking. Matt was friendly and they got along well until the end. Valerie said it was almost like he realized he was being nice to her, that he had let his guard slip, and so he made some nasty comment.

"It sucks that we're not friends," Valerie said. "It sucks that it has to be so adversarial. You never want anything adversarial around your kid. Ever since he met Pamela, he's acted like we were never friends, like we were married for five minutes and it was a tragic mistake."

So when Fern asks if she and Matt were ever friends, Valerie is sure to tell her that they were. When Fern then asks if they're friends now, she can only say that they're trying.

She and Tony still try to be flexible with the scheduling and the arrangements. They don't ever want to get to the point where they're being nitpicky about which day is which household's. She said it works well for everyone to have Fern about half the time.

Still, she doesn't always feel that Matt and Pamela have a lot of tolerance for Fern. She thinks that they prefer the girl to spend time alone in her room with her Gameboy, her TV and VCR, and her CD player for company.

And Valerie worries, too, that Pamela's influence isn't what she would pick for her child. At Matt and Pamela's house, Fern was listening to bands like Destiny's Child and Backstreet Boyz by the time she was seven years old, something Valerie remembers distinctly that she and Matt had agreed they wouldn't allow until the girl was older.

Fern has told her mother that she should buy her clothes at the Gap and Banana Republic, like her dad and Pamela do. And one day, Fern innocently said, "Mama, you're white trash."

Valerie said as nonchalantly as she could muster, "That's funny. Where did you hear that?" And Fern said, "I'm not going to tell you because you're going to get Pamela in trouble."

Valerie knows that Fern loves Pamela, and she's made it pretty clear to Fern that she doesn't share her feelings. But she's also made it clear that she doesn't have to, that Fern can have different feelings about Pamela and that it is OK.

Thinking about Pamela can really make Valerie steam. For Valerie, it is hard enough that she feels she has to defend what she does with her child. But she gets really agitated when she has to defend her basic motherhood. Valerie feels Pamela isn't just trying to be a good stepparent to Fern, she's trying to be a mother to Fern. And worse still, it seems to Valerie that Pamela feels she's a better mother to Fern. It used to make Valerie wish that Pamela would get hit by a bus.

But outside of this kind of raw emotion, Valerie said that, really, Pamela is probably the best she could hope for for Fern. She's good to the girl and Valerie knows that Pamela goes out of her way for Fern a lot. And, Valerie said, although Pamela can be elitist, she isn't mean, so she appreciates that.

"She's kind of the Brownie-leader type," Valerie said. "I know they do a lot of projects and activities. She's very activity-based. It's kind of like she's leading a cruise ship instead of a life. So, I think it could be much worse."

Her biggest concerns are Pamela undermining Valerie's role as mother and then just the peripheral stuff that she hears Fern pick up from the other household. Like the ideas about where to shop. Or the time that skinny little Fern came home and was complaining that she was fat. Or the idea that because Matt and Pamela are active in their church they are somehow morally superior to her and Tony.

Cautiously moving forward

Valerie is happy that things have settled some between the two households. She said she doesn't want to do anything to upset the recent cooperation. Over the past two years, the whole family system has gone through major changes. Valerie now feels that the two households are finally starting to get in sync, finally starting to work together again with Fern as the focus.

Valerie seriously considered pulling out of this book because she wanted to make sure she didn't rock the boat. She didn't want to have any setbacks because of any of the things she said during an earlier time when she was feeling more frustrated with the situation. There was a time when she thought that life would be easier if both Matt and Pamela just quietly disappeared.

These days, her life is much more stable. Most of the old crowd that she and Tony used to hang out with late into the night don't call or come over much anymore. Valerie has to work early in the morning every day and they have become much more domestic, concentrating more on their family and on raising her daughter.

When Valerie sees Fern now, her bouncy, bright, beautiful girl, she feels good about her life. And Valerie is starting to enjoy the benefits of living in a stepfamily. She says she and Tony have a pretty cushy parenting life. They get to have Fern in their lives, they influence her and love her and have time together. And they also have time when Fern is off in the other household, time to be alone as a couple. All in all, she thinks it's a good arrangement for everyone involved. She wouldn't change it if she could.

PAMELA KERTZ

GROWING UP, PAMELA learned to put on a smile when she felt angry, learned to drop things when they got too tough to talk about.

There's a picture of her when she was six standing with her brother and sister in their family's home, all with their arms at their sides, barely touching each other. Their hair is perfectly combed, their smiles more requested than happy. The back of the picture says "1/31/75 New Gowns and Haircuts." Her family, no matter the screaming and fighting that went on in the home, was always the perfect family in public.

Pamela laughs and says that sometimes she thinks it was the perfect training for becoming a stepmother. But Pamela is doing what she can to create a life that is real and rewarding for her stepdaughter, her husband, and herself. And it is harder work than she ever imagined.

Pamela moved from St. Louis as a little girl, shortly after her sister died from a rare disease. Pamela spent the rest of her childhood in the suburbs of Dallas, about halfway to Fort Worth. She finished high school and college there. Then she met her husband and they moved to Seattle, Washington. The marriage wasn't working and when Pamela's parents came to visit, she told them she was going back to Dallas with them. She moved in with her brother until she could get back on her feet. She was thirty years old.

Should she or shouldn't she?

She had been in Dallas six weeks when her brother and his friend invited her out to dinner. At the last minute, they mentioned that there would be another man there with his little girl, Fern. She was cold to the idea. It was just too soon. In fact, at that point she didn't think she would ever date again. She was feeling pretty down on men in general and certainly not up to anything that resembled a date. But they assured her it was just a group going out for dinner together, a very casual gathering. So she went.

She doesn't remember much about Matt that night. He was polite, the dinner was fine. But she does remember Fern.

"I did not spend a lot of time interacting with her," she said. "She had little butterfly clips in her hair and she was dressed up all cute. I later found out that her mother had gotten her all dressed up because Matt had told her we were all going out for dinner."

After that initial meeting, their mutual friend made sure that Matt had Pamela's phone number and the calls began. Sometimes they'd talk for hours. They'd talk about the marriages that they'd both left behind, about what they liked, and the things they wanted from life now.

They went out with their mutual friend again, this time without Fern, and saw a movie. And all the while, Matt was trying to convince Pamela that they should go out by themselves. Pamela was still conflicted about the whole thing. It felt too fast, but Matt was a kind man who was certainly persistent about getting to know her.

"We'd probably talked about thirty hours over the phone," she said. "That was real comfortable for me. We learned a lot about each other over the phone. He'd call and say 'I just got Fern in bed and I thought I'd call and see how you're doing.'"

Pamela would cancel date after date. But there was still the phone.

"We were talking on the phone one night and he invited me to go out and I was like, 'All right, I'll go.' The day came, and I just couldn't do it. I called him and I thought, if he picks up the phone, just hang up, but if it goes to voice mail . . . I left him a message telling him 'I just can't do this right now.' He still called me. He called and we talked about it. He said, 'I understand.' I was angry. I was thinking, 'You're supposed to be mad at me and not be so understanding.' But he would never give me a reason to not like him."

Their first date they went bowling, ate sushi, and had a great time. But that, Pamela thought, is that.

"A week or two later, he invited me over for dinner," she said. "I had already decided that I wasn't going to go out with him again. We're on the phone and he's inviting me over for dinner and I hear myself going, 'Yeah, that'd be great.' And I'm thinking, 'What are you doing?' I thought, 'I'll just cancel.' Then I thought, 'No, I can't cancel again, he'll never call me again.'"

When she got to his apartment, Pamela saw that Matt had been paying attention. There were purple flowers on the table—her favorite color. He made mushroom risotto and stuffed squash for dinner.

A few weeks later they went to a Christmas party together. Fern was there, but was mostly running around with the other children. They all got to know each other pretty quickly though, and started falling into a routine.

"We started spending a lot of our weekend time together. It was just kind of like the three of us hanging out to begin with and you know, I think she was very open to having someone around and she wanted her dad to be happy. She knew that someone else would make him happy, that helped make it an easier transition for her," Pamela said.

Pamela would come to Matt and Fern's apartment after work. Matt would make dinner and Fern and Pamela would color or play a game together. She thought that the little red-haired, blue-eyed girl was good-humored and affectionate; Pamela liked spending time with her. It all felt very natural and comfortable. One night, Fern asked Pamela to give her a bath before bedtime. She did, and after a while, Pamela became the one to do the bedtime routine with Fern.

Sometimes, Pamela would correct Fern and Matt would correct Pamela. They had arguments about how to discipline Fern, but never in front of the girl. They had talked about how important it was to be a united front with Fern. But especially in the beginning, Matt and Pamela had plenty of discussions about what to expect from Fern.

Pamela and Matt also talked a lot about what they should expect from each other when it came to Fern, who would do what, how they would handle different situations. Matt was very clear about who was the first priority in his life—and it wasn't Pamela. But she could deal with that. She thought it showed his true character that he put his child first. It seemed admirable to her that a man would think of his child before himself and she thought she wouldn't want to go out with a man who didn't make his child a priority. Pamela saw that Fern goes to her father for important things, that she really loves her father, that he is her bedrock. She found their relationship warm and close.

For the most part, Pamela felt that she fit nicely into that mix. In the beginning, Fern would be at her mother's house and Pamela would think, "Cool, we get a night off, we're only part-time parents." And the burdens seemed manageable in relation to the good things. But there were many moments of doubt before she finally committed to the relationship. She knew she loved Matt, she knew she loved Fern. But she also was beginning to realize that this wasn't going to be just another love affair, or just another marriage, if it got to that point.

There were so many parts that were hard—did she really want to get herself involved in all this? She'd always wanted children, but this wasn't what she had in mind when she thought about starting her family. The doubts really weren't specifically about Fern, but about the situation.

It didn't encourage Pamela that her parents were completely against the idea of a relationship with Matt. Her mother, particularly, thought that there was no way this marriage could work. It was too soon after Pamela's divorce and besides, what was Pamela thinking getting so involved with this child? Pamela's mother was appalled that Pamela would pick Fern up from school, go to her games, take her shopping—basically do all the everyday things that parents do. "She always said, 'That's not your responsibility. Why isn't Matt doing all of that?' But if I'm going to be involved with Matt, I'm going to be involved with Fern."

In the end, she decided to take the plunge.

"Part of it is that Matt is just such a great guy that it didn't seem reason enough to walk away," Pamela said. "And then, I'm a real big believer in fate and I feel like everything happens for a reason. The odds of Matt and I even meeting each other are amazing considering where we were just a year before. There's a reason that our paths crossed and a reason that I was supposed to be a part of Fern's life. That really helped me to realize that this was my place, this was where I needed to be."

Finding her place

But this was early on; this was before Pamela realized that by marrying Matt, she'd also connected her future to Valerie's life.

Pamela watched Valerie as a parent, heard some stories from Matt about Valerie not keeping her commitments. She worried that Fern wasn't getting the mothering she needed. Especially in the early days, she saw a mother who didn't show up to her child's soccer matches, who didn't seem particularly interested in keeping the schedule that she had with Fern. Besides all that, she was the kind of person who was heavily tattooed and pierced and hung out with people who stayed out all night at bars and listened to Marilyn Manson. Pamela didn't think she was a good influence on Fern. She worried about how the instability and uncertainty in Valerie's life would affect the girl.

During that same time, Pamela delighted in Fern and they grew close. Fern was five-and-a-half and Pamela feels like it helped that Fern was so young when they got together. As a teacher, Pamela had the summer off and Fern would stay with her every day while Matt and Valerie worked. Fern lives about half time at both her mom and dad's houses, although sometimes her dad and Pamela have her more. Fern grew to love Pamela. Sometimes, she called her "Mom." From day one, Pamela never told Fern what to call her—she figured it was up to Fern to decide. But certainly, she was doing all kinds of mom-like things, so it didn't feel foreign when Fern called her that.

Still, Pamela was conflicted. She didn't want to take Valerie's place, or even have the perception that she wanted to, so she felt a little guilty about the name. On the other hand, Pamela was feeling good about how strong their relationship was growing, and that the name Fern called her by shouldn't make any difference. Considering everything, it mostly just felt good when Fern called her Mom. Until Valerie found out. Pamela remembers Valerie throwing a fit and telling Fern that no one else is her mom and that she wasn't allowed to call anyone else Mom. Pamela was horrified.

One of the things that Pamela says over and over again is that the adults in Fern's life need to act like the adults. She says that Fern didn't pick this situation and so it's up to the adults to make it the best they can for her. But in this situation, Valerie was taking out her own pain on Fern. Fern was put in the middle and her loyalties were torn.

"A seven-year-old doesn't really know what it takes to be a mom," Pamela said. "I thought that was really horrible. We've talked about it. I think there's a lot of guilt that's got to be difficult for Fern. That's what upsets me. You know, it's just an unfair position for her to be put in."

Pamela and Valerie never talked about the situation with each other. There were other problems that Pamela had with Valerie. She felt that Valerie was disrespectful to her in so many ways—often treating her like a hired babysitter instead of an important person in Fern's life. She started to feel resentful about how Valerie would call and change the schedule at the last minute and expect that she and Matt would accommodate her. She worried that Valerie was hanging out with people who weren't good for Fern, that Valerie wasn't giving Fern the kind of attention that a young girl needs. Pamela never brought these issues up with Valerie directly.

"If I'm upset with her, I don't talk to her. Kind of that principle, 'If you don't have anything nice to say, don't say anything at all,'" she said.

Connected futures

Fern's birthday is in the summer and when she turned six, Pamela planned the party. Fern wanted to invite her mom, so Matt did.

"It's not what I would have wanted," Pamela said. "I just have to realize that I'll always be an outsider in a lot of ways when it comes to certain occasions and events in Fern's life. Fern's mom came and brought her boyfriend (now husband) and you'd think that she'd planned it, because she just ran the whole thing. Fern was happy and that was the point. But it was hard.

"This past summer I put my foot down and said, 'No, I am not planning the whole thing and putting it all together and then taking a complete and total backseat.' In years prior, I'm sure Matt planned and paid for it and she came, so that felt very normal for them. I didn't want to come in and shake it all up, but you have to find your place. Matt has had to say, 'This is one tradition that, whether you like it or not, it's going to be part of what we do.' And I've had to say, 'Whether you like it or not this is one thing that is important to me and I've always thought of it as being part of a family.'"

Pamela doesn't remember the exact moment when she realized that she had, in effect, linked her future to Valerie's. But she gradually started to feel differently about being a "part-time parent." She had always enjoyed the breaks at the beginning, but after a while, she felt that sending Fern to Valerie's house was just the wrong thing to do for the child. Pamela started to pressure Matt about getting more time. She thought that he should go back to court and try to win full custody.

These days, Pamela is settling into the idea of the long haul with Valerie. She's seen some changes over the past year since Valerie got married and has had the same job. She knows that Fern loves her mother and she respects that.

She doesn't want to fight with the other household; she just wants what's best for Fern. She's happy that there have been slow improvements over time in the two household's relationship. She's hoping that things just keep getting better.

TONY DIAZ

TONY'S FAMILY HAS embraced his stepdaughter with open arms. Tony's mother loves the girl and they spend a lot of time together. Their personalities just clicked, and when they get together, it's like everyone else in the world ceases to exist.

This kind of support has been great for Tony as he takes on the role of stepfathering Fern. It is not always easy to figure out what to do, but Tony, in his quiet and supportive way, is there for the girl.

"I don't have any experience, I'm still learning, I hope I'm doing a good job," Tony said. "I'm not trying to replace Matt. I don't want to cut Matt out of that. I would like to fulfill the role to help Fern out and guide her."

In the beginning of their relationship, Tony would attempt to get Fern to do something and they'd get into arguments.

"She would be acting up and I would respond in kind," Tony said. "Valerie would have to separate us. I try now to talk things out or rationalize with Fern. She's pretty sweet. We're building up something."

After a while, Valerie saw that it wasn't really helping Tony and Fern's relationship for her to come in and sort it out for them. So now, she let's them figure it out themselves. But she still sometimes offers Tony some not-so-subtle hints. Like the time they were shopping for shoes and Fern's constant fidgeting was starting to annoy Tony.

"You'd think she was seven," Valerie pointed out. Of course, at the time, she was.

One of the hardest things about living in a stepfamily for Tony is balancing his reality with the rest of the world's reality. Fern loves Tony and Tony loves her and Tony feels great about that. But sometimes, the outside world just doesn't accept his version of this reality. It's not just teachers and dentists and other strangers. It's even Fern's other parents.

"That is the hardest thing. I feel like I'm a family with Valerie and Fern and even with Matt and Pamela," he said. "But they don't always recognize me as a parent. I don't always feel like a parent."

"And then I'm always having to double-check with Valerie and that makes me feel less competent."

As time goes on, Tony is feeling stronger and better able to care for the girl and for the family. His family, his stepfamily, is starting to work.

5

CULTURE, CLEANLINESS, AND CUSTOM

❦

*T*HERE IS LITTLE else that causes the demise of stepfamilies or conflict between already-divorced parents as much as our habits, our traditions, our day-to-day operations in our homes.

Do you leave wet towels on the floor or is it important to hang them up? Can children watch TV after school or should their homework be done first? Should children bathe every day, or is a couple times a week enough? Are McDonald's, Cocoa Puffs, and Twinkies a regular part of your diet, or are you a vegetarian who eats pure, organic foods? Are you Catholic, Protestant, Jewish, Muslim? How old should your child be before she gets to watch *Silence of the Lambs* or *The Omen*? Should your new boyfriend stay the night when the children are there?

These are the kind of things that make raising a child in a stepfamily and between two households a challenge beyond anything that most people can imagine. Once, most children were a part of one household. And no matter whether the arguments were about food, clothes, music, religion, or sex, the children and the adults developed patterns over time, no matter how healthy or dysfunctional they might have been. Either they sat down for dinner together every night, or they didn't. Children could voice their opinions when they wanted, or they couldn't. Parents screamed, or they never raised their voices. The family prayed at bedtime, or they didn't. In most families, these things become habits over time.

After divorce and remarriage, a lot of new players enter the old family dynamics. There are two adults in a home in which there may have been one for some time. There may be new siblings. The new family members might have a hard time with the old family habits. The old family members may find the new ones' habits odd or uncomfortable.

These are big changes for everyone. Each family member has to adjust to the new circumstances. The stepparent, especially the stepparent without any children of her own, is walking into the most difficult circumstances. Most stepparents don't really understand that there is more to the package deal than just the children. The family's history and interactions with extended family from the ex's side can be enormous forces to confront before finding peace in her own household. She will have to figure out how to balance her own needs in a family that already has its way of running things. The parent in this newly-formed family has to accommodate a new partner looking over her shoulder, or a new partner of her ex. Parents in both homes may worry about their child's relationship with the new stepparent or the new stepsiblings. The children have to figure out how to live with more than one household, more than one set of values, more than one set of ideas about where wet towels go.

The amazing thing is that lots of people have been able to do this happily. But those first couple of years can be killers, so you might as well expect some hard times and try to hang on to your hat.

Inner circle conflict

In stepfamilies, the practical difficulties of living with people that everyone has are compounded by emotional alliances and insecurities.

So it's not just "Your kid leaves his dirty dishes in the sink and it's driving me crazy!" It's "Your kid leaves his dirty dishes in the sink and it's driving me crazy AND why don't you do something about it AND don't you care if something is bothering me?"

It's not just "Why do I have to clean my dirty dishes now?" It's "Why do I have to clean my dirty dishes now? AND we never had to do them right away before *he* got here AND why do you let your new husband tell you what to do? AND it's probably because you love him more than me."

And it's not just, "Try to lighten up on her, she's only eight years old."
It's "Try to lighten up on her, she's only eight years old AND she's already
been through so much AND you're so critical of me and the way I parent,
why don't you ever just help me?"

So a seemingly simple issue like dirty dishes can turn into a big, nasty
blowout in short order. The fighting and the nastiness really have little to
do with the dishes and a lot to do with people feeling vulnerable or disrespected in their position in the family.

Successful stepfamilies—families that live together contentedly—have
a number of tricks they use to settle their cultural differences.

Don't change too much too fast

Everyone is under a lot of stress when a stepfamily is formed and starts
living together. Often, one partner moves into another's home.

This sets up all kinds of "turf" issues and creates a sense of invasion on
the part of the family that lived there first. And even when those who lived
there first are welcoming (though they often aren't), the newcomers may
feel as though it's never really their home. It is almost always easier, if
financially feasible, for the whole family to move into a new home.

A new home allows everyone to start fresh, to decorate together, to sort
out who will do what chores and who gets what room. If it works well, the
major project of creating a new space together can be a uniting transition
for a new family.

When a parent remarries, children often have a new school to adjust to.
And a newly married parent may ask the other parent for a schedule
change in time with the child, prompting anxiety in the other household.

A stepparent may be sharing a home with children for the first time in
his adult life. Even people who have been around children their whole life,
such as teachers, find living with someone else's child a completely different challenge.

The parent who is used to the single-parent life will have to adjust to
another adult not only watching how she does things, but likely wanting
some changes in the way things are run around the house.

It is a lot for everyone to take on. So as tempting as it may be to entirely
redecorate the house, to wipe the slate clean and start over, try to take it
slowly. We are creatures of habit and our habits are our comforts. If we
have to change them, it is hard and it takes time.

Playing cards every night might not seem like much, but it is these little moments that make up any good relationship between a parent and a

child. Stepparents will help everyone if they try to honor those moments between a parent and a child. And parents will help everyone if they try to remember that stepparents often feel like an outsider in their own homes.

Celebrations tend to raise some of the strongest feelings about customs. Rituals and traditions take on an almost holy status around holidays and birthdays. As with most things in stepfamilies, figuring out how to concoct the right mix of old and new takes a while. And since holidays only come once a year, it may take years for everyone to feel as if the stepfamily has its own way of doing things. Talking and listening to each other will help everyone understand what rituals are important, which should go, and what new things the family wants to make its own.

Find out what is realistic to expect

It is important to watch out for some common, but unrealistic, expectations. Stepparents are often expected to jump right into the existing framework of a family and be happy. This expectation can come from the parent, the stepchild, the parent in the other household, and even from the stepparents themselves. But stepparents have needs too, and they won't be able to simply walk into a family's life and have no needs of their own.

Another unrealistic expectation is that everything has to change. Stepparents can't expect that people who have always lived their lives a certain way are going to be happy to throw out comfortable old ideas and habits.

Children, especially, are comforted by consistency. Coming home from a weekend at their other parent's home to find their bedroom completely redone would be a very rude and unwelcome shock, not a delightful surprise.

Do your best to make sure your family doesn't fall prey to these unrealistic expectations by learning more. You're not the first family to walk in these treacherous woods. If your stepson's filthy bedroom is making your head hurt, find some good books about what you can realistically expect from someone his age. If your husband seems to think that the only problem in the house is your problem, then encourage him to read books like this one, go to a stepfamily couple's group, or listen to a tape from the Stepfamily Association of America. (See Resources Section) If you worry that you won't have time for both your new wife and your children, talk to some people at stepdad support sites on the Web. Even if no one else in your family is interested in learning more about this stuff, do it for yourself. These are hard situations, and most of these kinds of families just don't make it without some kind of support.

EXTERNAL CULTURAL CONFLICT

IN ALL LIKELIHOOD, you are going to have disagreements with the other household about how your child should be raised. Some of the disagreements will be huge systemic differences of belief, such as religious values. Others will be smaller, more practical matters, such as whether your ex should stop for ice cream on the way back to your house right before dinnertime. Often, since there is already a warehouse full of bad feelings on both sides, what kind of music a child listens to or how often she needs to bathe end up being major points of contention.

What's worth fighting about?

If you want to work with the other household, and have peace and happiness not only for yourself, but for your children, the question becomes what can you let go?

In your house, your children can eat whatever they want when they are hungry. When they go to your ex's, his new wife has an allotment of snacks that the children can eat only at snack times. Or your daughter comes back from your ex-wife's house after three days without a bath and in your house, she bathes every night. In your house, the children can't watch TV until after dinner and homework are done, in your ex's, the TV is on from the moment they get home from school.

These are the kinds of cultural, household-specific things that can drive you nuts. They are also the kinds of things that you just have to accept if you are going to parent your child well, much less keep your sanity.

If you make "let it go" a permanent part of your vocabulary and start to see that your children can handle these differences, and often even grow from these differences, you will be one big step closer to making things easier—not just for the children involved, but also for the other household, and ultimately, for yourself.

I am talking about the kinds of things that are not really going to hurt a kid. They are things that you would do differently, things that you may want your child to do differently, but which are not going to harm the child. Sure, you can get yourself all worked up about whether your child will learn proper hygiene if she has a parent who does not bathe her for three days. But the fact is, it's not going to harm the child not to bathe for three days.

On the other hand, if you decide that you are going to point out to the child every time she comes home that she has not had a bath, you are likely to harm her.

You don't even have to say something rude or outwardly criticizing. You could simply state, "Oh, you've been gone for three days, have you had a bath?"

Kids are smart. This girl knows you disapprove of the fact that her other parent didn't make her bathe. She may start to feel dirty and embarrassed to come to your house. She will almost undoubtedly feel defensive of her other household, and she may begin to resent your implication that her other parent isn't doing a good job.

I know your intention is to instill in her the value that you have of keeping clean, thereby promoting a feeling of high self-esteem, of well-being. But that is not what she's getting. Instead, she feels icky and stuck between two adults who do things differently.

Ultimately, the child will grow up and choose whether she is going to bathe every day or not. In the meantime, she is learning that there is more than one way to live a life, more than one way to run a house, more than one way to think about things. Not a bad lesson in itself.

Separate the big things from the little things

Of course, we can't always just let it go. There are some things that aren't as innocuous as whether or not your child gets to have Twinkies at the other house. The point is that you have to separate out the big things from the little things and that is often hard to do. You really have to ask yourself if the disagreement is worth the cost of rocking the boat, both with the child and with the other household.

And there are some situations that are worth it. Some things are just too serious and you cannot let them continue without trying to do something about it.

When my stepson was five years old, his mother decided to become a Lubavitch Hassidic Jew. She hadn't been raised a Jew and until this point had led a wholly secular life, but she and her new husband became a part of this very traditional, very strict community. She decided that my stepson would wear a yarmulke and a tzitzis (the fringed shawl); he would wear the long side curls and he would observe the Jewish laws.

We could handle this, we thought, although it was probably tough for the child. He was put in a kindergarten where all the children grew up together, all knew Hebrew. He was the outsider. One time when he made Christmas cookies and brought some to his mom, she told him that they weren't kosher and she threw them away. Frequently, he would run into our house, whip off his yarmulke, and say, "Dad, can I have some bacon?"

And we would sit down for a very non-kosher meal of eggs, hash browns, and bacon. I am sure that we drove my husband's ex crazy. But we were as respectful as we could be, not believing in the same thing she did. Then she decided that my stepson would be circumcised at five years old. Ouch. We didn't believe that the procedure was in his best interest, so we got a court order to prevent it. We figured that if he wanted to do that when he was older, he could make that decision himself.

My husband and I had been very uncomfortable with the changes that my stepson's mother was forcing on him, but we really didn't have any say about what she did in her home. But when it came to something that we felt would damage his health and well-being, we had to try to stop it.

I say try, because, ultimately, you have to remember that you can't control what goes on in someone else's home.

When it comes to situations in which the child's actual well-being is at stake, as we believed it was in the above situation, you need to act in your child's best interest.

Obviously, when it comes to physically or sexually abusive kinds of situations, you need immediate and swift intervention through the legal system. But for the most part, I'm not talking about these kinds of things.

I'm talking about things like how your ex does not generally seem interested in your child's soccer games. For two years she has not shown up to games and you have to go to your ex's house to get your daughter for practices, because your ex will not bring her.

This is a good example because this might annoy you on many, many levels. You might think, why isn't a parent interested in her own child's activities? Why do I have to do all the work to have my daughter play soccer? My daughter is really hurt by her mom's seeming lack of interest.

You may have a whole list of complaints about the situation. And it may be that in the end, you will not be able to change it.

But in any case, you have decided that you need to try. What do you do?

It might be tempting to call her up and tell her that she's just a slouch and a bad parent. Or to remind her that she's personally flawed when it comes to taking care of people and that is why you are not married to her anymore.

Yeah, that might feel good. For about three seconds. Then she will start to tell you all your faults and you will get right back into the same arguments you have always had. The issue that you called about will be lost. That is one way to guarantee that nothing will change.

Regulate your emotions

There is a far better strategy. If your relationship is rocky, any criticism is not going to be warmly received. And it is really not your place anymore to criticize your ex. She doesn't answer to you; she doesn't owe you anything. That is what it means to be divorced. A parent needs to answer to her child, not you. If she does harmful things to that relationship, she will have to answer to the child for them.

So, if you have decided to talk to the other household about something you would like to see happen differently, it helps to come with a humble attitude, and not a blaming and expectant attitude. You simply don't have the right to make demands on your ex anymore. The best thing you can do is to try to respect that the ex's household is its own entity and that whether you like what happens there or not, it is really not up to you.

In the soccer situation, you can respectfully give your opinion about what it means for your child if her mother doesn't show up to the games. You can point out the hardships that it causes for your household to have to do all the transportation and arrangements. You can ask for things to change. And then it's up to the other household to decide what to do.

I find that the more room people are given to make choices about their lives, especially given good information mixed with a dose of generosity, the more likely they are to respond in a cooperative way. ("Your daughter is hurt by what she sees as your lack of interest in her soccer games. It's difficult for me to always get her to soccer immediately after school on Thursdays. I wonder if there's some way to make you more comfortable participating in this aspect of her life?")

But even the most respectful and thoughtful approach doesn't guarantee that your ex will change what you want her to change. Accepting difficult situations that you can't control, especially when you feel like the situation negatively affects your child, is one of the most difficult things about living in a stepfamily.

A different kind of parenting

It is crucial to consider how you talk to your children about these difficult situations between the homes. Children are constantly looking to their parents for cues about how to respond to a situation. Even teenagers. It is one of our biggest roles as parents, to expose our children to our way of living in the world and to differentiate for them what we think is important. That is how our culture survives. That is how our families become who they are. But in stepfamilies, the whole thing gets very complicated.

If one of your main jobs as a parent is to frame the world for your child, then what do you do when the child's other parent lets them down or does something that you feel is dead wrong?

Instinct and habit may tell you to point out the fault and tell your child it is wrong. If a teacher told your daughter that she would meet her after school to go over some math and the teacher didn't show up and the next day said, "Oh, well, I had something else to do," you would likely tell your daughter that the teacher should have been there or at least apologized.

But when the person doing something you dislike, or something that is clearly wrong, is the other parent, your job as a parent shifts. You have to learn how to differentiate between supporting your child and venting your displeasure with her other parent on her.

If her dad cancels a camping trip the night before they were supposed to go, most of us would feel very angry for the child and worried that the child will feel rejected. But it will not help the child to start pointing out how wrong it was for her dad to do that to her. She already knows that. She'll have to sort that out with her dad. You can be there if she wants to talk about feeling hurt or disappointed. And usually, the only way your child will come to you with those kinds of feelings is if she feels like you will be sympathetic without making the other parent into the bad guy. What is helpful for the child is to support her by acknowledging her disappointment. "Gosh, I'm sorry that happened. That must be disappointing."

What isn't helpful is pointing out the fault of the other parent.

"Wow, I can't believe Dad did this. It is wrong to cancel at the last minute."

The important thing is to allow your child to feel what she is feeling without imposing your own feelings on the situation. Your child doesn't need to hear about how you are feeling. That is something you can talk about with your spouse, your friends, or other adults.

When my stepson was about six years old, he was scheduled to see his mother and she called at the last minute to cancel. She was having a lot of trouble in those days and often didn't keep her time with him. I remember him getting on the phone with her, crying and begging her to see her for just ten minutes. It was a truly pathetic sight and I felt so hurt for him.

And I was furious with his mother for treating him so shabbily. I wanted to encourage him to let him know it was perfectly understandable to be upset with her. He was saying over and over that he wanted to see her and in the background of his angst, I almost shouted at him, "Go ahead. Tell her that, tell her."

But my own anger at her just made him defensive for her. Of course. He loves his mom and he just needed someone to help him through his disappointment. I felt it was very wrong for a parent to blow off her child, but he already knew that, and he didn't need to hear my anger about it. At such an emotional and difficult point, it was not a time to teach responses to problem behavior. It was a time to listen and love. I should have just held him and let him cry, telling him I was sorry he was so disappointed. But at the time, I couldn't look past my conflicting values with his mother to simply comfort him.

We want our children to have our values. And they will, if they choose them. But they don't always, even if they live only with their biological parents. We win some, we lose some. The fact is that children are influenced by all kinds of things in their lives, including both parents or sets of parents, like it or not.

Children are master adapters (if the grown-ups help)

The most important thing to remember about this whole issue is this: Children are amazingly adaptable. They can adjust to a new adult in their home, take on new siblings, navigate between two homes, and still be fully functional, well-adjusted, interesting, and kind children. But it doesn't just happen effortlessly. It takes the adults' help.

How you respond to the other household plays a huge role in how well your children manage the differences between the two. Your children will likely be able to navigate two households with ease if they don't feel that they have to defend one to the other.

Your children will have their own thoughts and opinions about what they like and dislike about each household. And there may be times when things in the other household will be very difficult to stomach.

But if you think your ex is a terrible parent, be careful with those thoughts. When you are so certain about what you think of the other parent, you may begin to believe that your child feels the same way. Do not fall into this very poisonous trap. The fact, almost certainly, is that your child loves you both. Even if mom is a drunkard. Or dad is a slouch. So any critical discussion about the other parent is hurtful.

And children can figure out different rules and different belief systems if the adults present the differences constructively. In schools, different teachers have different rules and the children manage just fine. It's the same thing for two different homes. When I talk to children, they are quick to point out the differences in their two homes. ("At my mom's house we only eat healthy cereal like granola, but at my dad's house we have a bunch of different cereals, like Captain Crunch and Count Chocula.") When their parents can describe these differences neutrally and uncritically, the children adjust to differences.

You might say, "Well, Mom does have different cereals, doesn't she? That's one of the ways our homes are different, isn't it?"

Think of your children as multicultural. They can move deftly between cultures. Have you ever seen a teenager talking to his friends, "Yo, man, waz up?" and then turning and talking to a respected adult? "How are you today, Mrs. Zenith?" They are pros. They can handle all kinds of changes and differences between the households when both of their households remain respectful of each other and don't criticize each other.

The challenge for adults is to figure out how to talk to their children about their two households as if they are two cultures, without judgment or criticism.

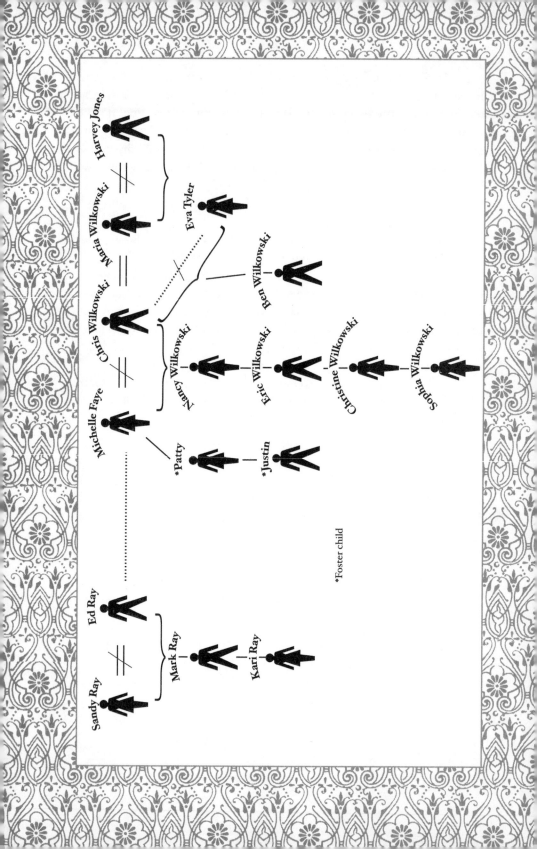

Sandy Ray ≠ Ed Ray

Mark Ray

Kari Ray

Michelle Faye ≠ Chris Wilkowski. = Maria Wilkowski. ≠ Harvey Jones

Eva Tyler

*Patty

*Justin

Nancy Wilkowski.

Ben Wilkowski.

Eric Wilkowski.

Christine Wilkowski.

Sophia Wilkowski.

*Foster child

6

THE WILKOWSKI/FAYE/RAY FAMILY SYSTEM OF NORTHERN WASHINGTON STATE

❦

CHILDREN/STEPCHILDREN:

Nancy Wilkowski, the sixteen-year-old daughter of Michelle and Chris, primarily lives with her mom, and stays with her dad and stepmother a couple times a month.

Eric Wilkowski, the fifteen-year-old son of Michelle and Chris, primarily lives with his mom, and stays with his dad and stepmother a couple times a month.

Christine Wilkowski, the fourteen-year-old daughter of Michelle and Chris, primarily lives with her mom, and stays with her dad and stepmother a couple times a month.

Sophia Wilkowski, the twelve-year-old daughter of Michelle and Chris, primarily lives with her mom, and stays with her dad and stepmother a couple times a month.

Ben Wilkowski, the eleven-year-old son of Chris and Eva, primarily lives with his mom, and stays with his dad and stepmother a couple times a month.

Mark Ray, the twelve-year-old son of Sandy and Ed, primarily lives with his mom, sees his dad several days a week.

Kari Ray, the ten-year-old daughter of Sandy and Ed, primarily lives with her mom, sees her dad several day a week.

DADS:

Chris Wilkowski was married to Michelle for ten years and had four children. Chris had an affair with Eva, had one child (Ben), divorced Michelle, and married Maria.

> Ed Ray divorced Sandy because he was having an affair with Michelle. Ed hasn't remarried, but is still in a relationship with Michelle.
>
> **MOMS:**
>
> Michelle Faye divorced Chris after learning of his affair with Eva, then had her own affair with Ed and has continued to see him in the seven years since his divorce.
>
> Sandy Ray divorced Ed after learning of his affair with Michelle and hasn't remarried.
>
> **STEPMOM:** Maria Wilkowski is stepmom to Chris's five children for past seven years.
>
> This family struggles with establishing clear boundaries between the two main households. Although the fights have lessened in degree and number, this is still a high-conflict family system.

*C*HRIS WILKOWSKI THOUGHT his affair was behind him, although he knew that the woman had gotten pregnant and had a baby. So he wasn't prepared for how his life would change the day a deputy showed up at his doorstep to serve him paternity papers.

Chris read the affidavit and looked at his wife, Michelle, sitting at the kitchen table, drinking her coffee. How would he explain this to her? How would he explain to their four children that they had a little brother? Explaining the situation to his wife was the hardest thing he'd ever done. But it was only a taste of challenges ahead.

Shortly after Chris told Michelle about the affair and the little boy, they decided to get divorced. Chris didn't want to continue his relationship with Eva, the other woman, but he did begin to see his son, who was already three years old.

Between juggling that relationship and having his four children on the weekends, Chris met Maria, who would become his second wife and stepmother to his five children. Chris figured that somehow his new family arrangement would work out all right.

"Quite frankly, I didn't really know what was going to happen between Maria and the kids," Chris said. "I've always been one of these guys — I'm a fixer. I want everybody to get along. My hope was they would fall in love with Maria, and Michelle would be cool with it, and we'd all live happily ever after, and we'd all ride off into the sunset together or something. Oh, yeah, right. It didn't even come close to that."

Instead, he and his second wife fought about his first wife and about his children. He and his ex fought about the children and about his second wife. The children fought with their parents and even more bitterly with their stepmother.

The journey isn't over. But they've learned to tolerate things in each other that even a couple of years ago would have caused major upsets and screaming matches. After seven years, their lives have calmed considerably, but Chris still sometimes marvels that he and everyone in his family made it through.

"I'm really surprised I didn't end up in an insane asylum or with ulcers 24/7. I'm telling you, the fights between me and Michelle, and Michelle and Maria, and Maria and I, and me and Maria and Michelle. Phew. There were so many times I thought 'This is so not worth it. I'm done.' And Maria said, 'No, because if you don't go through it with me, you'll have to go through it with someone else.' She had the insight."

CHRIS AND MICHELLE — A TEN-YEAR-FIGHTING-UP-AND-DOWN-EVERY-DAY MARRIAGE

BACK IN 1985 when the couple married, they never could have imagined the complex story that has become their lives. At twenty-two and nineteen years old respectively, Chris and Michelle were young—just babies, they both say now. They married when they got pregnant with Nancy, their oldest daughter. Their marriage was one of high passion—lots of screaming, blaming, unhappiness. They fought about money, because there never was any. They fought about the work of caring for the children and the house, because there was always so much of it. They fought about the long hours that Chris worked as a cop and a fireman. And when they were done fighting, they had lots of great passionate sex.

Chris and Michelle both grew up in northwestern Washington, not far from the beautiful craggy shoreline of the Pacific. They lived paycheck-to-paycheck in small towns out in the country, driving old beaters, scraping by with hand-me-down furniture and clothes.

But it wasn't so bad. They had their family. They had lots of friends and threw many parties. There were always children around and their family created their own way of stuffing Christmas stockings, their own way of talking to each other, their own memories. But as time went on, it became more and more difficult for Michelle and Chris to do anything but fight.

When Chris dropped the bomb about his affair, he and Michelle decided that their divorce was probably long overdue. Chris moved out in June of 1994. The children were eight, seven, almost six, and four; the surprise addition was a month shy of his third birthday.

Weekend visits got cramped with four or five kids jammed into his one-bedroom shoebox apartment. But Chris was nearby and could see them a lot. He also saw a lot of Michelle and for a while he still hoped that his marriage could be salvaged. Until he walked in on Michelle kissing his best friend. That's when he knew that his marriage was really over.

A double betrayal

For Michelle, the marriage was over even before Chris had moved out. Their conversations centered mostly on who didn't do what around the house. She didn't feel connected to him in any loving way; she just resented having him around taking up couch space.

When Michelle began acting in community theater, it opened up a whole new world for her. Not only did she find more to life than her marriage and family, she found Ed. She and Ed worked on several productions together and their families became friends. Ed and his wife Sandy had two young children and the families started spending lots of time together. Michelle cared for their children while Sandy and Ed worked. The families celebrated birthdays together, had barbeques at each other's houses. Their children played together. They considered each other close friends. When Michelle and Chris broke up, Ed and Sandy were there to help with the children, and to provide a shoulder for support.

But Ed and Michelle were secretly building more than a friendship. They sought each other out as a refuge from their troubled marriages. In each other, they discovered themselves differently. Sandy scoffed at Ed's interest in the theater. Michelle was not only respectful of his interest and skill, but impressed by it. Ed talked to Michelle about ideas, about things that mattered. And for Michelle, she finally felt like *she* mattered.

But all their feelings weren't good or easy. With one decision, Michelle and Ed betrayed their spouses and their friends. Michelle knew that she hurt Sandy, but in her mind, Ed and Sandy's marriage was over; she didn't feel like it was her relationship with Ed alone that caused its demise, in the same way that she knew that Chris's affair wasn't the only reason that her own marriage failed. She thought that Sandy didn't want to face the fact that her marriage was going to fail with or without Michelle's influence.

In any case, Michelle had a lot of things besides Sandy to think about. If Michelle's marriage to Chris had been stormy, it was tame compared to the kinds of fights and disagreements the divorced couple had after Chris began dating and then married Maria.

Michelle suddenly had to send her children over to the home of this woman who seemed unyielding in her quest to rearrange Michelle's entire way of parenting with her ex-husband. The woman exhausted Michelle, who thought Maria didn't understand the first thing about children or the way that families work.

Michelle was fiercely defensive of her position as the mother to their children and as Chris's primary responsibility. It took her a long time to sort out that Chris's emotional responsibility to her had vanished with the marriage.

SANDY AND ED

ED AND SANDY used to live in a house in town, with a big yard and friends all around. They did a lot as a family, considering that both Ed and Sandy worked full-time jobs.

So when—during Sandy's pregnancy with their second child—Ed started pursuing the theater, it was a point of conflict. Sandy thought Ed was spending too much time away from the family. Ed thought Sandy was unsupportive and hypercritical. But a bigger issue soon divided them. When Sandy started receiving calls from friends asking about the relationship between Ed and Michelle, she had to face some facts. After a long time of believing that Michelle and Ed were just friends, Sandy finally realized that Ed was having an affair. Sandy made it clear: Ed had to make a choice between his family and his girlfriend.

In a decision he's regretted every day since, Ed chose to leave. When he was married, he and Sandy did family things—played games, went on trips, hung out with other families, went fishing and camping. Ed misses that life. He hasn't found anything to satisfactorily replace it.

MICHELLE'S LIFE NOW

ED DOES STILL see Michelle, but he is conflicted about their relationship. So, for the most part, Michelle makes do on her own. She now lives about two hours north of Seattle. A few miles down a rolling country road, a row of trees marks the farm where Michelle, her four children, and her two foster children live. The dog that primarily lives outside barks his warning when a stranger removes the chain from the gate to drive in.

The driveway is a dirt path that quickly turns to mud in the rain. The family's garbage is piled up in plastic bags next to the dog pen, waiting to be taken to the dump. A child-sized picnic table sits near the long, single-story home. Bushes hang heavy with untrimmed branches; the back porch is covered in leaves and toys, not yet cleared from winter and ready for the summer use. Overgrown grass and the worn-out siding show the signs of a house that needs more attention than the single mother of six is able to give it. Life on the farm held great promise for the girls — they each have a horse in the barn and they tend to the chickens and sheep that another renter on the property raises. But the work is more than any of them counted on. The manure quickly piles up in the horse stalls; chickens break loose and have to be courted back to their pen. And there's the task of organizing and accommodating seven people in one house. Plus, each of the four older children in the house has a cat; and there's the inside dog.

Inside, a woodstove sits in the living room, sharing the space with a worn couch and a couple of big leather chairs that duct tape helps hold together. The TV sits along a wall and all the furniture faces it. The TV is often on and it's here that the family eats dinners of Hamburger Helper and canned plums.

The living room is the main gathering place in the house. There's usually one child or another playing on the carpeted floor, sometimes with one of the cats that sneak in through the constantly swinging back screen door. There's a buzz of activity most of the time; it's the kind of intense home that can overwhelm people without children.

The four older children are still adjusting to having the two younger foster children in their home. The older ones, especially Nancy, are frequently in charge of the youngsters. They impose time-outs, offer advice on how to be gentler, on how to get along. Nancy has told her mother that the introduction of these two small children in their home is the best form of birth control for her. Still, even if Patty and Justin can be trying, the older children are the first to support Michelle's occasional talk about adopting them.

Rules are a big deal in Michelle's house—everyone seems to know what they are and points them out to each other frequently. Sometimes, it seems that Michelle is the head boss and the older children are her managers. Michelle, her cup of coffee constantly in hand, listens patiently as one child explains another's infractions and the resulting consequences. Michelle is the final arbiter—she discusses the rules with the child and decides when the time-out is over. Each of the six likes to be alone at times. Eric, a video-game pro, logs hours on Zelda Majora's Mask. Sophia retreats to her room sometimes. But most of the time, the children move as a group, as a force. The older children don't hesitate to run out in the yard and play ball with the younger children when they're asked. They eat together, they argue together, they play together, and they talk together.

The activity of so many people makes Michelle's house feel chaotic, but also warm and welcoming. Here, life is casual and no one is too picky. Napkins from the pizza shop double as toilet paper. People cozy up with their dinner plates around the TV. The phone might not be working because the bill didn't get paid, but they figure it out.

There are photographs of the family, of the kids, everywhere—stacked in albums, framed in the hallway, pinned to the door, lying on the table. Craft projects and artwork from ten years and four children's art classes share the wall space and sit on the end tables.

Since the divorce, Michelle and the children have lived in four different places. She's hoping to keep the farm, but the rent just doubled and she's thinking she may have to come up with another plan.

Michelle considers Ed her boyfriend, but they don't live together and Michelle is mostly a single mom. She doesn't get much of a break from the children these days; Chris and Maria are taking them less and less.

Working four days a week and taking care of six children, Michelle doesn't spend much time contemplating her life. She just keeps moving, loving her children, and doing what she can for them and for herself.

. . .

CHRIS AND MARIA'S HOUSE

ABOUT AN HOUR and a half north of Michelle's, Chris and Maria live in a small city in Washington's tulip country. Their house is spotless. They consider it their hypoallergenic haven.

Maria recently discovered that she has asthma, and that's partly the reason. But her house has always been this way. The real reason is that Maria likes things clean and orderly. She recognizes her obsession with cleanliness and organization, particularly around financial issues.

This is, of course, both Maria and Chris's home, but they readily admit that it's really Maria who decides what happens and how things will be in their home. And in their home, order rules. Maria would never run out of toilet paper.

The yard is practical, low maintenance with rock gravel instead of grass. Their single-story home is neat and well cared for. The vehicles in the driveway are shiny and clean. The whole place has the feel of people who don't have children. They both consider their house a quiet shelter from the stresses of their lives.

Inside, the kitchen is spotless, the counters cleared of papers and clutter. Maria meticulously maintains the pantry—there are shelves of food that Chris is free to help himself to and shelves of food he has to save for certain meals. Chris and Maria have a machine that makes their own soda. It's cheaper.

In the living room, the striped couch matches the striped chair. A watercolor print hangs on one wall; the entertainment center includes a stack of videos that the couple watches curled up on their rare nights when Chris isn't working. The carpet is neutral, and the furnishings sparse. Chris and Maria's wedding picture sits on a bookshelf.

The five children have a single room that they share at Chris and Maria's house, although there's nothing in the room to identify it as the children's room. Maria remembers that their mother was upset because Maria wouldn't allow the kids to have their room their way.

"And I'm thinking, 'Chris, you and I use the room the majority of the time and they have rooms that they decorate at their mom's house and I don't like the way they decorate,'" Maria said. "Chris goes, 'It's your house, do what you want.' Michelle just got mad. She said, 'It's the kids' home, too, they should be allowed to do whatever they want.' I'm like, 'OK, it's their home but it's *my* house. I pay the mortgage. I pay the utility bills. When they're paying that, they can tell me what they want.'

"I did some compromising. I got a big bulletin board but then all we heard were fights. 'Well, I want to decorate.' 'I want this on there.' 'I don't want that on there.' 'I want . . .' And finally I took it down. I'm like, 'Unbelievable. It's coming out. We're going to do it Maria's way.'"

"I don't think the kids really care what's on the walls when they're with us. They're not there to see the walls, they're there to spend time with Dad."

ONE FOOT IN FRONT OF THE OTHER

EACH PERSON IN this family system has been through messy, painful, and difficult times in the past seven years. But somehow, Chris's hope that it would all work out is starting to come true for him. The children are growing up, the households are working together, the mom and the stepmom are able to be civil, even friendly to each other. Chris feels like his life is finally working.

Not everyone in this family system feels as good as Chris does about the way things are. The kids miss their dad. Michelle still feels that she does most of the raising of their kids. But everyone agrees that things are better now than in those turbulent early years of forming their stepfamily.

MICHELLE FAYE

MICHELLE FAYE WAS nineteen years old when she got pregnant with her first baby. She and Chris had dated in high school and reconnected when he returned from the service. They were young, they were in love and then, they were pregnant.

Michelle remembers good things about those difficult days of having babies. She's still very grateful that she was able to stay home with them when they were little—something Chris's long hours provided. And she feels that there's a connection between her and Chris. Even if they aren't married and sometimes want to strangle each other, there's enough that they have lived through together that she still feels a bond with him.

"We grew up together," she said.

Michelle spends most days and nights raising the children alone. She's easy and patient with the different demands that six children place on her. She's a snuggly kind of mom. Her twelve-year-old daughter Sophia curls up next to her on the couch to eat her cookies. She tells her children frequently that she loves them and she talks to them as if they matter. But it's a lot of work to raise six children alone and she gets tired and cranky, too.

Chris and Maria are supposed to have the children two weekends a month, but more and more that just doesn't happen. Michelle feels that Chris—under Maria's influence—has all but backed out of the children' lives.

There are a lot of the same difficulties for Michelle that there were when Michelle and Chris were married. The house is still owned by someone else and is still far from spotless. The bills are still past due and the furniture is still old and tired. Stress is still a powerful force in the family, but now it feels like it's just Michelle's family. Chris disparages the struggles he once shared with her. Now, Chris has money, cars, his own house. He has great contempt for the way Michelle lives, the way she raises their children. She thinks it's terribly unfair. Michelle points out that Chris and Maria have a two-income household, and most of the time, they don't have children around. So they have a lot more money and a lot more time to do what needs to be done.

But whatever tensions there are between the homes, Michelle has come a long, long way from the days when she couldn't even stand the thought of Maria in her children's lives. There was a lot to sort out when Maria hooked up with Chris. Early on, an incident set the tone of the relationship for years. Everyone in the family remembers the infamous dirty handprint. The children were at Maria and Chris's house and one of the children left a dirty hand mark on the wall.

"And I said, 'Jesus, Maria, if they touched the walls . . .' and I picked up a sponge and she just freaked because it was a *dish* sponge and I wasn't supposed to use a dish sponge on the wall. You can only use wall sponges on the walls, I guess.

"If the wall is dirty, you wash it. Better yet, give them the sponge and have them wash it," Michelle said. "Then it's clean. End of story. You don't need to scream at them about it for twenty minutes because they touched a wall. But that's my belief, that's not her belief. She was raised in an entirely different background. You had furniture you sat on and furniture you didn't and you never ate in the living room. She's a whole lot like my mother-in-law and I never got along with her at all."

Michelle said she's had to adjust to Maria's ways even though neither of them chose each other to be attached to for the rest of their lives. Their common link is Chris. But Michelle said she never would have picked Maria for a friend, much less another parent for her children. Still, she's gotten to the point where she can see some advantages.

Michelle knows, too, that her children see the differences in the two women. One night, Nancy, her oldest daughter, ran out of the medication she takes for her epilepsy. Michelle was supposed to get more, but she forgot. Nancy was upset and as she stormed out the door she yelled back to her mother, "I'll learn how to be a nice person from you, but I guess I'll learn my responsibility from Maria."

"Personally, I'd rather be nice than responsible," Michelle said. "But that's my personality. If she can learn both, that would be great. Responsible and nice. We've got a good package here."

The differences between the two women used to grate on both of them. Michelle is always late, Maria is always on time, Michelle isn't good at managing money, Maria manages people's money for a living. Michelle is laid back, and Maria is stressed out. Michelle is hopelessly disorganized, Maria is amazingly efficient.

"We have this complicated schedule and Maria always gives me a copy of it on the first of the year, which I always lose by January 15th," Michelle said. "She gives me another one in February."

But the things that once made her scream don't bother her nearly as much.

"We've all calmed down," Michelle said. "There's a lot less threat. When you first get divorced you feel like this person's going to take over. Moms have lots of kids and that's OK, each kid knows you love them. But each kid isn't supposed to have lots of moms, because they might not love you as much. It's backwards. And if they have another mom they might find out that I'm doing things wrong, or that I really don't know what I'm doing, that I'm faking it. That's a hard thing to share. And you'd never admit that when you first get divorced. But that's what you're feeling. This person has moved in with your husband and is sleeping with your husband is living with your husband and now, she's taking your kids, too. And he likes her more than he likes you. Even if you left him, he's still with her. And what if he takes the kids too and I'm all here by myself?"

"There's all this rivalry in the beginning. And then, you all settle into roles and you realize that it's not so bad if they like their stepmom," Michelle said. "And sometimes they don't like their stepmom. They argue with her, too. They don't like her, too. They don't listen to her all the time, either."

The other side of the family

Michelle has had plenty to sort out in her relationship with her boyfriend and his whole side of the family as well. From the beginning, her relationship with Ed wasn't easy, but it gave Michelle something she was missing. Michelle went right from high school into her life as a wife and mother; she didn't go back to school until recently, when the children were older. When she began acting again, it was something completely different from her role in the home. It was exhilarating; it was hers.

Michelle watched Ed with his family, with his wife, and she wanted that kind of attention for herself. He was a warm, inviting contrast to her life with Chris, which was rapidly deteriorating. Then Chris was served the paternity suit.

Ed looked better and better. But Ed was married and started pushing his wife to go to counseling. They went, but he couldn't get past her critical remarks and she couldn't get past his work in the theater and in the end, they didn't work out their differences. Michelle knows Sandy blames her for the collapse of their marriage.

"In her eyes, if I hadn't been in the picture he would have come around and done what she wanted him to do," Michelle said. "Ed and I had started talking more and talking about the fact that not being miserable wasn't the only thing, there was such a thing as being happy. We needed to be happy in life."

They flirted, they kissed. The attraction was strong but they tried to do what was right. When Michelle divorced Chris, she dated a couple other people, but her heart was really with Ed. She'd cut it off with one man because she'd think, "I really love Ed." But then she'd tell herself she was crazy, waiting for a married man, and she'd try to get on with her life. When he separated from his wife and filed for divorce, she was thrilled. Finally, she thought, they could have a chance. She had it all figured out.

"I'm seeing that I'm divorced, he's getting divorced, we're going to have the Brady Bunch," Michelle said. "We're going to get married and we're going to have these kids and that's what's going to happen."

But pretty quickly, Michelle saw that she and Ed had vastly different ideas about what their future together looked like. At the last minute, when signing the divorce decree, Ed agreed to a clause that would change everything. Sandy wanted to keep Michelle away from her children and she requested an agreement not to expose their two children to any dating relationship for two years after the divorce. Ed signed it. Michelle had cared for the children while Ed and Sandy worked, she was close to them and her children were close to them, too. But then she was cut off. She was furious that Ed had agreed to Sandy's request, furious that she was being kept away from the children. She basically considered the whole situation Sandy's declaration of war.

For a solid year, the two women raged at each other. Looking back, Michelle can see that she behaved badly. But at the time, she felt as if she was on the defensive. She'd come home and her children, who arrived before her, had listened to the answering machine spew curses and names about their mother from their "aunt" Sandy. If Sandy saw Ed's car at Michelle's house, she'd call and scream. Sandy had her children call and ask their dad where he spent the night. One time, Sandy came to a school performance that her own children weren't in and sat right behind Michelle, Chris, and Maria and talked loudly about sluts and whores breaking up people's marriages. This is a rural area, a small town where everyone knows everyone, and Michelle felt that Sandy was doing her best to make sure she suffered.

Michelle screamed back, told her to stop calling, put traces on the calls, and hung up on her. And then she lost a part in a play that Ed was directing because Sandy told Ed that he'd better not cast Michelle or there'd be hell to pay. This was just going too far. In response, Michelle did something she still wishes she could undo. She took the key to Sandy's house, the one she was entrusted with in more amicable days as a babysitter, and went in to Sandy's bedroom. She brought her perfume, the one that she knew Sandy hated, and sprayed it all over Sandy's clothing. It was a clear message, a distinct violation.

Michelle tells the story under the cover of night. I can't see her face, but I can hear her embarrassment, her shame. "It was the worst thing I ever did in my life," she said. "I regret it. That's the crazy stuff, the stuff you say, 'Oh my God, how could I have ever done something so stupid?' I'm a rational person. I'm a sane person. I'm a good person. I don't do these kinds of things," Michelle said. "I was so livid at this woman who controlled our lives so much. I guess I deserved some of it because I was with her husband. But I saw it as 'their marriage was over; they were moving on,' why can't she just let it go? I didn't see it as my fault."

There are other issues that Ed and Michelle continue to try to sort out. A huge one was Ed's allegiance to his first family. It blew up over Ed saying that he was spending the night at Sandy's house on Christmas Eve.

"That was really hard the first few years that happened," Michelle said. "Ed and I had some hellacious arguments about that very issue. 'You're going to spend the night with your ex-wife? WHAT?' and he'd say, 'But I'm sleeping on the bottom bunk of Mark's bed. It's their holiday. They're little, they need me there.' And that made sense, but it still hurt. It was still real hard. 'I want to spend holidays with you, I want to be with you, I want to have our family here.' With Ed's kids, Mark and Kari, I never wanted to take them away from their mom, but I wanted to have that every other year thing at least. I wanted to bring them over and have them here and have them know that Santa Claus came to Dad's house, too."

It wasn't easy; it still isn't. When Ed goes off on a vacation with the children AND his ex-wife, it takes strength and lots of deep breaths to be able to say to herself, "Well, it is best for the kids." She finds herself asking the same question over and over again. "What would I want Maria to do?"

The fact is that she doesn't have any choice. If she wants to see Ed, she has to live with his decisions. He's made it clear that his priorities are with his children and with his first family, not with her. They see each other when they can. He comes by late at night after work a couple times a week. But he lives forty-five minutes away and sometimes he just doesn't want to make the drive. He brings the children over sometimes, but he also reserves some time that he can spend with his two children alone.

Michelle accepts all of this most of the time. And then she gets angry and wants to know where they're going, what are they doing together? What is she doing here? She lives with a certain amount of anxiety about her life.

"What if his kids hate me, what if their mom tells them horrible things about me, what if they make their dad choose between me and them? Well, their dad's going to choose them and then I'm out. And if Ed and I don't make it, I lose his kids and him. That's scary.

"And what if Ed just decides this isn't working and he can't be away from his kids and he decides to go back to her someday? There's all that threat. They could work it out; they could end up getting back together because they have that common bond of the kids. And Ed and I don't have that."

She doesn't have answers to these questions right now. She does love Ed and his children. She knows he's important to her children. She'd like nothing more than to join households and figure it out together. But for now, she just keeps waiting.

CHRIS WILKOWSKI

CHRIS IS A big, affable guy. He laughs out loud and talks in a voice that matches his five-foot, eleven-inch, 245-pound frame. Chris was in ninth grade when his family moved to a small Pacific Coast town where he met Michelle. They've been tangled up in each other's lives in one way or another ever since.

Chris remembers the day Michelle told him that she was pregnant with their first child. He had returned from the army and they were still young, but the whole situation seemed so right to him. Chris remembers picking Michelle up and twirling her around in the parking lot. He was so excited, and he remembers the sense of clarity that he had about his life that day. He was going to marry the woman he loved, they were going to have a baby, and they were going to have a family together.

Chris and Michelle married and continued to have babies. He said that the one thing that they always did well together was sex. But he says now that he mistook good sex for a good relationship. Their relationship was passionate, exciting, and dramatic, at both ends of the emotional spectrum.

After a few years, Chris met Eva through a phone date line and had an affair that he says was purely sexual. Chris said the relationship lasted only a month, but she got pregnant. She told Chris she was going to have the baby and move to Florida. Chris said she didn't want him around, and he dropped the issue. He did see the baby, Ben, when he was a year old and Eva gave him occasional updates about the boy, but after a while, he just fell out of contact with her.

His marriage continued its steady decline. And then the sheriff showed up with the paternity suit for Ben. He told Michelle what had happened and she went silent. The next day, she asked him to leave her alone for a while so she could think. After a couple weeks of serious tension in the house, Chris asked Michelle if she wanted a divorce. She just nodded her head. They planned on the divorce and Chris moved out into a nearby apartment. But he was still hoping that he could repair the damage done and reunite with Michelle. Until he walked in on her kissing his best friend Ed.

"I just had to get away," he said. "I left and thought, this is over, I'm out, I'm done. This just wasn't going to happen. Michelle was going to be with Ed. I called my friend Brian and said, 'I have to get drunk.' We just went and got polluted."

After that, Chris continued to work long hours as a firefighter and he saw his children a couple evenings a week and every other weekend. He said he never skipped his time with his children. But every time they went home, his apartment was eerily quiet.

"I was using women like Kleenex," Chris said. "I was cutting a wide swath through western Washington. At one time, I was sleeping with four or five women at one time. I was lonely and I couldn't stand to be alone. My ego had taken a big hit and I was trying to prove that hey, I've still got it, I was thirty-two years old and I could still run with the big dogs."

Then he met Maria over the phone through a date line. The first time he saw her in person, she drove the hour down from her town to surprise him at work. He took her for a ride in a police car. Later, after they'd spent many more hours on the phone, they went on their first official date. They went out to the beach on the ocean and Maria took pictures. They got Arby's and ate in Maria's car. Chris kissed her and she didn't complain. Very soon after that first date, they talked about, and then became, an exclusive couple. Up until then, Maria had spent little time with the children. After about six months, Maria moved into Chris's apartment. And then the fun really began.

"I knew there was going to be some anger on the kids' part. I told Maria, just like I told everybody I was dating at the time: Don't attempt to come between me and my kids or the relationship between me and my ex-wife," Chris said. "Maria was the only one to call it bullshit. 'You can't continue to do what you're doing with Michelle and expect me to be OK with it.' It was the boundaries thing. She was ready to do battle with my ex-wife for me. That made me feel good. It makes me feel good now. But at the time, it was 'Don't meddle, it isn't your place.'"

Today, Chris trusts Maria to make those kinds of major decisions about his ex-wife and kids, or the running of the household, with his best interests at heart. Maria deals with the money, Maria decides what they can or can't buy, where they can or can't go, whether the children will or won't get any "extras" on top of child support payments to Michelle. She tells Chris what he can or can't eat, whether he can or can't go out for lunch. Initially, Chris was taken aback by Maria's expectations, but after a while, he began to see the payoffs.

"She made me give my checkbook to her. She told me 'Don't buy any-thing' and I think I'd gone to Subway or something like that and I'd put the receipt out there on the counter where I always put my receipts for her. She comes in and says, 'Don't do this, I told you not to do this; you do this to me every time. If you do it again, I'm taking your debit card.' And she was dead serious and I knew she was dead serious and I was kind of pissed because I'm thirty-eight years old and if I want to go to Subway, I will. But on the other hand, if there's anyone who has her pulse on the money, it's Maria. Some people call it controlling. It can only be control-ling if I allow it to be. I'm comfortable with it. If it's stupid and it works, it's not stupid. I don't feel stupid."

"In five years of marriage, this may sound incredibly shallow, so I apol-ogize," Chris said. "But we have stuff. With Michelle, we never had stuff. We had stuff that people gave us, hand-me-downs. Michelle and I never owned a house together. Maria and I have cars that we can get in and drive wherever we want. I wanted an SUV for, God, fifteen years. Now I have one. I don't know how we do it with our budget, but we do. And it's because of Maria."

It's also because of her that he says he's the happiest he's ever been in his life. He says that without her, he never would have been able to survive the trials of becoming a stepfamily. As it is, he's shocked they've fared as well as they have.

"If Maria had not come into my life, I have no doubt in my mind that I'd still be bouncing checks, I might have even gone bankrupt. I would still be acting the same way toward Michelle and there may have been at some point a reconciliation and then another split up because Michelle and I are exactly the same people we were ten years ago. I really think that God put Maria in my life to give me that perspective.

"It's not just material goods, but the way that I feel right now. The fact that Maria and I have lived through this and lived through stuff that would have wrung another couple out and not left anything else. And here we are. I feel like our relationship is one hundred and fifty percent stronger than it was five years ago."

They have worked consciously to ensure that their marriage is their pri-ority and that they're paying attention to making it strong.

"Neither one of us ever want to go through this pain again," Chris said. So when Chris noticed that he was working close to seventy hours a week and that when he was home, his children were often there, he made a change. He still works a lot, but he tries to limit it to sixty hours a week.

"The time that we spend together, we spend it *together*," Chris said. "Now that may be going to the mall and walking around or out here pulling weeds or spreading gravel or something like that. But we've decided that our relationship comes first.

"One of the things that Michelle doesn't understand is that kids are born, you raise them, and then they go away. And your marriage is forever. I kind of took the view on our marriage that Maria and I are going to be together a lot longer than we're going to have the kids. In that respect, I didn't devalue the kids. But my relationship with the kids is temporary because they're going to grow up, they're going to have families of their own, they're going to move."

What this means in practical terms for the children is that they see their father a lot less than they used to. But Chris feels that he's got a good relationship with his children and he knows that part of that is letting them go off and do teenage kinds of things when they need to. He and Maria try to support the children's activities. One of their favorites is the marching band competitions that Nancy and Eric are involved in. It's a traveling competition that hits several towns. Chris and Maria don't miss any of the competitions and they usually make a weekend of it with the children.

Things with the children are going along well, Chris said. Every relationship in the stepfamily seems to have improved dramatically in the past couple years. He is feeling less and less like the man in the middle who has to make everyone happy. He wishes he had given that up years ago; Michelle and Maria might have figured out how to get along a lot sooner.

A recent incident showed him how much has changed. As Nancy was getting ready for her first prom, Maria offered to help pay for the dress. Michelle and Maria met at the mall with Nancy and they shopped for the dress together. It was a momentous outing. Chris couldn't believe it was actually happening and he was nervous.

"The whole time I'm at work and I'm like 'Pant, pant, pant,' because I know I'm going to get a phone call, 'That bitch!' But I didn't know which one I was going to get the phone call from," Chris said. The phone call never came. Instead, the two women put their differences aside for the space of an hour. "Maria pointed out that we're going to have to deal with Michelle for the rest of our lives in one respect or another. We've kind of said to ourselves, 'OK, Michelle's a part of our lives but kind of like the way my cousin is a part of our lives.' We don't talk to her; we get a Christmas card from her. Deal with her when we need to. And that's it. And I have stopped trying to make everybody happy. Maria's biggest thing in the beginning was 'It needs to be a business relationship.' I resisted that. I thought, 'I can't have a business relationship with someone I've been intimate with since high school.' But to keep my sanity and maintain my marriage, that's exactly what it is. And while Michelle and I can joke, we don't joke about a lot of things anymore. We don't chit-chat because I limit my time that I spend with Michelle."

ED RAY

ED RADIATES A quiet warmth and sincerity. He's not a New-Age-sensitive-guy, but he's kind and gentle in a down-to-earth way. He feels things intensely—he is almost somber until he smiles—and he has a strong sense of right and wrong.

So when you hear that he cheated on his wife and divorced her because of the affair, it seems incongruent. It does to him, too. Which is probably why he's spent the last seven years hitting himself over the head for it and trying in whatever way he can to show that he really is a good guy.

"I never thought that I would be somebody who had an affair on his wife. I was never like that. I'd always been in long-term, monogamous relationships," he said. "But it happened."

It happened and changed his life more dramatically than he could have known.

"I wish I could just snap my fingers and go back six or seven years and make it all different," Ed said. "I'd stay married. I probably think more about that than the kids do. I hate my life now. Life was good; we had a home. I had friends, we did things. I don't have any friends now. It's just survival.

"Maybe that's part of not moving ahead with Michelle, showing Sandy that this is not about greener pastures. Our marriage was . . . well, we put on a good façade. I know that she loved me, but there were a whole lot of times I didn't feel loved."

Ed grew up among the Pacific coast mountains and loves the outdoors. He's usually in jeans and a sweatshirt; he looks comfortable. He's been smoking for twenty years; you can hear it in his voice and see it in the lines on his face. He might be what the Marlboro Man would look like if he began to lose his youthful glow and ruggedness. He looks tired.

Running a print shop a couple hours outside of Seattle, Ed struggles to make a living, to pay his child support and still have money for the basics. Last year, he squeaked by on $12,000. He just tries to make it work from one day to the next. In a lot of ways, he'll tell you, it's his own fault and really, what he deserves.

As a younger, single man, Ed had performed on the stage. After he married and started having children, he let his passion drift away. But one night, the family ordered pizza and when the pizza was delivered, the box had a flyer calling for people to audition for a play. Ed auditioned and got the lead role in *You Can't Take It With You*.

At first, Sandy was excited, too. She thought his rediscovered pursuit of acting was fun. But she soon began to wonder out loud why he needed to do something that, in her eyes, had no benefit to the family but took up a lot of Ed's time. She became resentful of his time away, of the whole theater life. She criticized Ed and scoffed at his work on the stage. Ed felt like she was overly critical of him in general, and it seemed that nothing he could do pleased her. But theirs was not a screaming, fighting marriage. Ed likes to smooth things over. He hates fighting more than most anything. So their marriage continued, in muted anger and resentment.

Still, he was determined to stick to doing what he loves.

"It is important to me and something I don't want to ever let go," Ed said. "Outside of my time with my kids, it's the happiest I am."

On his third production, he played opposite Michelle in *Egad, What a Cad*. The two became friends and their families started spending time together. As their families became close, an attraction developed between the two. It was powerful. They could talk for hours and she seemed to understand him in a way that Sandy couldn't—or wouldn't.

Both Michelle and Ed were married, both had children. Ed knew that any possible relationship was fraught with unsolvable problems. He knew it was against everything he believed in. And so for months, while there was flirting and fun, there wasn't anything else going on except continuing their relationships with each other's families. But the attraction stayed alive and real. For the first time in years, Ed felt a woman looking at him with admiration, kindness, and acceptance. Here was someone who believed in him instead of cutting him down. Here was a like-minded person who thought he was great. It was an enticing combination.

"After rehearsal one night I was saying good-bye to her and we ended up kissing briefly," Ed said. "And it actually kind of freaked us both out. We didn't really do anything for a while. We were talking about it one night and I told her I thought it would be like having a Lay's potato chip, once you have one, you can't stop.

"We really fought this relationship. I know that sounds lame. But it was very passionate. And we've been trying to break it off ever since. Or maybe I have been."

When Ed talks about his life, it is hard to remember that he's been seeing the same woman for seven years. She doesn't rate very high on his list of priorities. Ed and Michelle aren't married and they don't live together. Ed does stay over at Michelle's house a couple times a week, but they don't see each other every day. When he talks about their relationship, it's with heaviness and almost a sense of resignation. It's as if he doesn't want anyone to think he enjoys it too much. He thinks he loves Michelle, although he's not sure that he knows what love is.

"I really don't know why we are together sometimes," he said. "The whole emotional roller-coaster and the stress between me and Sandy and me in the middle of Sandy and Michelle and Michelle's needs and wants and desires. It's usually more work than reward. Then I get there and the relationship we do have is good. We do have a lot of common loves and passions and we connect well when see each other.

"My relationship with Sandy is still very important to me," Ed said. "It's immobilized me, paralyzed me as far as moving one way or another with Michelle."

And so for now, he keeps coming back to the one thing he knows. He has his children a couple nights a week, he knows their lives, what's happening in school, with their friends.

"All I know is that my children love me, always will. It's totally non-threatening; they love me. Period. That's what keeps me going, seeing that look in my daughter's eye, that hug and that kiss," he said. "I'm not responsible for anybody else except myself and my kids. I don't have to do anything for anyone except my kids."

But even as he says this, he knows that he works particularly hard at keeping his ex-wife happy. His guilt about cheating on her hasn't diminished. He rarely confronts her on any issue and is clear that his first family is still his first family.

"I take a real hard stance with Michelle in regard to decisions I make with Sandy and my kids," Ed said.

Ed said that he and Michelle have had many heated exchanges about her role in his life. With Michelle, he's learned to be open about how he feels, about what he expects, and what he wants. With Sandy, Ed doesn't take hard stances. He doesn't want to fight with her; he doesn't want to cause any problems. He left her seven years ago because he felt like nothing he did made her happy. But in a lot of ways, he's still trying. He wants to make sure she knows that he's not going to "run off to be a father to somebody else's kids," something that she accused him of years ago that still plays fresh in his mind. Ed still loves Sandy. He said he always would, even if he had a hard time with her criticism. He still wishes every day that he could just have his life back, his family back. But Ed has never brought up the idea of getting back together.

"I probably know it's too late," he said. "The sacrifices at this point, I'm not prepared for. I'm not talking about Michelle. I could live with that. If I thought it could happen and it would be a positive thing and we could make it work, I could leave Michelle. But I couldn't do theater. And I'd have to do the church thing—and I'm not there. And it's not worth it to be a hypocrite.

"I only want the best for Sandy. I want her to have happiness. I care about her. The most I want from her is, I guess, her compassion. Something she didn't ever show me a lot of anyway, so I don't know why I'd want it. Just some understanding. Yeah, I fucked up. But I'm not a bad guy. And I try to be a good father."

Ed knows that Michelle would love to marry and try to build a home together. Their children are close and both sets of children love their parent's partner. But there's a lot that keeps him more comfortable in limbo. His business has done badly and his financial situation is tough. With the financial stress, the logistics of raising two children between two homes, trying to fit in the theater work and having a relationship with Michelle, he feels like there's not enough of him to go around. And marrying Michelle would add to his list of responsibilities considerably.

"I don't want to be a stepfather to that family," he explains. "I love them and I've known them for a long time, but I just can't take that on. And to be her husband would mean taking on all that. And I would do my best. But life is finite. I have energies that have to be spent in other places. I can't move forward."

MARIA WILKOWSKI

MARIA FEELS BITTERSWEET about the way her life turned out. She was married before, but her first husband had an affair and left her for another woman. He's now married to the woman.

"It's hard. She has my life," Maria says quietly. "She's a stay-at-home mom, she's got the children. He's making good money."

She knows she'll never have her own children. Chris said that they would when they married, but then he changed his mind, deciding that five was enough. Not having her own children is hard for her, but she loves her husband and she likes her life with him.

The real bitterness comes from dealing with her husband's ex-wife and children. The ex-wife, especially, has put a heavy burden on what she considers an otherwise happy marriage. Never would she have believed that her life would have been so entangled with someone she so dislikes. And if she knew in the beginning what she knows now, she wouldn't look back, she would run, run, run.

In the beginning especially, Maria was waiting for Chris to step up and stop acting like he was still married to his ex and still catering to the children.

"I kept thinking, 'He's doing this wrong, he'll eventually wake up and see what he's doing wrong.' But by that point I was so in love with him and I don't give up on my relationships if I see that they're fixable. And I thought this was fixable."

Now, Maria says, seven years later, it is fixed. Chris's allegiance is solidly with her. Maria believes strongly that that's the best for everyone. If the parents are happy together and the children see the peace, they'll feel happy, too. Chris, who initially balked at the idea, has come around to Maria's way of thinking. But the couple still spends a lot of energy on Chris's ex-wife.

Maria is continually frustrated by what she sees as Michelle's lack of responsibility, lack of initiative, lack of organization, and lack of cleanliness. Michelle drives her crazy. And the children, whatever their good traits and however much Maria likes them, remind her of their mother.

Maria doesn't have any problems with Ben's mother, Eva. She has gotten into disagreements with her about scheduling and other practicalities, but the two women get along fairly well for the most part.

As a service manager for a brokerage firm, Maria dresses for the job in sharp business pants, formal blouses, conservative jackets. Even on the weekend, her clothes are neat and trim, a pale yellow polo-type shirt with navy pants. Her shoulder-length hair is layered and neat, her makeup minimal.

When she met Chris, she had never dated a divorced man. She didn't know what it meant to be a stepmother. She knew it would be hard. She knew, too, that she would be making some sacrifices. "When I married Chris, I knew that I'd have to work," Maria said. "I traded my sports car off for a van. I knew that there were things that I had to do because I married a man with five children. He knew I didn't want to work outside of the home. I wanted to be at home, take care of the kids. He and I talked about me possibly watching the kids so that Michelle could get a job. He would still pay her the full amount of child support but I would be the babysitter during the workday. That didn't pan out. So now, Chris also feels bad that I have to work to support him and his children. He wants me to be able to do what my dream is and stay home, cook, bake, sew, volunteer."

One thing that she did know right away was that Chris had some things to learn about how to deal with his ex. When Chris and Maria started dating, Chris hadn't been living with Michelle for about a year, but they were still working on the legal end of the divorce. Like a lot of people who divorce, both Chris and Michelle think of their divorce as starting from the time Chris moved out, not when the papers were finally signed. But Maria still felt like she had to fight for her place as a legitimate partner for Chris, and ultimately, another parental figure for the children.

"The first major fight was when I showed up for parent-teacher conferences," Maria said. "Michelle blew a gasket for interfering with their family time. She was thinking I was trying to come in and be a mom for their children. She thinks Chris owes her. She still does. She would have emergencies when she knew that he and I had plans. Her favorite line to me was, 'I'm the wife and I have the right to immediate access to him. He's my husband.' They weren't living together as a married couple. At that time, he was willing to do whatever he could to make her happy. He would just do anything possible to pacify her, which made me upset. She put the kids in the middle a lot. She told him that the kids couldn't come over with 'that woman' there.

"We had instances like that all through it. I was at the point when I didn't trust him at her house. He used to go to the house and play with the kids and give them the false hope that mommy and daddy were getting back together.

"At the time, I thought, 'I can change him,'" she said. "I used to work in day care and I saw divorced families and they weren't doing family things together. They would use the day care as the exchange. He was still treating Michelle like a wife. I didn't like that. He wasn't showing any signs of cutting the strings. She wasn't showing any signs of letting him cut the strings."

For one thing, Maria thought, Michelle was just too geographically close. But that was to change. "In 1999, we had an opportunity to live in Mount

Vernon in a town home," Maria said. "It was about two hundred dollars extra a month. We were going to be moving about sixty miles north. We weren't asking Michelle and Eva for transportation. It became very inconvenient for the moms because Chris couldn't drop everything and come by; I couldn't be an instant babysitter. We saw the advantage of an extra bedroom, a yard where the kids could play. The moms didn't see it that way. Some of our motivation to move *was* to get away from the moms. We were just too convenient for them. They were able to drive by on the weekends and see who was over, look right into our apartment. When we moved to Mount Vernon, our stress level went down. Way down. We didn't have to deal with them dropping by and saying, 'Oh, Eric had to use the bathroom.' It was hard for Chris, but I'm like, 'You know, you're a part-time dad now. There's a reason that they're the custodial parents.'"

But there were times when Maria was so exasperated with Michelle that she pushed Chris to go for full custody of the kids.

"When they were younger and Michelle was complaining about money, I told Chris, 'Let's just go for custody,'" she said. "'We can take that money, get a bigger place, I could stay home, we'd have all kinds of money. We'd have all the kids as a tax write-off. We wouldn't be paying into the IRS.' Chris's just afraid that a child dispute thing would make it hard on the kids, so he's never gone for custody. Although that's been our threat when Michelle complains about money. 'Oh, just give us that thirteen hundred dollars a month. We'll make it work.'"

Money is a defining issue in Maria's life. She said she learned to like nice things when she was growing up. She was raised in a well-to-do family and she's proud of what she has accomplished with Chris, despite the hefty monthly payments for child support. Since Maria handles all the money, Michelle never asks for money over and above the child support anymore. But Maria knows it's still the biggest power issue between the families. Michelle is always broke, and Chris and Maria always have money. Maria thinks that Michelle does need more money, but her solution is to get something better than a part-time job. More importantly, she should learn to manage the money she does have.

"I'm sure that when Michelle got our W-2 in the mail this week she's going to flip a gasket," Maria said. "Our gross says $119,000. But if you take away the $20,000 we pulled out of retirement plans, that's what? $99,000. Take away my income, that leaves Chris at $60,000. So, child support's based on his. Unfortunately, mine's in there. Last year was $101,000. But part of that again was we had pulled some money out of retirement plans to pay for braces and Ben had some medical expenses we had to pay.

"If it was taking away from her child support or if the kids weren't getting extra things, I would feel bad. But she gets her child support and so I don't feel bad that we have a house and two vehicles."

Maria often talks of the children's visits in the past tense. Part of the reason for that is the schedule has changed so much since they had the children consistently every other weekend. The official schedule is that Chris and Maria have the children two weekends a month, but the reality is that they see them a lot less frequently.

When a couple of the children accused Maria of being physically abusive, the adults all agreed on new rules: The children would only come to Dad and Maria's house when Dad was home. And since Chris works long and irregular hours, the children don't see much of them any more.

For Maria, it's a relief. There are a lot of things she likes about the children, and she cares about them. But there's a lot about their visits that is really hard for her, too. Maria used to get so angry with the children. She'd fly into rages and release nasty bundles of pent-up anxiety and frustration on the children. She was so stressed-out she started having panic attacks. Her doctor prescribed Paxil, an anti-anxiety treatment, and she's been on it ever since. She said the medication has changed her entire way of handling things with the kids. She's much calmer and much more able to let things go. There have been some things she's really enjoyed about being the children's stepmom. Like when Nancy or Christine confided in her; they'd tell her things that they don't tell their mom and dad. Or when she acts as the negotiator between the children and the parents.

"You know, telling Michelle that you can't walk your thirteen-year-old daughter into school the first day of junior high. You can't do that," Maria said. "Or that you can't hold Eric's hand at school. He's a fifteen-year-old boy; you can't do that. That's been kind of fun, being Nancy's ally, being Christine's ally."

Maria and Chris have a rule about what the children can call her.

"We tell the kids they can call me 'Mom' but they're not to call me 'Mommy' and they're not to call me 'Mother,'" Maria said. "Mommy and mother are reserved for Michelle. But there are times when Nancy will roll her eyes at me and go, 'Oh, Mother.' And I'll say, 'Stepmother to you.' We make jokes of it. They call me Mom when they want something.

"I'd love to be called Mom. But when I'm called Mom, it's usually when they want something or when they're trying to be cute. Kind of like the

'I love you, Maria,' after I give them money and then two weeks later, 'I hate your guts.' And I know they do that to parents, but for some reason it just hurts more when they do it to me. I don't have that—'I know they love me because I'm their parent.' I'm the conditional. The in and out. I'm not a guarantee."

But she's been parenting the kids for a long time. She hopes she helps.

"I hope I'm being a positive thing in their lives," Maria said. "You know, simple things like, 'OK, your mom cleans this way, but here's a different way to clean.' 'Your mom cooks this way, but here's another way to cook.' 'Your mom manages money this way, but here's another way.' And I do it by example, I don't sit down there and say, 'Your mom does it all wrong.' I do it by example."

She said she never tries to pull Chris away from his children, although she knows that sometimes it looks that way. She is the one who suggested foregoing the weekly visits with the children, but she said that their schoolwork was suffering with the long commute on weeknights and something needed to change.

"And Chris, when I first mentioned it, thought I was pulling him away from the kids. I said, 'OK. I need you to not think emotionally. You have to think practically for your children.' And so when he thought of it that way it was easier for him to see it. When we presented it to the moms, they were still emotional and we couldn't get them to think practical, so that was hard. And I think the kids may have viewed that as 'Well, Maria wants Dad to herself.' But it wasn't that, it was the schoolwork.

"It looks like it's Maria. They don't realize that it's a dad and Maria decision, or sometimes a Dad decision. There are some times when he comes home and mentions, 'We should go down and see the kids.' I'm like 'OK, Let's go.' And then he falls asleep on the couch, you know, from working. I'm not going to wake him up. Then he'll wake up and say, 'We should have gone to see the kids.' And I'll say, 'you needed to sleep.' He doesn't get mad at me because he was tired.

"Like I told the kids, they're more than welcome to call. They can call collect. If they really miss Dad, call and we can work something out. And I know some of that hurts Chris because they don't call. They don't call and say, 'Dad I miss you.' We get phone calls from Michelle, 'The kids really miss you.' It's not the same thing hearing it from the ex-wife. Chris would rather hear it from the kids. Chris is more willing to switch his schedule around if it was the kids. But when it's Michelle, it's like 'Oh, God, it's the ex-wife wanting me to do something she wants.' So there's less enthusiasm to switch. And plus, Chris, you know, during the week, works now to bring home that income for us to survive."

SANDY RAY

ON ANY GIVEN night, Sandy is taking her daughter to basketball or her son to soccer. They have church group activities and play card games with family friends. In between working a full-time job and splitting the children's time between her home and their father's, she wants to make sure that every moment she has with them is time spent really with them, doing things that matter.

Mark, her oldest, is just becoming a teenager—listening to rap music and testing the limits of good taste with some of the lyrics. Kari, her youngest, is ten and talks to her mom about things, something her mother hopes will last through the upcoming teenage years. Sandy likes her family time. She just never imagined that she'd be having family time as a single parent.

Her life with Ed began when Sandy was twenty-two and he moved in to the townhouse complex next door. The entrances to their apartments were right next to each other, so they met and started to get to know each other. They were in a circle of friends that got together and played games, went dancing, and went camping. Both Ed and Sandy loved to fish and they always made the opening day of the fishing season. They married in August of 1987, a year and a half after they met. Sandy was happy and excited to start a family. Less than three years later, they moved to a small town about two hours north of Seattle, into the home they would live in for the remainder of their marriage. Their first child, Mark, was born two weeks later.

"We had fun. We continued the games, the camping," Sandy said. "We had good friends, Karen and Bill. We did everything with them. She had a son that was born June of '89 and Mark was born March of '90, so they played together. I worked; he worked. We did the family thing."

They decided to have another baby and it was in the middle of her pregnancy that Sandy feels like their lives turned and never went back. They ordered pizza one night and on the pizza box there was a call for auditions for a local playhouse. Ed tried out and got the lead role. After that, he became very active in the theater. Sandy tried to be supportive but it ended up being too much work. "When Ed was doing theater, it put a lot of strain on me. I took the kids to day care, then I picked Ed up—I was on the road every morning from about 7:15 A.M.," she said. "And then I'd get home at 6:30 P.M. and he would go to the theater. I was exhausted. And he'd just leave."

When their daughter was born, it didn't get easier. She wanted Ed home more. They left the children for ten hours a day, five days a week while they worked and she expected their family time to be spent together. She wasn't about to leave the children on the weekends so that she could go be at the theater with Ed. When they did do things as a family, they spent a lot of time with Michelle and Chris, who lived in the same small town. Soon, Michelle began to watch the kids while Ed and Sandy worked.

When Michelle found out that her husband had had an affair, she turned to her friends. "When that happened, Michelle needed help. And I was there for her 24/7," Sandy said. And so was Ed. When she needed groceries, they surprised her with some bags of food for her children. When she needed a babysitter, Michelle called and Sandy took the children. When she needed a shoulder to cry on, Sandy was there. The rainy night that Michelle called at 11 P.M. from a town twenty-five miles away because her tire was flat, Ed ran out to help her. After a while, Sandy began to get suspicious about Ed and Michelle's relationship. Why did Michelle always call for Ed?

"You know, I thought, she's got brothers, she's got a mother," Sandy said. "And you know, I needed him too. I worked all day; I worked all week. He worked in a sales job and the income wasn't coming in. So then there was a financial struggle. And he was out at night. He was out and not putting in even an eight-hour day. He was with her and she was constantly over at our house. We would just leave Michelle's house and get home and she would call."

One time, Sandy came home and she could smell Michelle's perfume on Ed's pillow. "I said, 'How did her perfume get on your pillow?' Michelle said she had to bring the kids over to our house for something and she said she laid Kari on the bed," Sandy said. But in a small town, people are quick to talk and Sandy wasn't the only one beginning to wonder what was going on. Ed and Michelle went out for coffee together, they were seen together more and more. "I was starting to get suspicious. And then people around me started saying, what's up with Ed and Michelle?" Sandy said. Michelle and Ed were going to open a day care together and they went to talk to a mutual friend about how to run a business. When they left, the woman immediately called her daughter, a friend of Sandy's, and asked if they were sleeping together. The woman called Sandy. Sandy assured her that nothing was going on, just as Ed had repeatedly reassured Sandy.

"People in the theater were saying, 'Why is he spending so much time with her?' I would say, 'They're just friends, it's no big deal.'"

Ed and Michelle got a paper route together at night. Michelle would show up two hours before they needed to be at the depot and leave her children with Sandy. And while Sandy watched all six children, her husband and her friend would go off together. Sandy knew it didn't feel right. But she wanted to believe her husband. She wanted her family to work, to be together, and to be happy. And she wanted so much to believe that Ed was as dedicated to that idea as she was. Ultimately, she started calling it as she saw it with Ed. And the way she saw it was that Michelle was pushing herself on her husband.

"Michelle would come over and I could just tell by the way they looked at each other," she said. "I told Ed, 'You're going to have to make a choice.' He decided to move out." Still, in Sandy's mind, her marriage wasn't over. She figured they'd sort this thing out, that Ed would come to his senses, that their family would be whole again. And besides, when he left he told her a hundred times that it wasn't for Michelle, that he still wanted to work on their marriage. "He said 'I'm not moving out to date her, we are just friends. We are just friends.' You don't know how many times I heard that," Sandy said.

Then one night, shortly after he had left home, Sandy was home and feeling sick and the phone rang very late at night. She answered and it was Ed, but he didn't recognize her sick voice. He had clearly dialed the wrong number.

"He asked, 'Is Michelle there?'" Sandy said. "I said, 'You fucker, this is your wife.'"

She felt betrayed by Ed, but in a lot of ways, she felt even more betrayed by Michelle. "I really bent over backward for her. I would never do that to a friend. I would never cheat with a friend's husband," Sandy said. "She's going to have a judgment day and I feel sorry for her." Especially because Michelle's husband had an affair, Sandy thought Michelle would have had more understanding and compassion about the effects on the family. Michelle was so immersed in their lives—the children knew and loved her, she was a part of their world. And now it seemed she was helping to rip the world apart. Sandy said that if Michelle had backed off, she and Ed would have figured out the problems in their marriage. But Michelle pushed hard. And Sandy also feels Ed is pretty easily persuaded. "I think I blame her more," Sandy said. "Because Ed is a softie, I guess. He's easy to control. He wants everybody happy."

As the divorce was filed, Sandy was trying to come to terms with the fact that it was over. But she still wasn't quite ready. She asked Ed to sign an agreement that he wouldn't have Michelle around the children for two years. She thought that maybe in that time Ed and Michelle's relationship would fall apart and that Ed would come home.

"If Ed and Michelle's relationship is going to last two years then I'm going to have to suck this up," she said. "Two years went by, lickety-split. And now they're still together."

Those first couple years, she and Michelle had a terrible time. Sandy just burned every time she thought of the two of them together.

"I would drive by and his car would be in her driveway in the morning and it was like, 'OK, it's over.' I would call him on the phone when I got to work. I even left a couple nasty messages on Michelle's answering machine. She knew that I wanted my marriage to work. Maybe Ed was telling her something different. I wasn't in reality. I was thinking, 'How could anybody not want to live with their kids?'"

Today, things are a lot different for Sandy. She's still at the same job she's had for eighteen years, running the front office of a large clinic of obstetricians and gynecologists. She said it's probably for the best that she and Ed broke up. She found the church because of it and she's raising her children in the Christian tradition. Besides, she just feels that Ed isn't interested in the family life or the same kinds of things she is. She wants more for herself and for her children.

"I want things in life. I bought a town home; he rents a room right now and he's fine with that. I want to send my kids to college; I want to pay for it. I want them so much to go to college," she said. "If you ask Kari what the life order is, she'll tell you, college, marriage, kids.

"I know the child support is hard for him to make. If I didn't need it, I would recycle it back to him. Or I'd put some in a college fund and at least recycle some of it back to him, just so he could live a little more comfortably. Right now, I'm worried about the kids living comfortably," she said. "I want them to do things. I want them to learn to ski. I want them to go places."

Still, just because she's gotten used to doing it by herself, she wouldn't say she's completely over the whole thing. "I've forgiven them both, but I'm still, I don't know. I've been through so much counseling. Sometimes I think, 'OK, I'm done. I'm over it.' And then things will happen. If the kids mention her name or if I drive by his house and he's not there. Even though I don't really care, I must a little. Because there are still times it gets me. It's just anger.

"Sometimes I just get angry because here I am, doing the homework, doing the laundry, making sure their immunizations are up to date, making sure they go to the dentist, making sure they have their lunch," Sandy said. "And he's up there with her, doing whatever. He's up there helping her with her kids."

It's especially hard during the holidays. "Now I have to share my Christmases. It's just to the point where I can tolerate him there so I do it for the kids," she said. She knows this is an unusual arrangement and she's not completely convinced it's the healthiest thing for the children to have them together for holidays and vacations. But she figures it's better to have them see peace. And there's a little extra twist in it for Sandy.

"If I was Michelle, it would piss me off. Maybe that's why I do it," she said. "Wouldn't it piss you off to have your boyfriend leave you and go to his ex's for Christmas?"

Even now, seven years later, there's a certain satisfaction to pissing off the woman who she believes destroyed her marriage. But she wouldn't go out of her way to do it. The biggest thing for her is that she would like to keep Michelle away from her children as much as possible. She makes sure she's at every one of her children's events, even on her off weekends at least in part because she doesn't want Michelle there, watching them.

"I don't like the way she acts. I don't like the way she talks to my kids, the way she acts with my kids. My kids will come home and say, 'I hate going over there, they argue so much,'" Sandy said. They tell her about high-drama episodes between their dad and Michelle with all the children crying and involved. She also hears that Michelle tells her children things that she doesn't want her talking to her children about—like the affair. Sandy said her children just don't need to be around that kind of stuff. At the same time, she doesn't want them to feel badly about spending time with Michelle and liking her.

"Kari loves Michelle. I hate it. But she'll know when she's older and has kids of her own," Sandy said. "You can tell I have resentment for Michelle. I don't hate her, but I don't want her in my kids' lives. I asked Ed, 'What keeps you with her? Do you know what hurts me the most, Ed? You try so hard with her. Why didn't you try that hard with me?'"

She still speaks fondly about Ed. She talks about the time that they and the children spent together at Disneyland two years ago. They stayed in a single hotel room; Ed and Mark slept in one bed, Sandy and Kari slept in another. They had a blast at the park and it was comfortable for all of them to be together again, just as it had been on other vacations since the divorce.

"When we got home, he went to church with me," Sandy said. "And he was sitting there in church with these really old, beaten up shoes. I said, 'Ed, buy another pair of shoes,' even though he was a month and a half late on child support. I should really get him some shoes. I think after that trip, I was kind of sad after that week was over. But then he went right on up to Michelle's. And I thought, 'I'm glad I didn't get him those shoes.'"

That was two years ago and she would have taken him back even then, if he would do the things that she asked of him. She has her list clear in her mind.

He would have to go to church.

He would have to quit smoking.

He would have to quit the theater work.

He would have to cut all ties to Michelle.

Now though, two years later, she thinks it's probably too late. She said she hates to see him so unhappy and she really hopes that things go better in his life, but that now she mostly thinks about how these things affect their children.

"You know what I'd like is for Ed is to be happy. Ed's not happy. He's miserable with her," she said. "Mark and Kari know their dad's not happy. I want him to be happy, but I don't want him back. Because he's still with her and he's really let himself go. His teeth are falling out. He just doesn't take care of himself. I couldn't trust him now. He's been with Michelle almost as long as he was with me."

Right now, she's comfortable with her life. She hasn't dated since her divorce and she pretty much concentrates on her children. She thought she might be remarried by now, but she's not in any hurry even to look around. She'd just like to get her children raised. She's grateful that Ed is a good father and that he's involved in his children's lives. She doesn't want that to be diminished in any way because Ed is overwhelmed by his work. For now, their relationship is pretty comfortable and she wants to keep it that way.

"I talk to him when I need him. It will be quick calls like, 'Have you heard from the kids?' or 'What time is Kari's game?' or 'Can you take them tonight?' It's pretty much business. The only time we'll hang out is on the holidays. And that will probably stop if I remarry."

Mostly she has what she wants from life. She has good friends who throw her birthday parties and hang out with her and her children. Her children both still like her and she's happy that they're doing well. Life turned out all right. But there are moments when she wonders what might have been.

"I always think 'If we didn't order the pizza that night . . .'" she said. "I wonder how our lives would have changed."

KARI RAY

KARI RAY IS a sweet-faced ten-year-old girl with a quiet way about her. She isn't quiet, really, she just looks as if she might be. Kari likes the fact that her mom and dad still do things together, like going to Disneyland on vacation or spending Christmas together. She loves her dad and wants to spend more time with him, but she's worried about what her mother might think.

"Sometimes, when it's my dad's weekend my mom wants to take me early and I don't want to go because I want to stay with my dad," she said. "But I want to go because I want to see my mom. Like this weekend, I'm going to be with my dad. There was a different plan and my dad was going to take us three weekends in a row. I don't know if my mom will be mad."

Kari doesn't remember much about when her parents divorced, but she's heard things. The pain and conflict over Michelle and Ed's relationship isn't lost on her. Kari said that the advice she'd give divorcing parents is this: If you think you might be about to get divorced, don't start dating until the divorce is final because the other person might be mad and maybe would have wanted you to come back.

"That's why my mom hates Michelle," Kari explains.

But Kari really enjoys going to Michelle's house. She likes Michelle, she likes Michelle's children, and she likes the farm and digging in the mud. She tries to reconcile her mother's feelings about going there.

"I like to go to Michelle's on the weekends. My mom used to care a real lot about my going to Michelle's, but now she doesn't," Kari said.

Which is a relief for Kari. When she thinks about whether she'd want her parents back together again if she could chose that, Kari doesn't take long to answer.

"No, because I'd have to stop seeing Michelle and I really like seeing Michelle."

ERIC WILKOWSKI

ERIC WILKOWSKI IS fifteen and it's obvious that he's been brought up around the stage. When he talks about his parents, his voice changes to fit each character as he sees them: His father is a deep, booming voice, his stepmother a shrill shriek, his mother yelling. He plays them each affectionately, without a hint of rancor.

"I live with my mom most of the time. I see my dad two weekends a month. I don't know what weekends. It could be one weekend at the beginning and the end of the month; it could be both weekends in the middle of the month. But he does come down sometimes to see us on weekends he doesn't have us because he misses us. And we miss him.

"I love my dad and all, but it would just be hard for me to see him day after day after day. I didn't see my dad that much when he and my mom were together, he would normally sleep because he worked graveyard shifts. But now on weekends when I see him, he's up and we IN-TER-ACT (He sharply claps his hands: *clap, clap, clap*). He's a real nice guy, if you're on his good side. And if you're on his bad side . . . He has this thing, he doesn't like to spank us, I don't know why, he just never has. But he makes us do pushups and we do like ten pushups and he says stop and he puts us in halfway down position. So we're not down or up resting, we're like this and we have to hold ourselves there. I think it was like an army thing because he was in the army.

"I would like to see my dad more than two weekends a month and when he comes down sometimes. Not every weekend of the month, but maybe a third weekend. He lives in Mount Vernon and he works eight hundred different jobs so he can keep the house and pay child support and stuff.

"It's bad because I can't really call him because, well, first of all, we don't have long distance and second of all, I don't really like calling Maria at work and saying, 'Hey, I want to talk to dad.' Because I don't like bugging her at work. It's not that I don't like Maria—I love Maria. But it's just that if she's at work and having a bad day, I'm not sure if she'll if she'll be snotty when I get on the phone and say, 'Hi, it's Eric.' I'm not sure if she'll go 'What do you want?' or she'll go 'Hey Eric, what's up?' Usually, though, she'll be like 'Hey Eric, what's up?'

"But it's just different for me. I want to see him. It's not the same talking to him over the phone; I want to see him face to face so I can say 'Hey Dad, what's up?'"

Eric was seven years old and doesn't remember much about when his mom and dad split up. "I do remember back then that they fought a whole lot. I do think it's better that they are divorced. I couldn't handle all the arguing and stuff. It would really drive me even more batty than I already am."

As it is, he thinks his life now is pretty good. He said there are all kinds of advantages to having two households and more than one set of parents.

"Two birthdays. Twice the Christmas presents."

He laughs.

But, he continues, besides those *important* things, there are a lot of reasons it's helpful to have two homes. He says he knows that he can go to his dad's house when he's feeling stressed out by the nonstop activity at his mom's.

"Like at the beginning of this semester, when my sister Christine and the two foster children were driving me insane, I stayed up at my dad's for a week. When I got back, I was talking to my mom and she said 'Sophia is getting lonely because no one is calling her "squirt."' It's nice to know that when I'm away, people will miss me. But it's also nice to know that when something happens, I won't just have two people, I'll have three people there.

"The week was relaxing. Completely boring, but relaxing. They don't do anything. I woke up at nine, tenish every day. I'd have a bowl of cereal and a Pop Tart. Maria went to work, my dad was sleeping. I did my homework. I got it done in less than fifteen minutes. I watched all the shows I can't watch down here at my mom's. It was completely relaxing. Every morning and every other night I'd take shower. I had time to take a nice long shower and I had time to let all the stuff of the day run off me. It was very, very peaceful."

But it's not all rosy having more than two parents. If there's three there to support you, there's also three to come down on you when there's trouble.

"Having your stepmom yell at you. Having your dad yell at you. Having your mom yell at you:

"'Grades!'

"'Homework!'

"'You need to get good grades.'

"'I'm going to pull you out of marching band.'

"'I'm going to pull you out of marching band.'

"'I'm going to pull you out of marching band.'

"All three of them say the same thing."

Eric doesn't seem conflicted about his relationship with his stepmother. There are some things about her that bug him, but he loves her anyway.

"Maria gets mad over little things. She used to. I'm glad she doesn't anymore. I remember this one time. We'd take showers and she would put our towels on the rack. And we'd take one, take one, take one, and then Nancy would have the last shower and she would normally have the bigger towel because she was older. We never noticed the difference. So we all get done taking a shower and Nancy's out of the shower and she's got a small towel.

"Maria flipped out. 'Who took . . . ? You return . . . AAAAKKK blah, blah, blah!!!'

"I swear, glass shattered when she screamed. I'm not trying to dis' Maria. But when she's pissed you know because she sounds like a seagull.

"'WAAAA, WAAAA, WAAAA, WAAAA, WAAAA!!!!' That's no insult to Maria, she just does. It's scary when she screams. I love Maria to pieces. There's nothing to not love about her. She's clean, she's tidy. She's a little irritable when it comes to cleaning and tidiness.

"This is the only thing that bugs me, she needs to have everything in order and it has to be spotless. It's just annoying sometimes. We do our chores. Chores aren't hard. We switch off every weekend, when we used to go up every other weekend. We clean the bathroom, clean the litter box, clean the kitchen, wash the dishes, clean our room, clean the upstairs bathroom. You'd leave one speck of dust and she'd know it. Either she's psychic or it's her allergies.

"But she'd walk in:

"'You're not done cleaning up.'

"'What?'

"And she'd point exactly where the spot of dust was. 'Right there.'

"'HAAA!'

"'Can I go play now?'

"'Yes, oh, here's your allowance.'

"I get along with her. Before she did whatever she did to turn herself around, when she got mad she would call us names and stuff. Like when we didn't clean up right she would call us sloppy little pigs. But whatever it is, it's gone now. Because now we don't clean up a mess, yeah, she'll get upset and she may scream, but most of the time she doesn't, she just says, 'All right Eric, do it again.' She used to pinch us in the back of the necks like you do when you're upset like, 'Don't talk back to me.' She doesn't do that anymore. She doesn't do anything like that anymore.

"I see her as a parental mom. I see her as—she says it, I have to do it or else Dad's going to come home and he's not going to be happy with me. He's told us before, 'If it's coming out of Maria's mouth, it's just like it's coming out of my mouth.' And I would never—well I can't say never—talk back to my dad.

"But I also see her as a real reliable friend, a friend that I can rely on when I need to tell her something and I know she won't blab me out. Unless it's something, really, like, 'I murdered a guy and I dumped him in the river.' It's good to have her when I'm really upset. She's there to calm me down and hold me back."

7

$\mathcal{M}$ONEY MAKES
THE WORLD GO MAD

c⚘ɔ

$\mathcal{W}$HETHER A FAMILY system has a lot or a little, money can turn a stepfamily inside and out.

We harangue people in the other home for asking for more money or for not giving enough money. We harangue our partners for not standing firmer or for constantly harassing us to *do something* to deal with this money issue. We cringe when we hear our children say "Well, mom pays for everything," even though mom doesn't work and is living off alimony and child support payments.

Learning ways to regulate emotions during interactions about money will only help smooth over this very difficult area. A lot of the sting of these interactions could be avoided if you have a realistic plan that includes contingencies and room for change.

IF YOU HAVEN'T DIVORCED YET, GET SOME HELP

WHEN MOST PEOPLE with children divorce, it is almost impossible for them to imagine how their lives will change. Living as a family, no matter how unhappy or dysfunctional that family may have been, is really different than living in two separate households. Usually, all the income is used for the family. Whether it is two incomes or one person working outside of the home and the other caring for the children, in the end, the efforts are for a common goal—the welfare of the family.

So when people divorce, it is hard to imagine that there may come a day when a whole other family complicates that common goal. Most people, even in nasty divorces, want what is best for their children. And what is best for children is to have an ample amount of money to live comfortably and to provide opportunities for enriching their lives.

Unfortunately, after divorce, there often isn't enough money to provide these things for both households. If the financial situation was tight before the divorce, trying to take the same income and stretch it to cover expenses in two homes will only exacerbate the problem.

Even in cases where there is seemingly enough money to provide the children with what they need, money often ends up being a tangible thing to fight about when there are other unresolved issues for a divorced couple.

Parents who divorce often can't fathom all the issues that can come up for a divorced couple around money. When your son turns sixteen, you may assume that a car and insurance are expenses that you and your ex will have to accommodate. But your ex may be thinking that there is no way a sixteen-year-old needs a new car and that there is no way that he will be contributing to such an expense.

No matter how amicable a divorce may be, there are very few people who have the experience or insight to create a plan that will be flexible enough to incorporate changes and be clear enough so that everybody knows what to expect.

That's why getting help is crucial. If you're already divorced, changing the divorce decree may be difficult, but there could be a lot to gain if both divorced parents are willing to sit down with a smart financial advisor to discuss these issues.

IN THE BEGINNING, SIT DOWN AND FIGURE IT OUT

THERE IS NO one way that money should be sorted out in stepfamilies. Families have to figure out what makes them comfortable and what works in their own arrangement. What is critical is to talk about it up front, at the beginning. Sit down with some "homework" of financial planning books for stepfamilies, or with someone who has official expertise in this area. When you pick a financial planner, it might be tempting to go with someone you don't have to pay. But the reason you don't have to pay them is because they have specific products they want to sell you. Better to pay someone who has only your best interests in mind.

There are all kinds of things that need to be decided and every situation is different. Often, both adults come to the marriage with their own credit histories, their own debts, their own retirement accounts, their own medical and life insurance. Do you want to combine these things or leave them in separate accounts? Do stepparents want to contribute to the stepchild's college fund? Does the stepparent want to will his money to the stepchild? Will the stepparent's income be included in the calculations for child support to the other household? Legally, stepparents are usually not responsible for their stepchildren. However, for families with college-age children, no matter what the family decides about the stepparent's contribution, financial aid is determined based on both the parent *and* the stepparent's income.

And no matter what the agreement with the other household states, are there going to be side deals? Will you be comfortable if your spouse decides to give his ex some extra cash that's not part of the agreement? What if your husband decides he won't ask for extra money even when you know that your stepson's mother isn't paying what she should be?

There are sensitive issues outside of the two households, as well. What do you want to expect from stepgrandparents in the ways of money? Do you want stepgrandchildren to be treated as equals to grandchildren when it comes to wills and gifts? Treating all the children in a family equally may be the most fair and easiest solution for the children, but it doesn't always feel right to the adults.

It may lessen your anxiety about this issue to remember that there are very few obviously "right" answers when it comes to money in stepfamilies, and we all have to muddle through what makes the most sense for us.

STAY FLEXIBLE

IT MATTERS, OF course, what the divorce decree or the mediation agreement says. It matters, as well, what was agreed to with your current spouse. But almost always, that is not the end of the discussion or conflict about who pays what when. Which is why this is one area of many in stepfamilies where flexibility means fewer headaches.

Stepfamilies change more than first families. Children switch homes, and child support payments shift as well. When one parent loses a job, it affects the other household. When one parent has a new baby, the financial impact might be felt across both households. That parent may decide to become a stay-at-home mom and the household can go from a two-income home to a single-income home.

So however great your financial plan is today, it may not work tomorrow. You need to be ready to shift your expectations, your ideas about what works. Ideally, you should have a mediated agreement in place, which calls for periodic reviews to decide if the agreement is still workable for everyone.

REGULATE EMOTIONS WHEN POSSIBLE

THERE IS ALWAYS more heft to the money issue than the actual weight of the greenbacks. Money is power in this society, and in our families. Money alone may not make you happy, but if you don't have any, it sure can make you unhappy. And if you feel like your ex is living well, that his household is financially stable, while you are struggling, it's easy to become angry and bitter.

You need food, shelter, and clothing. It would be nice to have some money for extras, as well. Life in stepfamilies is hard enough without the added stress of financial hardship that often comes when couples divorce. There are a few things you can do that will help loosen money's grip in situations in which it has no legitimate ground.

One of the tragically common issues among divorced couples is the withholding of children unless the child support payments are made. You should do your best never to support your spouse in participating in such a despicable act. You need to remember that child support is not a substitute for a relationship with a parent. Visitation arrangements and child support arrangements are two completely separate issues.

Admittedly, if a parent isn't paying the required child support payments, the strain on the relationship between the parents can be enormous. But if a parent can't provide the money he is meant to, it doesn't make sense to cut off his ability to provide anything else to the child. Parents can give love, guidance, nurturing, rides to the dentist, companionship, help with algebra, stories about grandpa. Don't take away everything a parent can give to a child's life because he cannot or will not pay the child support. Every child needs what he can get from his parent, even if it is just a walk around the block. You can be angry with someone and still allow him or her to be your child's parent. Don't shut the other parent out over money.

Another hard pill to swallow in stepfamilies is that you don't get any say in how the other household spends its money. You get to only decide how you spend *your* money. If your ex is paying his correct amount of child support but you are still struggling to keep three children in decent shoes while he and his new wife go off on exotic vacations, this advice can be particularly difficult to follow. The same is true if you are paying your child support, an ample amount to buy the children what they need, but you see your ex mismanaging the money and unable to gain any solid financial ground. Your children are suffering and you have the unhappy choice of taking more income from your home to provide things for your children or to let them go without. You can try to discuss the situation with the other household, but in the end, it is your ex's household, not yours.

Finally, if everyone's basics are being taken care of, but money is still making you rage, you may need to consider the possibility that there's something besides money bothering you. Maybe you see your ex's smug face smiling happily with his new wife as they jet off to Hawaii and you wish you could have that happiness. You deserve it, don't you? More than him, right? Or maybe all the planning about money is one more reminder that you aren't in, and never will be in, a first family. Or maybe the issue of money is the one thing that makes you feel disrespected by the other household. In any case, it's good to know where the stress is coming from and to try to address it.

WHAT DO THE CHILDREN NEED TO KNOW?

ALTHOUGH THIS MIGHT appear at first glance like mostly an adult issue, it often comes up with the children. Children, especially as they get older, want to know who pays for what. Sometimes, they have ideas, right or wrong, about where the money comes from and where it goes.

Again, there aren't any obvious answers here. For older kids, it may make sense to show them how you budget for things, how you plan for vacations or school clothes.

The main thing to remember is that children should not join you in any negative feelings you have about their other parent. So if there is conflict between the two homes, leave children out of the conflict. If the child's other parent is telling him something blatantly untrue, such as he doesn't have enough money for his rent because he has to give so much to you, you are really put in a difficult situation. It is very tempting to explain to the child how the system really works, including the information about your ex's gambling habits. But you have to decide what you will gain. Will your child really understand complex money issues or will you be overwhelming him with too much information? It might be best to keep it simple. You could say something like "These are adult issues. I am so sorry you are thinking and worrying about this. It's OK to tell dad that he can talk to me about this." Children need to know that the adults in their lives are taking care of the adult business and money should be mostly adult business. As they get older, they may be able to understand more of the dynamics, but however you explain how money works in your household, you should never ask children to carry the weight of one parent's resentment of the other household.

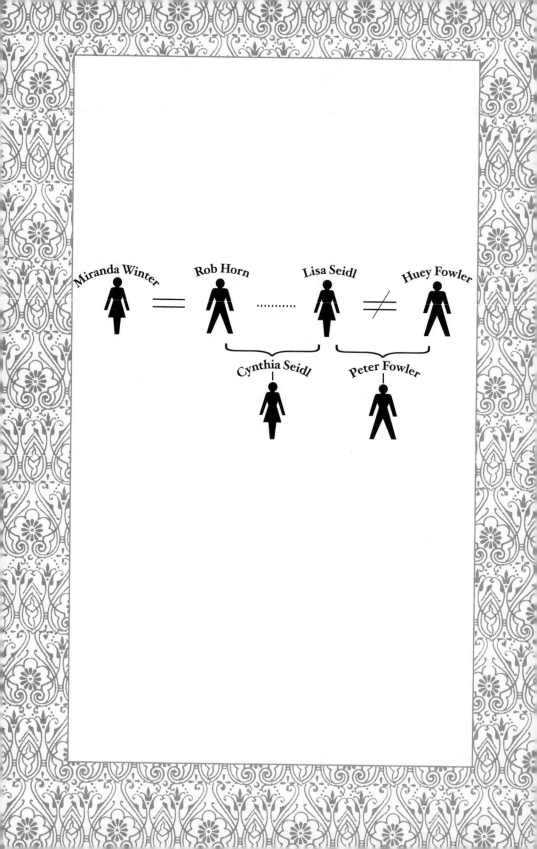

8

THE HORN/SEIDL/WINTER FAMILY SYSTEM OF MINNEAPOLIS, MINNESOTA

❦

CHILDREN/STEPCHILDREN:
Cynthia Seidl, the eighteen-year-old daughter of Rob and Lisa, lived primarily with her mother until she turned sixteen, when she moved in with her father and stepmother

Peter Fowler, the son of Lisa and Huey, is not technically a stepson, but adopted his big sister's dad and stepmom as his own "stepparents."

DAD: Rob Horn, never married to Lisa, saw Cynthia on weekends until she moved in full-time at age sixteen.

MOM: Lisa Seidl, married Huey when Cynthia was a toddler, was the primary caregiver for Cynthia until she was sixteen.

STEPMOM: Miranda Winter married Rob when Cynthia was a toddler.

STEPDAD: Huey Fowler, father of Peter, stepfather of Cynthia, and ex-husband of Lisa, declined to be interviewed for the book.

Biggest issue: When, at sixteen years old, the daughter/stepdaughter in this system switched primary homes, both families had to radically alter their relationships with each other. The changes brought to the forefront some issues that had simmered below the surface for years.

$\mathcal{M}$IRANDA WINTER WOKE up and knew life was different. It was Sunday, and just as he should be, Rob was next to her in bed, still sleeping. Usually she would have the day to enjoy him—her husband, yes. But more to the point, her lover, her confidant, her friend. Today she wouldn't get the chance to do that. The house didn't sound any different, but that's only because the girl wasn't awake yet. Teenagers sleep in if they can.

Miranda and Rob had lived through some difficult times together. Life can be complicated and they had had their share of sorting out to do. But Sundays were their day to retreat. It was their "don't pick-up the phone, don't answer the door, don't go out with other people" day. This was the time to maintain their bond, their commitment to a life together.

This Sunday, Miranda was annoyed. There wouldn't be any lovemaking, for one thing. That was important, but there was more to it than that. Sundays were supposed to be about romance, about connection between man and woman, about sharing their thoughts and feelings about the things that mattered in their lives. It had been this way for years. Now, there was an intruder in that time, and Rob didn't even notice. He didn't feel invaded; on the contrary, he felt happy about the whole situation. Miranda couldn't understand how he could give up their time together so easily.

Rob Horn didn't feel like he had given up anything. When he woke up, the world seemed a beautiful place. Miranda was already awake. Cynthia, his daughter, was in her room across the hall, and would be with them for the rest of the day. And tomorrow and for many tomorrows to come.

For years, when Cynthia lived at her mother's house and just visited, he felt like a part of him was elsewhere. Now, he knew how she was every day, he was part of her immediate reality and she was part of his. Sunday restoration would now include both his wife and his daughter—the two people on the planet who meant the most to him. He saw the three of them creating their cozy time together, talking, relaxing, restoring their energy to face the outside world. Rob felt that his world had been righted.

When it became clear that Miranda felt quite the opposite—that what was right with the world had been jolted—they had to figure out how to either reconcile or live with the different perspectives.

"There's a difference between how we're each feeling about the situation," Rob said. "I don't want Miranda to feel uncomfortable or stressed or disappointed that it's not the same. And yet, I don't want to deny that, to some extent, to me it felt recharging or rejuvenating. I don't know how to resolve this. We're having two different experiences. If it were cooking it'd be a dash of sadness, a little frustration, a smidgen of irritation, some resignation; there's a mix of things."

CHANGING ROLES

THAT WASN'T THE only thing they had to figure out. After fourteen years of marriage, after trying repeatedly to have a baby and being unable, after settling into a routine as the part-time parenting household, everything changed. Cynthia, at sixteen years old, moved in full-time.

The move was sudden, or a long time coming, depending on who you talk to. What everyone agrees is that Cynthia needed to leave her mother's home and that it was a good thing for her to live with her dad and Miranda.

But Rob and Miranda had lived alone together for a long time. They were used to their routines, their sounds and rhythms. Adding a new person, particularly a teenager, was a huge adjustment. Cynthia's entrance into their lives full-time meant huge changes for them practically and emotionally. Sometimes, those changes hit Miranda hardest.

It wasn't that Miranda begrudged Cynthia—she loved Cynthia and wanted to provide the best that she could for her. Miranda knew it was the right thing to do and she has an impeccable record of trying to adhere to her principles. She was taking a child into her home and she spent a lot of time thinking about how she and Rob could be a strong, stable force in Cynthia's life.

It's not that this was completely new territory for them. Miranda and Rob had always been involved in her life, had gone to her plays, had worked with her on school issues, had been there to guide her and be a part of her world.

But when Cynthia moved in, they had to realign their lives to accommodate the day-to-day work of raising a teenager. They all had to renegotiate their roles. Would Cynthia tell them where she was, with whom, when? Would they wait up for her until she got home? How did they decide who did what chores? The expectations that Rob and Miranda had were different from the expectations that Cynthia was used to.

There were big issues. Miranda and Rob both work out of their home, so they needed to do some creative scheduling and set some limits for certain areas of the house. At the same time, they wanted to ensure that Cynthia felt that she was at home and comfortable.

And there were small issues, such as when to change the lint catch on the dryer. (In Rob and Miranda's house, it's when you're done using the dryer, not when you are about to put a new load in.)

And there were seemingly small changes that were felt in big ways. Miranda and Rob started shutting the door to their bedroom, something they had never had to do. More than the stale air by morning, the closing of the door felt significant to Miranda because she had never had to protect her privacy in her own home.

There were intangible benefits, as well. Rob and Miranda wanted to provide a nurturing, receptive, and comfortable home for Cynthia. When the payback for that work rolled it, the taste was sweet. One concrete way that they knew they were on the right track was the late-night conversations.

Cynthia was a night owl and often when she would get home at 11 P.M. or so, she would come into Rob and Miranda's bedroom. She would sit on the bed or on the floor and they'd talk. And talk. And talk. Cynthia would tell her parents about the things in her life; they would listen. They talked about relationships, about sex, about spirituality, and politics. They grew ever closer to each other and their relationships were nourished by these late-night conferences. Miranda, particularly, felt honored that Cynthia would allow them to be such a part of her inner thoughts.

If the conversation wasn't personal, Miranda started excusing herself to get some sleep. It took some time, but the three developed their own ways to live with each other. After more than a decade of part-time parenting, Miranda and Rob were parenting Cynthia full-time and it was working.

Cynthia just knew how good it was to be out of her mother's house. It seemed to her that she could never do anything right in her mother's eyes. A lot of Cynthia's friends were getting into trouble, doing stupid teenager things, and Cynthia saw herself as basically a good kid. But her mother didn't see it that way. Cynthia knew from experience that there was no point in arguing with her mother when she thought she knew best. So Cynthia began lying and sneaking around, not talking to her mother about what was going on in her life and becoming more and more agitated at her home.

HOW IT ALL STARTED

CYNTHIA'S MOTHER, LISA Seidl, got pregnant at twenty-five when she was dating Rob. Lisa was happy to be having a baby, even if she wasn't sure what it meant for her life. One thing she did know was that she didn't want to spend the rest of her life with Rob. He was a nice enough guy, but not someone she wanted to marry. Getting pregnant didn't change her mind and she told him that they should stop seeing each other. Eventually, after a period of Rob's resistance, they broke up.

During the pregnancy, Lisa moved in with her boss at the time, Huey Fowler. After Cynthia was born, Lisa saw Huey and the baby growing close and she felt that they would make a good family together. Lisa and Huey married shortly thereafter. They did make a good family for some time; traveling the world, eating out, and having good times.

For a while, Lisa thought that it would be easier not to have Rob be a part of Cynthia's life. She was tempted by the hope of uncomplicating her life by shifting Cynthia's fathering to Huey, who was doing a lot of it anyway.

Today, Lisa knows that the idea wouldn't have been good for Cynthia. She is grateful for Rob's presence and knows that his relationship with Cynthia is an important and irreplaceable thing.

The reality is, Lisa said, that she didn't spend a lot of time asking these kinds of profound questions when she was raising her children. She was busy with the day-to-day work of running a household, loving two children, and trying to keep her marriage together. She was just trying to make it work.

Since Rob and Lisa never married, they didn't have a divorce agreement. Instead, they created a legal agreement that spelled out Cynthia's primary residence at Lisa's home and the amount of child support that Rob would pay. In the early days, Rob and Miranda had Cynthia only one day a week, with extra time in the summer and for vacations.

This agreement—akin to a divorce decree—would become a point of contention at a crucial time in Cynthia's life. Rob and Miranda considered it the formal framework for their relationship with Lisa. But Lisa had gotten used to working things out with Rob and Miranda over time; she doesn't even remember making the agreement, much less what was spelled out in it.

In the early days, there wasn't a lot of open tension. For many years, the families worked together harmoniously and dedicated themselves to making life for Cynthia whole between the two homes.

There is little else that indicates the tone of the relationship between the two homes so well as the fact that Cynthia's little brother would often tag along with her to Rob and Miranda's house. In an unusual stepfamily twist, when Peter Fowler saw his older sister going off to her dad and stepmother's home, he thought he ought to have his own stepparents.

There's nothing surprising about a child wanting more loving adults in his life. What is rare is that his mother let him go and that his "step-parents" were willing to be adopted. There was enough tolerance, cooperation, and sharing of similar values to allow that kind of crossover family bonding.

That advantage—having more than one home—is sometimes great for children when things get unbearably difficult at one home. As Cynthia grew older, she and her mother began to have serious conflicts. Cynthia started spending more and more time at Rob and Miranda's home—which was only ten minutes away. By the time she officially moved in, she was there almost every weekend.

ROCKY TIMES

CYNTHIA'S PARTING FROM her mother's home wasn't amicable. Cynthia had begun to stay out without her mother's permission. Sometimes, she'd disappear overnight or for a few days without telling anyone where she was going. Lisa was terrified about what her daughter was getting into. Lisa thought Cynthia was slipping into some scary behaviors and she didn't know how to make it stop. She began to push Rob to take Cynthia into his home.

By now, the relationship between the two homes had suffered some blows. Lisa and Huey had divorced, and Lisa no longer had access to two incomes to raise her children. She went to Rob and Miranda and asked for more money. They balked. Eventually, the child support was raised through discussion and without court intervention, but some damage had been done. Miranda and Lisa both felt mistreated and misunderstood.

Lisa, who had been doing the lion's share of day-to-day raising of Cynthia, felt that it was about time for Rob to step up and act like a fully-involved parent. Miranda and Rob felt like Rob had always been a stand-up dad and that, furthermore, Miranda had pulled her weight as well. They were offended by the suggestion that they weren't "real" parents. And Miranda also felt like Lisa was treating Cynthia badly and abandoning her in a moment of true need.

The rift between households still hasn't completely healed.

When Cynthia moved out, the tension between the two households escalated. Cynthia and her mother didn't talk for months. Lisa had imagined that her daughter would be visiting on the weekends, but that didn't happen. Lisa tried to call Cynthia a few times, but Cynthia didn't return her calls. Lisa was dismayed, but she also figured that her daughter would return when she was ready.

After almost two years with very little contact, they see each other about once every couple of months, usually for dinner or coffee. Their relationship is strained, but they are both still engaged. Lisa chalks a lot of the problems up to a teenager's normal developmental distancing from parents.

A HAPPY SEND-OFF

CYNTHIA GRADUATED FROM high school last year and Rob and Miranda threw an all-day open house party in her honor. Graduation ceremonies always mark the end of one part of life and the beginning of another, Cynthia's perhaps even more so. She had spent eighteen years living between two households, juggling time with the extended families of parents and stepparents, sorting out who expected what from her. Now, she was ready to step into the world on her own.

For the adults, too, the graduation party was a turning point. Lisa and Huey, now divorced for many years, were both there. Lisa came and hugged Miranda as she was leaving. There were aunts and uncles and grandparents and step versions of all the same. Whatever happened over the years, in the end, Cynthia had made it—they had all made it—with much to be happy about.

Cynthia held forth at her graduation party, characteristically waving her slim arms around as she talked and thanked people for coming. She was graceful in her short sleek black dress, proud and happy to have everyone there for her. Artifacts of her life so far, pictures from infanthood through the present, a book of poetry she edited, evidence of her work in plays and several organizations, sat on a table for visitors to look through. She seemed strong, rooted, and ready for the world.

Lisa is proud of her daughter and she said that raising her in two homes was mostly a good thing.

"I mean, there are certainly some negative feelings, but I'd say the positive feelings outweigh the negative," she said. "So it's not an unqualified 'Hurrah!', but it's generally worked out fine. I don't have any regrets. Cynthia's just a fantastic person. She is who she is."

A short time after the graduation party, Cynthia moved out of Miranda and Rob's home. Cynthia now lives in a house with three other young adults. They pay the rent, they buy food, they have parties and watch movies together when they're not working or going to school. She is relishing the freedom of not answering to anyone but her own conscience. Still, she knows that all her parents are out there for her. She knows that she can call her mom to help her move, she can borrow her stepdad's car, she can count on an interesting conversation over dinner with her dad and her stepmom.

Miranda and Rob are relishing this time, too. They know that their job as parents isn't over—that it never will be. But they also look back on what happened in this girl's life and feel good about what they did.

"It does feel like a particular vantage point right now," Miranda said. "We were all in it for the long haul we did a good job. It's like a sweet relief. It's joy. When I see Cynthia I feel this swell of happiness."

ROB HORN

ROB'S LIFE AS a parent hasn't always been what he would have designed. He would have picked, for example, a better way to find out he was becoming a father.

"Lisa and I went down to my sister's wedding and on the way back Lisa told me that she was pregnant, after a full Saturday of family," Rob said. "She also said in the same conversation that she wanted to end our relationship."

Rob was so upset he pulled the car over. It was a lot to take in all at once. He always knew he wanted to be a dad, but this wasn't what he had in mind. And what did she mean she wanted to call off the relationship?

That was almost twenty years ago, and although at that time he would have tried to marry Lisa and make their family work, in the end, he knew that wasn't going to happen. He tried for a long time to convince Lisa that they should stay together.

"As difficult as it felt at the time for Lisa and me to work out our differences, certainly I can't imagine that it would have been more difficult than splitting up because we still have to try to work out our differences but with two households and two other people involved," Rob said. "I mean, it's not like our differences went away just because we split up."

Rob said that sometimes people fool themselves into believing that divorce will bring some kind of closure in a relationship. He said that when children are involved, there is no closure.

"Well, you still have to deal with this person. It's just that now you have to deal with them via telephone, via letter, via court. And with other players," he said. "It doesn't make it easier."

During the pregnancy, Lisa agreed to go to counseling with Rob. Then she moved in with Huey, both Rob's and her boss at the time. She said it was just a matter of convenience, but she continued to tell Rob she didn't want to marry him. He still clung to the hope that they would reconcile.

"I was probably in heavy denial," Rob said. "She was living with our boss and telling me she didn't want it to work out."

Denial became more difficult as things progressed. When Cynthia was born, Lisa didn't call Rob. But when both Lisa and Huey didn't show up for work, Rob figured the baby must have arrived. He went down to the hospital to see her.

After a year and a half, Lisa and Huey married.

Over the first year and a half of Cynthia's life, Rob saw the baby sporadically, maybe a few times a month. Lisa kept telling him that she didn't want him involved at all, although she wanted him to pay child support. Then she said he could see the baby once a month. Then twice a month. Finally, they settled on a mediated agreement through the court. The plan was that Rob would see Cynthia once a week. But even after that, Lisa still had hopes of making a cleaner, simpler break from Rob.

When Cynthia was about two years old, Lisa was expecting another child with her husband Huey. She asked Rob to give Cynthia up so that Huey could adopt her.

"I didn't want to do that," Rob said now. "I still wanted Cynthia to know me. It doesn't change the fact of my paternity. It doesn't change her curiosity about her biological father. It doesn't change the fact that I wanted her to know me and not see me as a stranger. I said, no, I wouldn't do that."

Enter Miranda

During the pregnancy, Rob met Miranda. They were working together on the set of a play and became friends. She heard that he was going to become a father, but all the details of the events were in the background. Their friendship grew after Cynthia was born and over the year and a half that Rob tried to make it work with Lisa. At some point, Rob started to accept that making things work with Lisa wasn't an option.

But Miranda, the beautiful dancer with the sympathetic ear and caring heart, now, this had real possibilities. This could work.

"I got to really experience somebody who was interested in me," he said. "Someone I could really talk to, someone who had a great intellect. Our relationship grew."

During this time, Rob hadn't really thought about Cynthia and Miranda's relationship. Rob grew up in southern Minnesotan small towns, where everyone got married and stay married. As a boy growing up, not only did he not know any stepfamilies, he knew very few divorced people. The issue just wasn't on his radar.

"I was falling in love with Miranda, I hadn't had any idea of how this was going to affect her," Rob said. "She knew Cynthia existed, knew about her. Cynthia would come over, and sometimes we'd have Cynthia together. I knew that she was getting the whole package, but I didn't have a really good concept at the time what that meant."

Rob and Miranda got married when Cynthia was three and have been married ever since. And Rob was right, it did work. The two are well suited and have a solid relationship. Besides all the loving mothering that Miranda has done over the years with Cynthia, Rob is grateful for how she's helped him, as well. He is a better father because of Miranda.

"My relationship with Miranda has been really great in terms of helping me understand parenting and helping me understand relationships in general," he said.

Making it work through tight times

As the years went by, Lisa began to accept that Rob was going to be in the picture, as was Miranda. The four parents worked together to have an amicable relationship, not only for Cynthia, but for her little brother, Peter, as well. Rob said that overall, the parenting agreement and the personalities involved helped make a complicated situation work well. Any one of the four parents involved could have made it more difficult for everyone, especially the children. As it was, Rob said, they mostly did a good job together.

"We've been civil," he said. "There were clearly issues but my feeling has always been that what's important is the kids' development, what gives them a sense of nurturance and growth. My job is to help them feel strong, feel great, and help them grow up and be fully functioning."

One issue that came up and was difficult for Rob was the child support payments. If there was any conflict, at least until Cynthia was older, it was over money. Rob is an artist who has worked for twenty years in all kinds of media. Today, he runs his own animation company and is a partner in another company that does a lot of work with Web design. Things are fairly financially stable these days, but it was definitely not always that way. His income varies dramatically and some years he barely scraped by. Child support amounts are based on a percentage of income. At some points, his income was so low that his payment, according to the state guidelines, would have been virtually nonexistent. But he and Lisa had agreed to a rock-bottom minimum payment in the legal contract. He always paid at least the minimum, and as his income increased the percentage of his income for child support grew to a substantial amount each month. Rob would not include Miranda's income, which upset Lisa. But Rob felt that he lived up to his commitment to Lisa, raising the child support payment each time she asked.

"In our circumstances, even though all of us have had a middle-class lifestyle, none of us have earned scads of money," Rob said. "So, yes, there've been times it's been tight. Raising a kid does take money. And I see Lisa's point that it would be nice to have more money. You have a limited supply and you have to live within a budget, you can't do everything you'd like to do. And then I see my side of it. I'd like to provide more money, but if I don't have it, I don't have it. I can't just make it up."

When Cynthia moved into Rob's house at sixteen, Rob didn't expect Lisa to pay support. He knew that she didn't have the money to spare, and he was doing well financially at the time, so he didn't press the issue. He thought it was the right thing to do. But he sees money as an issue that often drives men out of their children's lives.

"It's not really a surprise to me that a lot of men don't stay involved when they don't have physical custody," Rob said. "There is a huge cultural push, it's not just legal, but there is an emotional, cultural push and bias and I think a lot of guys say, 'Forget it, it's just too difficult. I'll pay the child support, I'll visit once a month, I'll have the kids over for holidays and I'll leave it at that.'"

Rob was never inclined to bow out. He hoped that there would come a day when his daughter would want to live with him all the time. He and Miranda had talked about the possibility many times. When the reality came, he was ready for it.

His daughter moved in and he felt like he was able to help guide her, help her understand that he would be there for her. He was able to live day to day with her voice, her ideas, her mannerisms that sometimes mirrored his own so much it was uncanny. He feels he has been able to pass on his family's culture to his daughter, to show her their beliefs, their ideals, and their perspectives. He knows that his daughter is ready to greet the world with her feet firmly planted on rich soil.

Cynthia has seen a wide set of perspectives in her family, Rob said. He said this has its good and bad points.

"When there were different values, she would see that. She started to have some of that critical thinking. Given that she had these two different households, from birth really, that sort of stimulated a certain questioning or consciousness that has led to more maturity at a younger age."

CYNTHIA SEIDL

GROWING UP WITH two sets of parents, Cynthia puzzled over why her stepmother and stepfather were called "step." They were her parents, but there was something different about them. Using her five-year-old logic, she decided that at some point, her stepmom and stepdad must have been married to each other.

It took her a while to sort out all the connections; each adult in her life comes with a complete extended family. She has eight grandparents and scads of aunts, uncles, and cousins. All these connections have enriched her life.

"My biological parents split up before I was born, so I didn't really know anything different," she said. "My mom got married before I can remember. And in fact, my dad got married at the earliest edges of my memory. I have a vague recollection of going to a studio apartment of Miranda's or something, but I don't remember their wedding. I don't remember when they weren't together.

"It seemed very normal to me until, well, I don't even know when I kind of realized that it wasn't typical. Certainly, at least up until school. It never struck me as weird. I remember realizing that everybody else thought I should think it was odd."

For all kinds of reasons, she sees having two sets of parents as a benefit. There are multiple Christmas, Easter, and Thanksgiving celebrations, there are many more presents for her birthday. There's more family around and more people to hang out with, there are even different ways of cooking in all the families. As a college student, she appreciates her stepfamily situation greatly.

"It's a distinct advantage," she said. "If I went to a state school for four years, I would not have to take out any loans and I find that to be a huge, giant good thing. It makes it more realistic for me to go to graduate school or have a second major."

When it really mattered, she was grateful for her stepfamily situation. It made it easier to leave her mother's home, and in the end, Cynthia sees that as the thing that is bringing her and her mother back together again.

Adolescent rebellion

Cynthia isn't all that tall. But her five-feet-seven-inches are seemingly elongated by her thin, flowing limbs. Her nails are clipped neatly at the end of long fingers. Short deep-purple dreadlocks, often covered in a hat or bandana, set off her high cheekbones. If you catch her at the coffee shop she goes to several times a week, she'll be in the back smoking section, the girl with the long navy blue overcoat and the newspaper in her hands. She is confident and at ease speaking on subjects ranging from her family to the arts to the political state of the country.

She wasn't always at ease with herself. In middle school, she says, she was a weird child. She was very quiet and ended up being a bit of a loner. As she went into high school, she did what she calls the "image experimentation thing." She went through dreading her hair in her hippie throwback pothead phase, and through "Goth casual"—think lots of black. She's never had the time, energy, or money to make a big effort with make-up and accessories. In her sophomore year and the summer after, she went through the rave craze with beads in her dreads, huge pants, and lots of bracelets.

It was during this phase that the relationship between her and her mother deteriorated to the point where Cynthia was very stressed out and getting into trouble. Cynthia was lying to her mother, sneaking out after curfew; she sat around smoking pot in parks in the middle of the night, drank with friends, and walked through the city streets. The more her mother forbade her to go and tried to lay down the law, the more Cynthia resisted. Cynthia shut down all but absolutely necessary communications about her life. Sometimes, she would disappear for a few days and her mother would be livid. At one point, her mother told her she couldn't go to a rave—an all-night dance party. When Cynthia went anyway, her mother waited until Cynthia got home and then called the cops. They came and issued Cynthia a ticket and a court date. The whole incident didn't bring any peace between mother and daughter.

"My mom's attitude was sort of like, 'Do what I say,' Cynthia said. "And standard sixteen-year-old rebelliousness made me do the exact opposite whenever it was humanly possible. Some of it wasn't for any reason; it was just to prove to her that I could. I snuck out all the time. She was not willing to flex anywhere."

The move

When the opportunity came to move to her father and Miranda's home, Cynthia took it. She felt, to some degree, that her mother just wanted to wash her hands of her, of the whole situation. She was really grateful that she had somewhere else to go.

"In Lisa's mind, it was my choice to leave," Cynthia said. "In my mind, she was making me leave. Rob and Miranda were like, 'We want you to live with us.' So, kind of in their minds, they were asking me to live there, in the way they phrased it to me. That may have been like a conscious effort to make me feel like I was wanted somewhere. That's the kind of thing that they would do. Which is totally cool. It definitely helped at the time."

Still, she had her concerns about moving in. Cynthia was used to lying about where she was going, what she was doing, and who she was with. She was used to lying even when it wasn't necessary. She had a completely covert life and she wasn't sure how that was going to play out in her new home.

For one thing, she just had a different relationship with Rob and Miranda. When she stayed over on the weekends, she didn't sneak out to meet her friends. There were different boundaries there and she wasn't in a power struggle with Rob and Miranda. She was worried that things might go badly there, as well.

It took her some time to realize that she didn't need to lie to Rob and Miranda about what she was doing, or about who she was. She remembers one time that she had a date with a guy and instead of telling Rob and Miranda about the date, she told them she was hanging out with two other friends. While Cynthia was out on her date, Miranda happened to run into the friend that Cynthia had claimed she was seeing.

It didn't go over well. Rob and Miranda didn't yell and demand explanations of her, but they sat with her and wondered why she didn't just tell them the truth. Cynthia tried to explain that her mother would not have approved of her dating, so she just thought she'd better not tell them. Rob and Miranda assured her that they can deal with the reality of her life and that they didn't want to be lied to.

Later, Cynthia felt comfortable enough to bring her boyfriend, with some other friends, home on her birthday for a key lime pie that Miranda made. It was a relief to Cynthia that they were not only OK with her relationship, but they were interested. And it was a relief that they didn't do anything embarrassing when he came over like say, 'Oh, so *you're* the boyfriend.' Cynthia started to feel respected and she started to trust that she could talk to Rob and Miranda.

"Their attitude toward parenting is really much more intelligent as far as parenting teenagers," Cynthia said. "Because you really can't just tell a teenager not to do something. It's a relationship where you have to make some compromises. My parents' (Rob and Miranda's) attitude was sort of that it wasn't going to be the end of the world if I was going to a rave or something as long as they knew I was getting a sober ride home and that I was going to be home by this time and here's where I was going to be and this is my friend with a cell phone and if it's an absolute emergency, you can call them. Don't call them if it's not an emergency, but if it is, you can call them.

"Rob and Miranda never gave me a curfew. It was never, 'You can be out until this time, no questions asked,' it was more along the lines of 'As long as we know what you're doing and who you're doing it with and how you're getting home, that's cool. And if you can't get a ride and you're not going to a big, fat frat party you can borrow the car. As long as you put some gas in it and we know when you're going to be home and you knock on our door so we know you're alive.'"

The ironic thing was that after moving in with Miranda and Rob, Cynthia didn't feel like she needed to go out as much. She worked nights, and then most nights just came home. At eighteen, Cynthia now feels really close to both her dad and Miranda. Miranda, especially, she said, is so in tune with what's going on with her that sometimes it's spooky. ("She's freaking psychic, it's weird. She always knew when I was lying, when I was keeping something from them," she said.) Cynthia is still very concerned about disappointing Rob and Miranda. When she failed two college classes, she disappeared for a bit instead of facing their disappointment. But she's learned that there's not much she can't talk to them about, and she usually comes around to it.

"My dad and my stepmom are so cool," she said. "They keep each other grounded, they have a really good relationship. I like it; I like hanging out with them. They've actually taught me a lot, they sat down and talked to me about things like relationships and they've demonstrated things, like about communication."

A new start with Lisa

After getting more grounded herself, Cynthia was able to get reconnected with her mother. For a time after she moved in with Rob and Miranda, Cynthia didn't have much to do with her mother. She felt hurt by her and didn't really know how to deal with that pain.

Cynthia doesn't remember how things started to get better, but eventually she and her mother started meeting over dinner and talking. They have coffee together; sometimes they go to family gatherings.

They have never talked directly about those dark days. Their relationship still isn't easy, and it isn't intimate. Cynthia said it will take both of them some time to figure out how to interact differently. When her mother starts to criticize a decision that Cynthia made or tries to tell her what she should do, Cynthia feels a familiar tension in her body.

"I revert right back to being really defensive," she said. "Just like 'I don't want to talk about this right now. Let's talk about it later.' Then we'll never talk about it. That's always the way it's been."

Like when she decided to get an apartment with a long-time friend that her mother knew as a younger, less responsible, child. Lisa told Cynthia she thought that sharing an apartment with that friend was a bad idea.

"I told her I didn't have any choice, because I thought that would make her leave me alone," Cynthia said. "She forgets that she hasn't interacted with any of my friends in three years. A lot of things have changed. And, yeah, they were teenagers when she met them. They were immature high school students. And of course, if they were like they were three years ago, I wouldn't want to move in with them. But, they've grown, just like I've grown. She's watched me, she's seen me grow up, she knows I can handle it. But she's not putting it into a context where my friends have done that as well."

She struggles to prove to her mother that she's capable, that she's responsible, that she's a legitimate adult. Cynthia doesn't usually feel resentful or bitter about what happened between her and her mother.

"Three hundred and sixty days of the year, it's fine," Cynthia said. "A few days out of every year, it will just flare, I'm annoyed. It's usually when I'm irritated. Because I never got an apology or a discussion.

"Part of it is the way she grew up. She's that Wisconsin Irish Catholic, and so there's a little of this 'I'm the adult and I'm right.' When I give my opinions, she doesn't see any merit in them. When I have lived in the adult world for a reasonable period of time, or when I have had kids, or when I have had a long-term relationship, it's possible that we can talk about this."

And she's off

Cynthia is going to college and loves to talk about the way the world is structured and why things work the way they do. She can look at families that way, as well, and she thinks that working in psychology in some way would be interesting. She's also politically minded and can see herself working with an organization like Amnesty International. She wants a family, she wants to travel the world and explore different cultures. She knows that her interests and her skills didn't just happen by accident.

"Rob and Miranda made a conscious effort to make me think about society and politics and what's wrong and what's right and what's actually true versus what people tell you," she said.

All of her family, in some way, contributed to her ability to cope with lots of different kinds of people, lots of different kinds of situations. Whatever she ends up doing, she's pretty happy with the way life has set her up so far. She's a fairly sophisticated and thoughtful person about the world she lives in and the relationships she chooses. She can adapt easily to significant changes, she knows there isn't just one way to do things in the world. She's not sure she'd have these skills if she hadn't grown up the way she did.

"Living in a stepfamily gives me more options," she said. "If even just from having the sheer numbers of family members."

MIRANDA WINTER

MIRANDA HAD SET out to change the world of stepfamilies. When she met and married a man with a daughter, she envisioned a welcoming ceremony dedicated to her inclusion into the parenting circle. She just wanted to sit around together with the other parents and formally acknowledge that she now be part of the twenty-year process of raising a girl.

Stepmom reality didn't quite live up to the vision.

Growing up as a stepdaughter, Miranda surprised herself by ending up in a stepfamily, determined as she was to avoid the whole situation. But she fell for Rob on the perimeter of his life as a parent as they worked together in political theater. And by the time the whole package became clear, she was already in love.

So she decided that she would change the way stepfamilies worked. Her stepfamily would have to be different. They were going to be smarter, to be more thoughtful, to be aware of each other's perspectives and be respectful of each other's lives.

They accomplished a lot of what Miranda had hoped for. But there were times when she just shook her head in shock. No matter how carefully she planned and how sensitive she thought she was being in building new relationships, she was sometimes blindsided by what happened. Before they married, as they entered their relationship, Miranda didn't know if Rob was going to get back together with his ex, she didn't know where she fit in this little girl's life, she couldn't believe that she was getting involved in another stepfamily.

"It was hell, basically, those first couple of years," she said.

But whatever the stress and anxiety of those first couple years, they pale in comparison to the past two when Cynthia, her sixteen-year-old stepdaughter, moved in and Miranda and Rob had to shift to full-time parents. There are many good things about the past two years. She feels good about her role in helping her stepdaughter. She knows that she and her husband have opened a new chapter in their relationship. The best thing about the past two years, though, is that they're over.

In the beginning, Miranda was buoyed by love and by her particular set of beliefs in the world. Miranda believed that sitting down with people, being honest and respectful could make even the most difficult circumstances workable. She lives in an inner-city neighborhood filled with artists, drug dealers, and urban renewal projects. Miranda's world is one of dancers, performing artists, painters, illustrators, therapists of all stripes, and radical politicos, writers, and actors. Her friends are gay and lesbian couples, war protesters, people who work for collectives, people who choose quinoa over McDonald's. She believes in ritual and in marking important moments and milestones in a life. She is at least as inclined to ask how a decision feels in your body as she is to ask if you would like something to drink.

When she married Rob, they invited their friends and families to the bluffs overlooking the ocean in St. Croix where they had an enormous bonfire and the sounds of a bagpiper and a violinist. They asked kin to contribute "kindling" and people brought all kinds of meaningful objects to add to the fire. A dancer brought a huge stack of (fake) money so they'd have "money to burn"; a photographer friend brought photos, so they would have silver in their ashes.

Her professional life, too, has been rigorous and full. She has acted, danced, and done performance art from street theater to the concert stages around the Twin Cities. She's done groundbreaking dance work, massage, and other bodywork. She has provided labor support at births and she writes poetry, professional essays, and aspires to playwriting. She's taken on national and local committees in her professional organization and helped formed their policies. She's taught experiential anatomy and physiology to senior medical residents at the University of Minnesota.

Principles applied to parenting

Over the years of parenting with another household, Miranda's way of living her life became evident. She came to the responsibility of parenting with her heart wide open, ready to embrace the idea of an extended family, ready to create a world where Cynthia felt loved by all her parents and not torn by conflicting loyalties. Miranda agonized over decisions; she worked hard to respect the people and the process of raising a child. She looked to Buddhism to find love for Cynthia's mother. Miranda took on a feminist model of championing Lisa's rights. She made sure that the child support was paid on time, she made sure that she and Rob considered Lisa's role as primary parent.

It worked for much of the time. They all—Miranda and Rob, Lisa and Huey—worked well together. So well, in fact, that Peter, Cynthia's brother, would go back and forth between the homes with his sister. And the whole group had family gatherings together. They went to the children's piano recitals and plays together. It felt to Miranda that they were doing the right thing for the children involved. Later, when Cynthia started having trouble academically, not for lack of ability but because of boredom or rebelliousness at the school's expectations, all her parents sat down with her to figure out how to help.

Things really started to unravel about the time that Lisa divorced Huey. Lisa not only asked Rob for more child support money, but she said things that Miranda had no idea were being harbored, obviously for years.

"I realize in hindsight that I was assuming a certain set of values and behaviors that were the right thing for the kids," Miranda said. She tried to live her life doing the right thing for the kids, whether or not those things were easy or comfortable for her. "It didn't feel optional to me. It felt like this was the minimal ethical responsibility," she said.

Although Miranda always wanted to be involved in Cynthia's life, as a stepparent, any involvement was completely elective. She did things with and for the girl because she wanted to and because she thought it was the right thing to do. But Miranda got the definite sense that Lisa simply expected her to take on the work of raising the child. Lisa didn't seem to acknowledge that Cynthia was her responsibility and that anything Miranda did was extra, a choice. It burned Miranda that Lisa had this sense of entitlement.

At one point, Miranda heard Lisa tear into Rob for not being a "real" father. She heard Lisa yelling at him and it hit Miranda hard. It was around that time that Miranda realized that not all the parents shared her assumptions about how to build the best possible circumstances for the kids.

Miranda still can't shake the image of Lisa sitting in Rob and Miranda's living room and asking for more money because she wanted to take more vacations. Lisa wanted to include Miranda's income as well, which Miranda thought was ironic, since there were times when Lisa had ignored Miranda's other contributions to the children. Miranda tried to stay respectful to what she saw as disrespect from Lisa. But Miranda felt that no matter how much energy and commitment she had for raising Cynthia and Peter, Lisa didn't recognize her as a key player in Cynthia's parenting. Instead of thanks or encouragement, there were times when Lisa openly dismissed her. Routinely, she would refer to their home as "Rob's house," not Rob and Miranda's house. It was those kinds of things that made Miranda cling even more tightly to the ideals of being there for the children.

"I was engaging in this overstretched, unsupported reach, with feminist analysis, we're sisters, blah, blah, blah," Miranda said.

But her attempts at treating Lisa with this kind of solidarity weren't returned. Lisa basically told Miranda that raising Cynthia was none of her business. This, Miranda thought, from a woman who pushes her kid out the door to live in my home.

"It just seemed like the height of hypocrisy to me," Miranda said. "Now, I sort of look at it and it's my way of dealing with a very difficult situation, to say, 'Well, at least I'm not going to cave in on my values.'"

Emergency medicine

Miranda would need to draw heavily on that strength to get through what was to come. As Cynthia got older, she started staying out without permission. She'd leave her mother's house and no one would know where she went. Lisa wanted Cynthia to live at Rob and Miranda's home. As soon as possible. Miranda felt like Lisa was being expedient and irresponsible. On the other hand, she was relieved to have Cynthia in a safer place.

"I was angry with Lisa," Miranda said. "She was treating Cynthia more like a peer than her charge. She was apparently screaming at Cynthia saying things like, 'You're going to make me lose my job.' Which seems really inappropriate. I'd overhear Cynthia say things like, 'Well, at my mom's house, I used to just go out and stand out on the porch. I was so emotionally overwrought I'd just stand out there and cry and chain-smoke.' Lisa and Cynthia were getting into some pretty unseemly, violating fights. It didn't seem right for a teenage girl. Once Cynthia left and said 'I'm going with some friends,' whatever. And after the whole thing passed, Lisa called the police and humiliated Cynthia. It just was very different. It seemed like her motives weren't about nurturing and caring and teaching and respect and unfolding. It was more about punitive revenge and feeling her own power. It scared me."

Still, Miranda wasn't thrilled to suddenly find herself the full-time parent of a sixteen-year-old girl who needed some extra attention. Lisa hadn't renegotiated the parenting agreement. Miranda hadn't created these problems and she didn't feel like cleaning them up. She didn't have any interest in taking Lisa's place as a mother. But it was clear that Cynthia was getting into trouble and needed what Miranda thinks of as emergency medicine.

"It was a state of heightened alert. Everything shifted. My commitment had to be to Cynthia," Miranda said. "Up until that point, I had really held out more for this mutual kind of thing. Once this thing happened with Cynthia, I needed to let go of contact with Lisa. I finally got it: 'You know, Miranda, she is not your responsibility.'"

And then she had to deal with her own internal struggles.

It wasn't going to be easy for Miranda to have her own baby, if she was able to have one at all. She and Rob had been trying for fifteen years. Miranda had had several miscarriages. One of the babies died almost five months into the pregnancy. It was an excruciating part of their lives and the whole subject of having a baby took on a sense of urgency as the years passed. If she were going to try any heavy-duty medical intervention, her time was limited. Just before Cynthia moved in, Miranda had wrapped up several things and felt like she had cleared her schedule. She was ready to decide about the interventions or ready to pursue her art with a single-mindedness not available before now. She felt like a 747 cleared for take-off.

But when things came to a head between Cynthia and Lisa, the flight was delayed. Miranda had to swallow hard. She knew the right thing to do for

Cynthia and so she would do it. The energy that she devoted to someone else's child wouldn't be going toward her own child, a child she had longed for over the years. She redirected the energy for her art into her parenting.

"Parenting Cynthia occupied that same space," Miranda said. "So now, I'm about to turn forty-two and I have some poignancy about that. Because I'm two years older, my body is that much different. People have babies in their forties all the time, I've always counted on that. What I couldn't have known is how much different I'd feel. I don't know if I will have missed my boat. There's sadness and shock. Resentment about certain things, certain components. Not resentment with Cynthia, just the situation itself. It feels harsh."

The girl came to them crumpled and dejected, closed up and in need of a heavy dose of love and affection. Miranda summoned her energy and started planning. She wrote a lengthy and involved document outlining her hopes and goals for the life that she, Rob, and Cynthia would now be living together. She wanted to do it right. The document was ambitious and idealistic. They would discuss science one night, anthropology another. They would do aerobics two mornings a week together, there would be a family night.

Miranda now chuckles about what she calls the "treatise." It never happened that way, of course. Her relationship with her husband shifted. Her exasperation with her husband's ex had sent her reeling. And getting used to a teenager in the house was a challenge in itself.

But parts of what did happen over the past two years were pretty good. She saw Cynthia go from being shut down emotionally, failing classes, not knowing if she was going to graduate, cynical, and tough, to graduating with college courses, getting straight A's, becoming interested in several projects, and becoming more open to the world, more engaged in family life, more confident of herself and her direction.

"The first time I heard her come in the house and yell brightly, almost in spite of herself, 'Hi!' I thought, 'Oh. All right.' It's a relief. There's been a lot of work. It's not been accidental," Miranda said. "That has been very affirming."

Today, Miranda can look at the whole experience of stepparenting with gratifying distance. The room where her stepdaughter had lived for the past two years became suddenly empty. The girl who came to them under duress had grown stronger and moved out on her own. Miranda could now see the good things, the things that worked in all the years of raising her stepdaughter. She felt accomplished.

There is one lingering string that Miranda would tie up if she could. She's let go of the relationship with Lisa. But there's still a part of her that would find it interesting and healing to have everyone in the family in the same room, looking back at their lives together. She hasn't given up on the idea of hashing it out and arriving at peace and reconciliation, she just isn't as invested in the idea as she used to be. She's learned to live with the loose ends.

She's had help getting there. About a year into Cynthia living with them, Miranda sought out a stepmother's support group when the weight of the changes in her life became overwhelming. Now, a year and a half later, she sat in a stepmother's meeting, feeling amazingly light. She couldn't wait to tell the others that there would come a day when it would be easier. Miranda knows her responsibilities as a parent aren't completed. And she knows that she'll continue to have Lisa in her life in some capacity as Cynthia gets older, graduates from college, possibly marries and has children. But thinking back on what she's lived through, especially in the past two years, she feels like anything else will just be cake. She has been transformed by the hardship, and she likes how she's come through.

"I'm like a nut at the bottom of a forest fire and my shell has been cracked. I'm just cracked open," she said. "I'm much more relaxed. Maybe now I can just laugh. I'm a nut who's more relaxed."

PETER FOWLER

PETER'S ROLE IS like many kids' in a stepfamily. His only technical connection to a stepfamily is that his older sister, Cynthia, is a half-sister. Her mother is also his mother. But her father is not his father.

He grew up in the same house with Cynthia until she was sixteen. They lived together with Peter's mom and dad. He remembers fondly the four of them playing games around the kitchen table while his mom made dinner. They were family; they were simply brother and sister. They have never differentiated themselves as "half" anything.

Peter said that his whole life he's been his sister's shadow, and that's easy to see in the dreadlocks that dangle over his thin, angular face. They often meet each other as they hang out at a coffee shop they both like. They went through a phase of rivalry, but today their relationship is tight.

There are a lot of children in Peter's position. They have watched their sisters or brothers leave their home to go off to their other parent's home. They have had to share their siblings with another household for holidays and vacations. There were times when Cynthia went to do something with her dad and he stayed home with his mom and dad. It can be a disorienting situation for a child that brings up lots of questions.

Questions like, "Why don't I have a stepmother?" or "Why doesn't my sister's father live with us?"

Peter didn't have these questions. Instead, with the help of the parents in his life, he created an unusual arrangement. When he was about four years old, he started asking to go with Cynthia to her dad and stepmom's house. He, in effect, adopted Rob and Miranda as his stepparents.

He would go over to their house with Cynthia on weekends. He was there for the special occasions, for Christmas and Easter egg hunts. And they were there for his special occasions, his school events. And for the everyday events, like dinner, as well.

He occasionally went on vacations with Rob and Miranda; he talked to them, he enjoyed having an extra set of people love him.

"They are like parents," he said. "They're really good people. They're really understanding and easy to talk to."

He adds, in a whisper so as not to offend his father in the next room:

"Sometimes more than my own parents."

Peter doesn't spend as much time with Rob and Miranda these days. Now sixteen years old, he's busy with school and friends and hanging out. Besides, his own parents divorced when he was about ten, so there are already two households that he has to fit into his schedule. But they still spend time together. He invited them to his parental dinner for his sixteenth birthday and when they couldn't make it that night, they had him over for a dinner celebration at their house.

Today, Peter is living with his father and he only sees his mom about twice a month. It bothers him and he'd like to see her more. He and his mother have always had a close, warm relationship. But his school, his friends, and his life are on the south side of Minneapolis; his mom is now living in north Minneapolis.

He, like his sister, feels that having so many parents has only made his life more full. In addition to what he calls his "blood-related" side of the family, he knows that if he ever needed Rob and Miranda for anything, they would be there for him.

Peter's connection to Rob and Miranda was possible only because everyone involved wanted it to happen. Peter counts them immediately behind his parents in the order of importance to his life.

"Rob and Miranda are my stepparents," he explains.

Lisa Seidl

Five years ago, Lisa's life started over. She got divorced after thirteen years of marriage. A few years later, her sixteen-year-old daughter moved out. When her son reached about the same age, he moved out to his father's house as well. Lisa quit her job after managing nonprofits in the arts for eighteen years and decided it was time to focus on her own life, her own art, her own thoughts.

It was an enormous shift from the role of mom and all that had encompassed: making the meals, trips to the doctor, the dentist, soccer games, piano recitals, the grocery store, hardware store, museums, clothing stores, the thousands of stops that make up the minutia of day-to-day mothering.

When her children were little this was a role Lisa took on without reservation. These were her children and she was their mother. When she got pregnant with Cynthia, unexpectedly, it felt natural, right, even though she was unmarried. She knew that her life would be changed completely, she just didn't know how. She did know that she didn't want to marry Rob. Thinking back now, she says she didn't spend a lot of time planning out her strategy for raising her daughter with a man in another home. She just lived her life, reacting to the events as they unfolded.

She felt comfortable enough with Rob's qualities as a human being to know that she wouldn't regret being tied to him for life. She thinks he is a good man and a good father.

Still, she hasn't always been happy with his role. For the first several years of Cynthia's life, Lisa said, it took Rob a while to warm up to the role of parenting. Lisa doesn't want to underemphasize his role or hurt his feelings, but she feels like he really didn't quite get it until he had to live it.

"The reluctance was more this naivety about what a full-time parent did and the amount of time and energy invested in that. He felt like it was his prerogative to put boundaries around that," she said. "As a parent, you can't really say to your child, 'It doesn't work for me to have you this many days a week.' 'It doesn't work for me that you eat this much.' 'It doesn't work for me that you're throwing up, I have a meeting right now.' Rob was very clear about what would and wouldn't work in his life. It was 'these days and these times.'"

Lisa took some satisfaction in having him take their daughter into his home full-time when she was sixteen. She felt like saying, "OK, now it's your turn."

The early days

While she was pregnant with Cynthia, she moved in with the man she would eventually marry. She married Huey when Cynthia was a toddler and set about creating a new family. Lisa says now that she remembers thinking that she wanted her daughter to be fully enveloped in this new family. She wanted her family to work in an uncomplicated way. Her husband seemed happy to take on the raising of Cynthia and Lisa entertained the idea of a single, happy family under one roof. She believes it when she hears Rob's memory of her asking him to bow out of Cynthia's life, although she doesn't remember actually doing it.

"It's like one of those things that I was thinking about and then thought, 'Oh, did I say that out loud?'" she said. She can see how that would have stuck painfully in Rob's memory. She's glad nothing ever came of it; but at the time, she was ashamed about having a child out of wedlock. She had a fantasy that if her husband adopted Cynthia and Rob bowed out, people wouldn't know that Cynthia was "illegitimate" and discriminate against her. Eventually, Lisa said, she accepted the complex reality and she's happy that Rob was there for Cynthia.

"Rob's being there made Cynthia's existence make much more sense. If she were missing a biological parent, that's a loss for kids," Lisa said. "Certainly, they'd overcome it, but it's a loss to have a biological parent step out. It certainly would be in Rob's case."

When Lisa divorced Huey after thirteen years, she was happy to see Huey maintain his relationship with Cynthia. One of the things that Lisa is grateful for in her sometimes-complicated family is that both fathers of her children have been graciously open and genuinely loving to the child to whom they aren't biologically connected.

And then there was Miranda. When Rob and Miranda married, Lisa had to digest having another adult in her daughter's life. She didn't have any distrust specifically of Miranda, but not knowing much about her, Lisa wondered about what kinds of values she had, what kind of family she came from. As she learned more about the stepmom, Lisa came to trust that they shared enough common ground to feel completely comfortable with Miranda parenting Cynthia.

The middle years

Parenting Cynthia between the households went relatively smoothly throughout Cynthia's grade school years. This family, more than most stepfamilies I talked to, came together at Cynthia or Peter's events. They spent time at each other's homes, and attended school functions together.

But there were a couple painful bruises along the way. Lisa still gets upset talking about money. Asking for money was an incredibly distasteful thing to have to do in the first place. But she needed to do it. If there had been a less excruciating way of getting money, Lisa says, she would have picked it. But worse than having to ask for it was the response she got when she asked. Rob didn't want to increase the support and Miranda was obviously peeved at Lisa for asking to have her income included in the calculations.

Lisa remembers particularly after she divorced Huey. The two incomes she had relied on for years were gone and Lisa was really struggling to provide basic things for her children. Lisa felt like the welfare of her child was at stake and she would have done whatever she needed to in order to provide a comfortable home. She felt that Rob had been underpaying his child support, but that when she could count on two incomes, it didn't matter. As she tried to make it on her own, she simply needed more money. The whole situation brought about an almost primal instinct to protect her daughter. Lisa remembers heated exchanges with Miranda and Rob about raising the child support.

She ran into Miranda at the grocery store and they argued about whether the support was adequate or not. Lisa was offended at having to justify getting her child's basic needs met. Eventually, the issue was solved through more discussion and the child support was raised.

The teenage years

After she and Huey divorced, Lisa began to look more and more to Rob to share the role of a primary parent with her. When things started to get rocky between her and Cynthia, she felt that it was time for Rob to step in and take over as the primary parent.

When Cynthia started disappearing, it scared Lisa to think of something happening to Cynthia, and that she wouldn't even know where to start to look for her.

"And I told Rob that if his taking Cynthia would stop the disappearing, that's what I needed to have happen, because I needed someone to stop this thing that was making me extremely afraid for Cynthia's well-being," Lisa said. "And Rob balked at that. He said that he and Miranda weren't ready for a teenager in the house. And the disappearing continued. And my stress level and fear and anxiety continued. I saw a counselor about it and I leaned on Rob harder.

"Finally, I said to Cynthia that if she disappeared one more time I was going to have her arrested. I told Rob that if Cynthia leaves to go to this event—she was going to raves that lasted all night—so if Cynthia goes to this rave I'm going to have her arrested. I told all parties what I was going to do. And when the time came, Cynthia went to the rave. I called the police, they came over and arrested Cynthia and Cynthia got a court date. And I said to Rob, you're going to court with me. I said, 'We've got a problem; you're going to court with me.'"

Thinking about that troubling and complex time, Lisa feels like Cynthia was both reacting against her and sending a message to Rob. Lisa thought Cynthia's acting out was a test for Rob.

"'Are you going to take me? Are you going to take me and be my dad? And how soon are you going to do it? And how bad do I have to be?'" Lisa imagines the message.

"I think Cynthia was pretty confident in the fact that I wasn't going to make her leave. I believe that she was telling Rob in a roundabout way about something she needed. About needing to know how much of a father he was for her. She couldn't ask Rob what she needed to know from him. She couldn't just ask him. Even if she knew it consciously, kids can't just put those questions to their parents. This is my interpretation."

And to Lisa, having Cynthia leave her home wasn't a failure; she wasn't backing out of her commitment to her daughter. It was just the right thing to do given the circumstances. Rob is the girl's father and there wasn't any reason that he shouldn't step up to that responsibility. Lisa was relieved to have the option.

At the same time, the separation was a sorrowful time for Lisa. When Cynthia moved into her dad's house, Lisa thought that her daughter would come back on the weekends, as she had done when the situation was reversed. But Cynthia wanted nothing to do with her. Lisa tried to call a few times, but Cynthia never called her back.

"Part of me was just devastated," Lisa said. "There really wasn't anything I could do about it. And I remember how much grief I had about that. I lost my baby."

Still, another part of Lisa remembered her own trouble with her mother at about the same age. She figured that the best way to get Cynthia back in her life was to let her go and hope that she would eventually want to come back on her own.

After several months, Cynthia did call her mother and they reconnected. They haven't plumbed the depths of those difficult times together, but they are building a relationship where Lisa is happy to let Cynthia call the shots.

Looking back

One of the hardest things about living in a stepfamily for Lisa is the feeling of being judged unfairly. She said that she never really felt understood by Rob or Miranda, that she feels like she had to defend herself a lot.

"Of course, a lot of this is in the past. The hardest part of it was trying to communicate the *real* reality of my life over their perception of my life. Because there wasn't enough interaction for them to really know me, especially Miranda, in a less than superficial way," Lisa said. "So anything she decided about me from that superficial knowledge was then her perception of me. I really had a hard time communicating to her that my reality was actually probably different. And I would go so far as to say that she probably had the same feeling."

She believes, for example, that having Rob switch from weekend parenting to full-time parenting was traumatic for Miranda. And she knows that the money issue caused friction between the homes. That did change for Lisa when Cynthia moved into Rob and Miranda's home. Lisa is satisfied with what she sees as an end to that whole sticky issue.

"Obviously it was no longer appropriate for Rob to pay the child support, since he was taking Cynthia. But he also went so far as to say in this last year and a half that I didn't need to pay him child support," Lisa said. "And so I felt that at that point there was a recognition, an acknowledgement that the arguing over the child support was inappropriate. It just felt good to me that he would acknowledge that he shouldn't have been so difficult. That's what I'm reading into it. Now it feels fair to me."

And even though she and Miranda have had some real bumps, Lisa has a lot of good feelings about Miranda. Lisa said she felt like Miranda's support was, at times, more what Cynthia needed, even though there were many times when Lisa felt she was the best support for her daughter. She's grateful that Cynthia loves Miranda. The thought of sending her daughter to a home where she didn't feel comfortable would have been very difficult. Overall, she's grateful for Miranda's presence.

"I'd say I'd put Miranda up with my sisters," Lisa said. "I talk about aunties and people who would go to bat for your kid. And it seems like girls and aunts have a special bond. I would put Miranda up there in the same place I put my sisters. I don't advocate every single factor of my sisters' lives; we're all different. But yet, in the end, they're the people that I think helped raise Cynthia. In that way, I would say she's like my sister."

Moving forward

Lisa doesn't worry about her relationship with Cynthia. As long as they're meeting together, Lisa sees the chance for their relationship to grow and change into something more solid and comfortable for both of them. But the terms of the relationship are under constant reevaluation. It still feels fragile enough that Lisa does a little internal jig when Cynthia calls her for help. At one point, she was going to pick Cynthia up for a family gathering and Cynthia cancelled at the last minute. After Lisa expressed her disappointment, Cynthia didn't call her again for two months.

"So, it's been two months and then Cynthia called me up and this is what she said, 'Will you come help me move?'

"And I said, 'Oh yes, of course.'

"'Please let me help you move.' I didn't say that but that's how I felt in my mind, 'Oh, please let me have an opportunity to help you move. I'm so sorry I know I was wrong.'"

Lisa's new strategy is to try to keep her own strong opinions about the world to herself and just listen.

"I just want her to talk to me. I just want to know about her," Lisa said. "And if I pressure her to do stuff or give her ideas, she usually kind of rejects them, so I don't. That's been our problem. If I try to control her in any way, now that she's an adult, she'll blow me off. That's her way of responding. If I don't treat her as a person in her own right, if I treat her as a kid, she stays away from me. I miss her a great deal and it hurts when she doesn't call or visit for a while. So, I'm learning. It's hard. It's hard to not tell her what to do or to give her advice.

"She's my oldest daughter, she's my only daughter. I do want to give her advice; I want her to be successful on my terms. And she is saying to me she doesn't want a life like mine.

"My mother had a stable fifty-plus-year marriage and I said, 'I'm not going to be like you.' And I wasn't. So the fact that Cynthia looks at me and says, 'I'm not going to be like you,' doesn't really bother me. I don't think she should be like me. I think she should be herself."

9

*A*LL THE WORLD'S A STAGE

❧

*Y*OU MAY BE, like most people, surprised by how difficult family interactions can become in stepfamilies. Surprised by the intensity of your emotions. Surprised by what other people do, and sometimes by what you do. Taking the surprise out of what to expect in stepfamilies can help your interactions tremendously.

Just as with any other difficult task in life, knowing what to expect gives the circumstances less power to throw us. Handling a toddler's temper tantrum is a good example. Think about what might happen if you didn't know that it is completely normal for toddlers, with minimal provocation, to throw themselves on the ground, to writhe around as if they were in tortuous pain, to scream and shake and finally collapse like a pile of jelly on the floor. You might be tempted to whisk your two-year-old to the emergency room and demand some kind of an explanation for her bizarre behavior.

In stepfamilies, some behavior may seem as bizarre as the two-year-old's temper tantrum. Situations can feel so desperate and so painful that it is hard to feel that there is any hope, or that life in a stepfamily will ever feel good. Having the perspective of how a typical stepfamily develops can completely transform your life. Given this understanding and some concrete tools, men, women, and children in stepfamilies have been able to face their challenges with renewed energy and watch their successes build upon each other. Just hearing that other people are having the same struggles, grappling with the same issues, can be very comforting.

"OH, I'M NOT ALONE?"

THOSE OF YOU who have recently reared babies are likely familiar with the *What to Expect When You're Expecting, What to Expect the First Year,* and *What to Expect the Toddler Years* series.

The books are divided up into months of life for the baby and each month discusses the things that your baby will likely begin doing some time around that month. The power of these books cannot be denied. Here you are, a new parent, and your kid starts banging her head on the floor, not angrily, just sort of testing out the strength of her skull, it appears. So you go to the book and look up the seventeenth month and there it is, "Head Banging." You read the information, you know how much to worry and whether to stop her, and you realize that you are not the first to have this issue.

Babies start throwing things on the floor, emptying shelves, being afraid of strangers, crawling, walking, and talking all on fairly predicable schedules. It is uncanny. You can track the development of a baby so easily because, by and large, humans tend to develop in much the same ways, within much the same time frames.

I kept searching the bookstore shelves for the book *What to Expect in Your Thirties,* so I would know whether I should be banging my head against the floor at this point, or if there were some other, better ideas. The book doesn't exist. Then I found something better.

Patricia Papernow, a psychologist in Massachusetts, wrote a book called *Becoming a Stepfamily: Patterns of Development in Remarried Families.* The book is so encouraging because it puts stepfamily lives in a larger context. It gives you new ways to see the same problem you may have dealt with, however unsuccessfully, a hundred times. Papernow uses the example of the toddler temper tantrum to help you understand how useful it is to have some knowledge about the road you are likely to travel in the stepfamily journey. She uses examples that are so vivid, conversational snippets and anecdotes so familiar, that the book rings true to those of us in stepfamilies.

In this chapter, I humbly try to condense Papernow's work and give some examples of why you need to have this big-picture framework for your everyday life.

Each stage is a guideline for the path of development that many families take. But as with most frameworks, the key to its usefulness is its flexibility. Papernow describes the early years of starting a stepfamily, the middle years of restructuring, and the later years of solidifying a family.

Some stepfamilies follow these developmental stages, well, by the book. It is more likely that your family will gain some ground on one issue and be stuck on another. And you may return to a stage as well. Just when you think you have gotten out of the chaotic years and that your family has settled down, some major family event, a graduation, a wedding, a funeral, can bring old disputes to the surface. Hopefully, every time you pass through these stages, you learn a little bit more, you become a little bit better at figuring out how to get through them the next time an issue comes up.

The Papernow stages

Papernow has seven stages of development and she gets into a lot more detail than I will here, which is why you need to read her book. Briefly, the stages are:

- ◆ Fantasy Stage: The adults are hoping to heal the pain of divorce or death. Parents may hope for someone to help them with the parenting, and someone to love their children. Stepparents hope to be all that and more. Children are usually hoping that their parents reunite and the stepparent goes away.
- ◆ Immersion Stage: People in the stepfamily are beginning to feel the difficulty of balancing already established relationships with new relationships. Often, the stepparent is the most uncomfortable at this stage, as they don't usually have as close a relationship with the child as the parent does. Stepparents may not understand what is wrong, but are very clear that *something* is certainly not right. Parents may be annoyed that the stepparent isn't joining the family more easily.
- ◆ Awareness Stage: Everyone is starting to figure out where the hard feelings are coming from. Stepparents are able to recognize that they feel left out, that the relationships already in place between the parent and child and the parent and the ex-spouse are difficult to break into. At this point, stepfamilies start realizing that their family needs

to do things differently from first families in order to be successful and happy.

◆ Mobilization Stage: This is where things can get ugly. Someone, usually the stepparent, is pushing for some changes. Immediately, thank you. The stepparent may feel that they finally understand what they need and they're not going to stop demanding until they get it. The parent may feel attacked.

◆ Action Stage: This is when things start to change to accommodate stepfamily realities. Parents and stepparents are better able to understand each other, to listen to each other, and to come up with ways to make their household run more smoothly.

◆ Contact Stage: Finally, things have settled into a comfortable, working rhythm. Relationships begin to grow one-on-one. Stepparents and stepchildren build their relationship, and parent and stepparent support each other.

◆ Resolution Stage: Solid relationships are in place and the family has its way of doing things. The stepfamily has formed and everyone has grown accustomed to the family's ways.

Therapists and psychologists now use Papernow's stages in one form or another all over the country to help stepfamilies better understand what they're likely to encounter. Here, I've broken the stages down to five more general stages and discussed them in a bit more detail.

STAGE ONE: FANTASYLAND

MOST MEN AND women in stepfamilies can look back to the beginning of their relationship and remember all the ideas that they had about the family they were starting to form. Most of us can only shake our heads now at our naivety or idealism.

You were going to make your family "whole" again. You were going to heal old wounds with love. Of course you would love your stepchild. You were going to be the best stepparent the world had ever seen. You were going to be better than the child's mom. You were going to finally have a father for your children. You were going to make sure that the children had a male role model worth emulating.

It is not that some stepfamilies don't end up achieving all these things (and more), but none of these things happens without serious work. All require understanding of the dynamics you are dealing with in stepfamilies. With more information, it becomes clear that some of these early fantasies are especially likely to set us up for trouble.

But in those heady first days of love, anything seems possible. Each family member is more likely to gloss over potential problems. If a stepparent is overly critical of a child, a parent may look the other way. At this stage, a stepparent is more likely to shrug off hour-long phone conversations between the parents. The child, too, has fantasies: usually that her new stepparent will go away and her original family gets back together.

You will notice, as you read through this book, that none of the families who participated is still in the fantasyland stage. Many people who are in fantasyland do not yet consider themselves a stepfamily.

I'd been raising my stepson for several years when I told a new acquaintance about "my son" and as we talked further, I clarified that the boy was my stepson. The man had an interesting reaction. He was a stepfather, too. But he had dropped the title of stepfather years before, and his stepdaughter called him "dad." "Drop the 'step,'" he advised me. "He's your kid and that's that."

At the time, I felt the same way. I had been a custodial stepmother for almost five years and my stepson's mother was only sporadically involved in his life. He felt like my kid. He still does. But the relationship is different. In those days, a part of me was hoping that he would grow to consider me his mother. I now see this as not only virtually impossible, but also disrespectful and even ignorant of the importance of his relationship, however strained, with his mother. It wasn't until I started to acknowledge that he and I had a *different* kind of relationship than one between a mother and son that I was able to embrace our relationship for what it is. The relationship is not less than the one I have with my own children. There is a certain inevitability about your own children adoring you, at least at some points. And I, almost always, adore them.

In contrast, the relationship between a stepparent and a stepchild does not begin with this inevitability, no matter how much you wish it were so. I am grateful that my stepson and I have grown to genuinely love each other. We have worked hard at this relationship. Everything that he and I have together, and there is a lot, is because he and I chose to build it. We couldn't have gotten to this place without everyone in the family realizing that the fantasy of a first family wasn't ever going to be a reality.

Facing that "simple" fact can take a long time for many people in stepfamilies. It may be that it is too scary to contemplate the fact that the stepparent and the stepchild do not immediately and naturally love each other, if they ever do. It may be that they continue to blindly hope that their family will just progress along as a first family, smoothing away the rough edges over time.

People reading this who are in fantasyland may be thinking something along the lines of, "Well, I'm glad my family doesn't have this problem. I know I love my stepkid," or "I know my wife loves my children."

This is one of those situations where more than one thing can be true at a time. Love often develops between stepparents and stepchildren. But the love doesn't just happen and rarely right away. The situation calls for a particular kind of acceptance that the love is not inevitable, but earned.

There are people who spend very little time in fantasyland. They gather information and experience from others and realize quickly that this family they are building is different from a first family. Beginning with this knowledge and context about stepfamilies makes it easier to confront and cope with the inevitable challenges as they come. Information about what to expect and how others have managed these changes makes the bumps less intense.

STAGE TWO: "WHAT DID I GET MYSELF (AND MY KID) INTO?"

IT BECOMES CLEAR, eventually, that something isn't working.

A new husband, looking forward to the honeymoon period, begins to realize that his wife doesn't plan on spending her evenings with him alone, but with her son and daughter.

A new stepmother may wonder how her husband can let his weekend-visiting teenage daughters treat him with such disrespect. She would never allow her son, who lives with them full-time, to say such things.

The children may like their new stepmother, but worry, often silently, that liking her might hurt their mom's feelings or make her angry.

A parent who had dreams of finally having the family she wanted may be disappointed that the new stepparent isn't stepping more gracefully into the role.

This is the time when the stepparent watches her stepson toss his coat on the floor and thinks, "How could such a great guy have raised his children like this?"

Or when the stepdad who finds his teenage stepdaughters' music appalling thinks, "Oh geez, I'm supposed to love these children? I don't even want to be in the same room with them."

A daughter says, "Mom, why do we always have to go out with him? Can't we go out alone?"

The parent says, "Boy, you have a lot to learn about parenting and living with children. You really need to lighten up."

Add in the everyday annoyances about dirty dishes or lost phone messages and soon there is plenty of discomfort, anger, and frustration to go around. Everyone starts to wonder if this new family is really going to work—or if it is even worth the effort.

Often, in this stage, family members remain fairly polite when dealing with these challenges. Family members who are most bothered by the family dynamics (usually the stepparent) may mention their discomfort. Or they may not bring it up at all and hope that the situation will change in time. Often, parents are the ones most likely to try to hold on to their fantasies of their new family. They have the comfort of their relationship with both their spouse and their child, so it's harder for them to see the difficulties.

Depending on personalities and situations, families can spend a lot of time trying to just accommodate each other and hope that the situation starts to feel better. People who find fighting distasteful or believe that it is their duty to sacrifice their comforts because they entered a stepfamily will often spend a lot of time in this stage.

Others, who are more comfortable with confrontation and are very vocal about their discomforts may move fairly quickly into the next stage.

Stage three: A chaotic time

WHEN FAMILIES GET stuck in this stage, and many families do for some time, it is easy to believe that this is what stepfamily life is all about: struggle, pain, and hardship. When you are in this stage, it is hard to believe that you will ever make it out. Still married, anyway.

The fact of the matter is, a lot of us don't. This is the make or break time for stepfamilies. It is the time when accusations fly, feelings are stomped on, people are fed up, and change is going to happen, one way or another. People who have blisters on their tongues from biting them so much, knots in their stomachs from the tension, who are feeling dizzy from all the deep breaths they have been taking while counting to ten have had enough. They start making noise.

How families act during the chaos stage depends on the family member's personalities and the situation. In northern Washington state, the Wilkowski family spent years screaming and shouting and having knock-down, drag-out fights. A family in Dallas screamed some, but their main mode of destruction was biting, sarcastic criticism. In Minnesota, a stepmother who remained quiet for years in her own private "What did I get myself into?" stage finally started speaking up, ever more forcefully, as she pushed her family into the chaos stage. Meanwhile, in Minneapolis, the Lennon/Urbanski family didn't scream or shout, but calmly and respectfully worked through the conflicting needs in the family.

However your family gets to or through the chaos stage, it is usually pretty easy to tell when you are in it, because your family life stinks.

During the chaos stage, all those thoughts that things aren't working right start to show up in actions. A stepmother may insist that her husband limit his interactions with his ex-wife—the children's mother. A father may respond that the stepmother is out of line and better just get over his interactions with the ex. Parent and stepparent may argue about discipline, running the household, scheduling, and money. A child might start acting out in school or at home, having academic trouble or withdrawing from favorite activities or friends.

When things are not working well in a stepfamily, it is very common for the stepparent to be the one pushing for change. Papernow talks about how families who combine under one roof often have "insiders" and "outsiders." Usually, the outsider is the stepparent. If both parents bring children to the marriage, there is often one sub-family that is more dominant, the insiders, and one that is more passive, the outsiders.

As the outsider in a family feels more uncomfortable, she will likely be the one asking for changes. The insider often considers these requests for change as attacks. And certainly, there may be attacks. But whatever the emotional tone of the requests, the underlying need is the same: There needs to be some accommodation made to create a working, stable new stepfamily.

This can be an emotionally grueling stage. But when you know it is predictable and that there are ways out, it takes away some of the really scary thoughts that hang over stepfamilies: I really am no good at marriage; I'm going to fail (again); how will my children ever learn to have a healthy relationship?

Everything in second marriages is weighted with these doubts and fears. The fear itself can be a major obstacle in getting everyone in the family to look at new ways of interacting. But you can fight the fears, and you can help each other through this very difficult time in some practical, concrete ways.

To rid yourself of this stage, you need to start listening to each other in new ways. Papernow says we need to become curious about each other in practical ways—what do we need from each other? From our family? What isn't working? Why and what can we do about it?

Adults who are not able to do this may want to consider getting some help. Those who can't get through this tough stage are laying the groundwork for a second divorce.

Conversely, if family members are receptive to hearing about disappointments and conflicts, the family will likely unite in ways they have not been able to until now. The parents will work together, sorting out what needs to change to accommodate every family member's needs.

Stage four: A working stability

Depending on how long and how bitter the chaos stage is, there may be a lot of work to do to get the stepfamily up and running smoothly. If there has been a complete breakdown of communication and hurtful accusations have been made, your work is twofold. You have to sort out what is not working and how to make it work, and you have to address the ways that your family communicates and listens to each other.

If the stepfather says to his wife, "I want you to spend some time with me at night and not devote the entire evening to Monopoly," but the mother hears, "Your kid is a pain to have around, why don't you get rid of him so we can have our relationship," then each person in the conversation needs to hear the underlying fears and acknowledge them. The husband may feel left out. The mother may worry that her son will feel like she is favoring her new husband. There are many compromises that could be worked out so that everyone gets a little bit of what they want, but first you need to be able to understand the complications of a seemingly simple issue.

If a parent and a stepparent can begin to understand each other's sensitivities, each is more likely to accommodate the other's perspective to some degree. The stepdad might tell his wife that he thinks her time with her child is really important and he is glad they have a good relationship. He would like to find a way to have some time for their relationship, as well.

The mother, her fears being acknowledged, might suggest herself that she and her son play their game every other night, or for less time each night so that there can be some couple time.

This is often the stage when the new stepparent and the stepchild create their relationship on their own terms. They may begin to settle their differences without the help, or sometimes interference, of the parent. A mother who quits trying to manage the relationship between the stepparent and stepchild may be relieved to discover that when she steps back, her husband and child sometimes figure it out themselves beautifully.

We can all have other discoveries when we try to see the situation from each other's point of view. When a stepfather knows that his stepson worries about his dad feeling replaced, the stepfather may back off and give the child some extra space.

When a mother knows her daughter is nasty to the new stepdad in the house because the girl is worried that her mom will like the new husband more than her, the mother may add an extra dose of love and assurance to her limit-setting.

When family members talk more openly and honestly about the unique aspects of their family, it becomes easier to smooth the wrinkles that caused such tension and stress in the previous stage. In this stage, family members become more comfortable and accepting of each other's differences.

What follows from that acceptance and understanding is that people start communicating from a different perspective, one that is sensitive to the history and alliances in a family. The parent, stepparent, and children begin to build "their family's way."

STAGE FIVE: COMMITMENT AND ACCEPTANCE

AFTER A WHILE, the way of the new family becomes more ingrained in everyday life. The issues or comments that once caused pain and conflict are either sorted out and resolved, or they don't have as much power to rile and anger people.

There's a sense of acceptance that things are the way they are. Not everyone appreciates all of the ways a family develops, but everyone accepts that the family is together for the long haul and this is the way the family works.

Most people in the stepfamily begin to relax and loosen up at this stage. There's no longer a sense of impending doom; these families have made it to a point where they feel solid and supported.

Family members can often look back and laugh at some of the times when they didn't believe that their family would survive the stress of creating a stepfamily.

Relationships that were once tenuous at best have become stable and respectful. Some relationships have bloomed into deep affection or love. There aren't all happy endings. But at this point in stepfamilies, even the most difficult relationships are now tolerated without such anxiety or stress. Family members who simply tolerate each other and don't have warm and close relationships don't threaten the whole of the family.

Making it to this stage gives families a solid sense of mastery, a feeling of major accomplishment. To get here often takes passionate dedication, but those who have made it say that there is real satisfaction in their success.

10

THE MORGAN/MERDAD FAMILY SYSTEM OF MESA, ARIZONA

◦✴◦

THE CHILDREN/STEPCHILDREN:

Hannah Merdad, the eighteen-year-old daughter of Stephanie and Warren, lives primarily at mom and stepdad's house, and sees her dad sporadically. Carl Merdad, the sixteen-year-old son of Stephanie and Warren, lives primarily at mom and stepdad's house, and sees his dad sporadically.

MOM: Stephanie Morgan divorced Warren in 1995 and started dating Randy when the children were nine and eleven.

DAD: Warren Merdad, divorced and remarried, is in the process of a second divorce.

STEPDAD: Randy Morgan married Stephanie when Carl was eleven and Hannah was thirteen.

A stepdad who leads classes at his church on stepfamily dynamics still struggles with his place in his own stepfamily after several years of marriage.

RANDY MORGAN HAD been married before; he had been a stepdad before. So he figured he had a good idea of what he was getting into when he fell in love with Stephanie.

He knew he was once again not going to be the "real" dad. He had never gotten to be the "real" dad. And it was something he had wanted. But he loved Stephanie and they both drew on their belief that God had plans for them in each other's lives.

In his darker moments, Randy sometimes wonders how God ever dreamed up this plan. Four years later, he says, God is still beating on him, trying to show him how to get it right.

Stephanie's two children, Hannah and Carl, were eleven and nine when Randy and Stephanie started dating. The children live full-time with their mother and see their dad sporadically. Visits to their father's house had been regular and consistent before he started his second divorce proceedings, but the schedule has been less consistent since then. Their father still calls them on the phone every day, just as he has since the divorce.

The children remember the loud and boisterous fights between their mom and dad. Although the children weren't thrilled about the divorce, the volume in the house did decrease when their parents lived in separate places.

When Randy moved in, life in the household became difficult for everyone. For the children, having another adult tell them what they ought to be doing was pretty tough to take. For Stephanie, having another adult come in and criticize the way she parented was equally difficult. And Randy sometimes felt like no one in the family, not the children, not his wife, wanted him there. He, himself, often wondered if he really wanted to be there.

People in this family have no problem saying what they think. Often, they scream what they think. They yell, they talk about everything, they analyze and criticize and complain openly, loudly, and without hesitation. They do not suffer in silence. So when Randy moved in, there was more fighting, more blaming and shouting. Several times, everyone involved thought that this marriage, too, was doomed.

It might have been if Stephanie and Randy didn't do something to help themselves. They were already heavily involved in their church. As the issue of stepfamilies began to overwhelm their lives, the church was a logical place to turn for help.

FINDING HELP THROUGH THE CHURCH

THE CENTRAL CHRISTIAN Church of Mesa, Arizona is a mega church with an enormous congregation. On Sunday mornings, the acres of parking lot are filled as many of the five thousand members come to services, classes, and small, specialized groups.

Randy and Stephanie realized quickly that they weren't alone in their frustration over their new stepfamily. They belonged to a small group of singles that were quickly pairing up and forming stepfamilies. With the help of another couple, close friends who had also remarried with children, Randy and Stephanie began a small group of their own. They dedicated it to learning about how to cope in stepfamilies with the support of faith in their lives.

The group took off as more and more people realized the support they got when husbands and wives, parents and stepparents got together in a room and talked about the challenges of combining families.

Stephanie and Randy have been working with the group for almost two years. Even as they're running classes and giving advice on ways to ease the transitions in these kinds of families, the two struggle to put the same advice to work in their own lives.

It is easier to see how others can do things differently than it is to apply the same principles to their own lives, they both acknowledge. But they also believe that without the support of the group, without the concrete education and advice that they have gained from studying about stepfamilies, there is no way their marriage would have made it through many turbulent times.

There are still loud arguments and disagreements about how things are done—especially how things are done with the children. But there is also a working stability, an acceptance that they are going to make it together, even if it is sometimes hard.

Some of the issues haven't gone away. Randy still sometimes expects that the children will do something without being asked, just because it has to be done. And Stephanie still finds the idea completely unrealistic. But today, the whole discussion takes place over well-worn ground. Now, they just smile or laugh because they know they disagree. And then they move on.

RANDY MORGAN

RANDY HAS BEEN around religious ideas his whole life. Growing up, some people in his family took him to the Mormon church, others took him to the Baptist church. By the time he was eight years old, he'd been baptized a Baptist. His father was constantly exploring all the different religions of the world and sharing his explorations with his son.

So Randy isn't didactic about his particular brand of Christianity. He just believes that God, in whatever form, is a powerful force not to be overlooked in people's lives. When he thinks about his marriage, he can't separate it from his faith. It helps him that he and Stephanie are answering to something bigger than themselves or their marriage.

"I don't know how marriage can operate successfully without some element of faith," Randy said. "Do I say that I've got this figured out? No, I'm a work in progress, I'm still learning. God's still beating on me. But I think it works better with some element of faith. It triangulates a little bit. You can try to do this thing on two wheels, it takes a lot of balance and it's kind of shaky, and when you're getting it off and going, you're going to crash a few times. Yeah, you can get it down the road, but how much easier is it to have that tricycle effect where you've got that triangulation of faith into a higher power."

It is one of the few areas in this sometimes-stormy marriage where there is no disagreement about how things should be. He's grateful that he and Stephanie have been able to draw strength from this common ground. As the stepfamily support group grew, Randy said that he's been able to use much of what they have learned.

Randy loves that he married a powerful, strong woman. She has definite opinions and she's quick to shoot them his way. Sometimes, the force of her comments is so strong Randy feels like he's trying to manage a gale-force wind. He's learned to separate out the delivery and sometimes even the content, and try to concentrate on the motives.

One night, Randy and Stephanie went out for dinner with some good friends. Randy drove over with the kids; Stephanie was in a separate car. When everyone sat down in the restaurant, one of the teenagers, in a huff, was still sitting out in the car. The teenagers had argued on the way over in Randy's car, but Randy didn't think it was a big deal. Stephanie, fielding the cell phone calls from her upset son in the car, was clearly annoyed that Randy hadn't intervened. "You don't even know the difference between fooling around and fighting," she said, her voice heavy with accusation.

Randy thought about it for a second, and decided to let it go. He says he's learned to use a little internal process of checking with himself before he responds to Stephanie's comments.

"What are you willing to die for?" he said. "What issue is so big that you're willing to trade off your relationship for? It's amazing what people are willing to die for. Are you willing to get divorced over it, are you willing to ruin the week, the month, the night, whatever?"

In the end, he can usually let things go because he trusts that Stephanie is coming from a good place, no matter how harsh her words are.

"If you're looking at content, you'd be offended," Randy said. "Her motive is pure, in every instance. Doesn't mean that she doesn't piss me off. Doesn't mean that I don't think that she's entirely wrong in content. Doesn't mean that she might not later agree with me. All that's different from her motive. Even in the heat of an argument, even when I'm so mad at her I could spit, I genuinely sense that she has my best interests at heart."

Randy doesn't attempt to pretend that just because he *knows* what works that he's always able to do it. There's a huge difference between knowing that you have to eat better and exercise more to lose weight and actually exercising and eating better. But Randy said that over time, with plenty of opportunity for practice, he's getting better at doing the right thing.

"Doesn't mean that sometimes I don't die for things that are stupid," he said. "All these things are in theory. Follow me around, very little of it is in practice. But it's much better than not having any theories and just wandering around bumping into things."

The sore thumb principle

Randy can have a very sharp tongue and there are times when he's unleashed it on Stephanie. But he's learning to really pull his punches, to try to resolve the issue without attacking her.

Randy and Stephanie have a lot of key phrases that they use to try to remind themselves to be caring, nurturing partners to each other. One of the things that they talk about not only amongst themselves, but also in their classes, is that all remarried couples bring baggage from their previous relationships. Most people have pain and tender feelings about certain areas of their lives that haven't gone well in previous relationships. In stepfamilies, this is certainly the case, as at least one partner has terminated a relationship with children involved. Randy said that he has to try and keep in mind Stephanie's "sore thumb."

"If I just tap your thumb it doesn't hurt," Randy said. "The physical act of tapping your thumb doesn't hurt. Now, yesterday, you were hanging pictures and you whacked the heck out of your thumb and it's twice the size that it normally is, black and blue. I come back and I tap your thumb. You go through the roof. You're ready to punch me out. Nothing different about the tapping.

"I try to get people to see that their past marriages give them sore thumbs. They may have particular areas where they're extremely sensitive to certain subject matters. If you had a husband who had been sexually promiscuous or did Internet porn or matters of such, the new husband tarrying a little too long at the Sears brassiere ads might invoke all kinds of fears and angers and everything else because of the sore thumb principle.

"If the thumb is sore, it's not the responsibility of the thumb holder as much as it is the person who might accidentally bump the thumb. And if they accidentally bump the thumb, they have to be ready, willing, and able, if they really love this person and really want to be relational, to realize that 'Yeah, it's an irrational reaction, but it's the only one they've got today.'"

So, Randy said, couples have to be aware of what is going to trigger escalated responses, rational or not, and try to accommodate their partners. The only way that the woman in the example is going to trust her new husband in this area is to see, over time, that he respects her sensitivity.

"If he wants to be married to this woman, he has to acknowledge the woman's feelings, he has to understand that the fear is real," Randy said.

Always the outsider

Randy entered a family with two adolescent children. He moved into that family's home, complete with memories and artifacts from the first family. When he moved in, he agreed to keep his dogs outside. He agreed to put some stuff in the garage for a while. A bunch of his stuff never made it past the garage.

Even four years later, the big picture of his wife's former parents-in-law still has prime wall space in the living room. The beautiful rug that they gave Stephanie and her first husband hangs on the same wall.

Randy isn't bothered by the pictures or presents from Stephanie's former life. The grandparents are still the grandparents to the children, he says, and besides, they have been incredibly gracious and welcoming to him. Stephanie doesn't have any troubles getting along with her ex-husband, now that they're living separate lives. And Randy thinks those are good things. He said that he and the children's father, Warren, have been able to form a relationship that Randy never expected. After Randy had open-heart surgery last year, he came to in the hospital room to find Warren sitting there. It was nice to have his support.

Still, coming into a house where everyone is used to doing things their own way took a lot of adjustment. Randy had ideas, too, about how things should run, about how children and parents should interact, about how discipline should be doled out.

But he found that in his new marriage, his new family, no one was very interested in his opinions. Even when he was defending Stephanie against something one of the children did, Stephanie would side with the child.

"The hardest thing for me is being the outsider, the fifth wheel feeling. I will never be a member of the family in full standing. It just isn't going to happen. There's no blood. Even with all my preparation, I was unprepared for that," Randy said. "I glibly believed that time and space eventually would produce a replica of a nuclear or biofamily that would be so real that you couldn't tell the difference. That was wrong and I don't believe that's ever going to occur. It's terribly lonely—this sense of being an outsider. There are these family blood relationships that are just stronger than anything I could have ever imagined. That's the biggie, just finally coming to grips with that it's always going to be that way."

Again and again, Randy has to go back and change his expectations for his life to make them more realistic.

No child of his own

When he and Stephanie first got together, they had agreed that they wouldn't have any more children. They talked about it extensively and came to the decision to get Stephanie's children off to college and spend their time together instead.

Randy said Stephanie wondered if he could really put away the dream of having his own child without resenting her two children. Randy said he could. And he's tried to, although there are times when he does have resentments. And as much as Randy likes their dad Warren, there are moments when the children head out with him that the stepdad has pangs of jealousy.

After a while, Randy realized that he was hoping for more from Carl than he was likely to get. Randy grew up idolizing his own father. He wanted to show Carl all the things that he was doing in his life, just the way his dad had shown him.

"I realized Carl and I were having some hard times for a while. I kind of came to the conclusion and I confessed it to Stephanie that part of the problem was this unmet expectation that he would be like I was with my dad," Randy said. "When Carl wouldn't come to work with me and he said what I did was dumb, I was very, very deeply hurt because I had foregone my opportunity to have a bioson and the stepson was never going to meet that expectation."

"I can accept Carl where he's at now. I went to Carl and I told him this," Randy said. "I said, 'Carl, this is why I think I've been so angry with you. This is why I've been so hard on you. I never got to have a boy of my own. Guess what, you're the only son I'm ever going to have. You didn't ask for that privilege. I acknowledge that, you didn't apply and get the job. Your mom kind of forced it on you. So I'm going to stop trying to be Geppetto and Pinocchio. And our relationship has gotten a lot better."

Randy said that the better he gets at recognizing his unrealistic expectations and letting them go, the better his marriage is, his family is, the better he can enjoy his life. And he's been very impressed with Carl. Randy said that when it comes to relationships, Carl, at sixteen, is more mature than he is at forty-seven.

"He has a compassion for me in my plight, which is really amazing," Randy said. "He understands and is concerned about my outsider status. To a sixteen-year-old's ability, he makes every effort to try not to put me out of things."

STEPHANIE MORGAN

STEPHANIE'S FIRST MARRIAGE had plenty of fights about the children. Stephanie believed that her first husband picked on their son, Carl. But even though she stood up for her children, she never really had any questions about their father's intentions.

"I knew in my heart how much he loved them, he loved them as much as I did," Stephanie said. "That was always there so I didn't have that struggle with whether he loved them."

In her second marriage, there's little that is certain when it comes to the relationship between her children and her husband. She believes that Randy wants what's best for her children, but she knows that there isn't that bond that comes from blood.

And so when Randy has complaints about the way her children behave, or the way that she responds to their behavior, it's very hard for Stephanie to listen without becoming defensive.

Not only does she love them more than he does, but she feels like she knows more about raising children and has a better understanding of what children do. Randy doesn't have a lot of tolerance for typical child behavior.

"You can look at it lots of different ways. A guy who has two kids and brings them here and adds them to my two kids, we'd have a lot more problems," Stephanie said. "But it's a very big problem, Randy not having kids, because he's sitting here trying to tell me how to raise mine. And he's totally unrealistic.

"He said 'Why didn't the kids do the dishes?' And I said, 'Well, I didn't ask them to do them,' and he said, "Well you shouldn't have to ask them, they should just come and do them because they have to be done.' I said, 'Whose dream world do you live in? I could get you a hundred teenagers, Randy, and maybe one of them would be that way.' He laughed. Two years ago, we would have gotten in a knock-down, drag-out fight."

Her daughter Hannah in particular clashed with Randy. Stephanie spent a lot of time trying to smooth over their disagreements. But most of the time, Stephanie thought that Randy really needed to be the one to change.

"He would say things like, 'How would you know Hannah, you're only thirteen,' when she would try to interject something," Stephanie said. "See, in our life, she was allowed to talk. I've always believed that children are allowed to have an opinion. If I'm going to make a decision, I'm going to make it. Of course, I was a little wishy-washy about that too. But they were allowed to voice an opinion. Randy doesn't believe that children have an opinion. That's one of the things we always fight about. He almost tries to treat children like they're a lesser human being. I was treated that way by my stepfather and so that doesn't go over very well with me at all."

"Randy has learned a lot," Stephanie said. "He has learned that his sarcasm hurts people."

It's one of the things that Stephanie loves so much about Randy, that they can learn together how to treat each other and the children better. Stephanie said that one of the things she would have done differently in the beginning is be more supportive of Randy in front of the children. She would have made her expectations that they treat him well clearer. But she was worried in the beginning. She knew Hannah didn't want her to marry

Randy in the first place, so she was always erring on the side of supporting Hannah. She says now that she wished she had said a lot more things like, 'Hannah, I don't care what you think, Randy is here to stay.' She would have told both of her children to thank him for what he did for them, to treat him more respectfully.

In another year or so, her youngest child will be moving out of the house and Stephanie is surprised by the suddenness. At times it seemed like she and Randy wouldn't make it until the children left. But considering how intense both she and her husband are, how strong-willed and stubborn, she thinks that they have done all right by the children and by their marriage.

She's said that when they no longer have the issues of day-to-day child raising, their relationship will have to be reinvented. She's excited about the possibilities.

CARL MERDAD

CARL REMEMBERS THE first time that he laid eyes on his stepdad, Randy. Carl was nine years old and Randy showed up at the door for a date with the family on the fourth of July. The boy was not impressed. Randy had long hair and a potbelly. Carl said he looked weird, like the kind of guy you just don't talk to.

"You could tell he'd had no friends in high school," Carl said.

It was the beginning of what would be a rough start with the children. Since his mom and dad separated about a year earlier, it had just been Carl, his sister Hannah, and their mom living their lives in the house. That was all to change over the next few months and it was hard getting used to another adult telling him what to do.

Carl does remember some good times in those early days. He has especially fond memories of helping Randy at the appliance store that Randy owns.

"When I started working at his store, that was cool," Carl said. "We were buddies, we were cool. I liked being buddies rather than now being stepdad and stepson."

In those early days of his mother's remarriage especially, Carl resented Randy's attempts to control him and his sister. He said that when his mother wasn't around, Randy would turn from a lovey-dovey husband into a tyrant. He'd go out of his way to try to make Carl or Hannah do some chore, usually something that they wouldn't have had to do with their mother around. Very early on, he remembers a particularly difficult night.

"One night, he was cooking and Hannah didn't want to help him cook, she's not a cooking person," Carl said. "He left. And mom wasn't home. He left us home alone for like five hours, just because he got mad. That was when they first got married. Hannah was thirteen, so I was eleven," Carl said. "She wouldn't cut the potatoes or the onions or something so he got mad and called her an ignorant teenager or something."

Over and over again, the fights came about either with the children or between the adults about what the children should be doing, about how Randy and Stephanie should handle it.

"For like two or three years, it was an adjustment," Carl said. "I can see that now. Before I was just like, 'I hate this.'

"I was mad at Mom more than him. Because, I figured, her first marriage was ruined and now her second marriage was ruined and I don't think she found the wrong guy twice," Carl said. "So I started to think maybe it's Mom and maybe she needs to change. I never thought the fighting would end. And then generally, it got better and better."

Carl remembers the fighting from his parents' marriage. He was nine years old when they separated. At sixteen, he has no wishes for them to reunite.

"I can't imagine if they were still together. It'd be unending arguing. They just didn't agree on anything so I don't know what the point of two people being together is," Carl said. "I was sick of my dad always getting yelled at and never sticking up for himself. He's so passive.

"Then Randy comes along and he doesn't take mom's crap. So I looked up to him, kind of," Carl said.

"He's a good influence on me," Carl said. "But we're too much alike. He doesn't take my crap and I don't take his crap so we're always butting heads. But it's always a playful kind of thing. We get over it in five minutes. We'll have an argument, I'll run to my room for five minutes, I'll come back down and we'll make dinner. It's no big deal.

"In my eyes, he's here to stay. I'll make the best of it. I hope he's here to stay."

Carl has seen a lot of marriages fall apart. Not only have his parents divorced, but his father's second marriage collapsed as well. Carl feels very close to Randy, he trusts him and says that if he ever needed protecting, Randy would be there for him. Carl says that even though their bond is strong, it won't ever be the same as the bond with his father.

He recognizes that Randy is much more involved in his everyday life than his father is, and sometimes he feels badly about that.

"I don't ever want my dad to be out of the picture. Like if I get married, I don't want to say 'These (Stephanie and Randy) are my parents.' I don't ever want that to happen," Carl said. "Yet, I want him to be there. I just want him to know his boundaries. Not like a bad thing, but I always hope that I remember them, too. Like he's my stepdad, I have a dad."

Carl thinks about why he worries about being too close to Randy.

"I don't ever want to get too used to Randy, I don't ever want to forget that he married my mom (not me)," he said. "Like I don't want to get too close to him, because maybe he'll leave. That might be."

As Carl looks at his life, things are going well. He's always been a top student, and he is well liked by the children at school, at least in part because of his stunning abilities in gymnastics. He's been practicing since preschool, putting countless hours in on the mats and bars. When he performs back handsprings and front flips it's an impressive sight.

Carl said that there's a lot to feel good about in his life. He's happy, for example, that not only do his mom and his dad get along well, but Randy and his dad get along well, too.

"We have what other people don't," Carl said. "There was no custody battle. Automatically, they want to share us. Most kids' divorced parents aren't friends, aren't chummy, they don't come over and hang out. We have that."

11

$\mathcal{W}$HOSE RULES RULE

ONE OF THE largest tasks we have in stepfamilies is disciplining our children well. The original definition of discipline is to train. But the word has garnered some unpleasant connotations in families. Parents and children alike sometimes confuse discipline with punishment, confuse power with teaching.

We are always training our children. Children are learning all the time how things work in their households, how to get what they want, how they should treat people. All parents, in step or first families, have to figure out if they are training their children to behave in the way they hope for.

We have all seen some version of the child in the grocery store, screaming for a cookie. The flustered mother denies the cookie before dinner, but becomes more and more impatient as the child's screams reach ever-higher octaves. Eventually, the mother says, "OK, here's one cookie, but only if you stop screaming. And that's the only one, so no more fuss."

Until the child finishes the first cookie, anyway.

This parent is training her child. Her child knows his mother's rules well enough to know that if he screams loud enough, he will get the cookie. The child is smart; he is playing by the rules that his mother has taught him.

But the mother does not see the success. She feels defeated and frustrated that her child throws such temper tantrums. She wants to train her son to accept no for an answer. Her actions, however, are training her son to throw tantrums.

Unconscious discipline is still discipline. And it is one of the toughest aspects of raising children in any family. But stepfamilies have additional work on top of this already intense parental challenge.

When a stepfamily is formed, a parent and the children already have in place their system of discipline, however effective or unsuccessful the system may be. When a stepparent enters the household, he sees the discipline system with fresh eyes. Almost always, the stepparent will see the system of discipline differently than the parent. The stepparent may demand changes. The parent may resent what he sees as an additional challenge to his authority. Besides, the parent may vehemently disagree with the stepparent's proposed solutions. And this doesn't even cover agreements (or disagreements) between the two *households* over discipline.

When it comes to discipline, the strategic question for stepfamilies is this: How can the adults involved in raising the children work together to form a consistent and thoughtful approach to training the children?

In an ideal world, the parents and the stepparents, realizing that a parenting plan would help them on this issue, would sit down before the wedding and hash out what they expected and how to reach those goals.

Sadly, most of us don't live in an ideal world. I don't want to be too cynical about this, though. If we only scoff at the possibility of creating a workable and functioning home, even between homes, we run the risk of closing the door to the possibility. It is more than a possibility for some families. Some stepfamilies are living the reality of working together, cooperating for the sake of the child and for the sake of everyone else's sanity. It can be done. It is being done in many homes. But it is still rare.

Sometimes, we just have to concentrate on what we can do in our own homes. If parents and stepparents are at completely opposite ends of the spectrum when it comes to discipline, there are still things that each can do to help themselves and their situation.

KNOW WHAT YOU WANT

DO YOU EXPECT children to be seen and not heard? Or do you want to raise your child to have strong opinions that he is not afraid to defend? Do you consider a teenager's under-the-breath comment, "Whatever" to be a major form of disrespect or are you unfazed by your kid stomping off complaining about your "stupid house" and your "stupid rules?"

Especially if your household is full of conflict over discipline, you may have to back up to the beginning and ask yourself and your partner what you hope will result from your "training." It is pretty tough to be training someone in a job if we do not know what the job entails. Do you want your child to become a courteous person, become a respectful person, become an honest person?

While you are making up your wish list, it helps to think of a child as an adult in training. Maybe they are not completely courteous, respectful, or honest right now. But they are still in the training program. They are allowed to screw up. It does not mean that they will never become the person you want them to become. When you are disappointed in your child or stepchild's behavior, it helps to keep a long-term perspective. They are works in progress. In the meantime, finding the good things about them right now and encouraging their successes will help other areas progress that much more rapidly.

It may be that the parent and the stepparent have very similar goals for the child, but disagree about how to reach them. Parents and stepparents need to spend some time thinking about how they want to run their house. You might think about breaking behavior down into three categories.

- There are behaviors that are unpleasant but not worth fighting over, like eye-rolling, talking back, and bickering between siblings.
- There are behaviors that might be negotiable with the child, with the parents as the final arbiter. (It may be OK to scream if you are angry, but go somewhere where people don't have to hear you. Or take five minutes to be angry and then come back and figure out what needs to happen.)
- There are behaviors that are completely unacceptable. (Any violence against another person or destruction of property.)

As a parenting team you must figure out where your comfort level is with the variety of behaviors that children throw at you. And sometimes, you will not know what feels right until you have tested it out for a while. That is why it is always a good idea to keep the conversation about discipline an ongoing one.

UNITED WE PARENT

IN EVERY HOME, it is important for parents to be united about what is acceptable and what is unacceptable. Children are professional loophole finders. If there is a weak spot in the parents' rules, children will find it and exploit it. Not because children are devious, but because they are smart and they figure out how to manipulate the world to get what they need, or simply want.

In stepfamilies, presenting a united front to the children becomes even more critical. There are already obvious alliances between the child and the parent and obvious opportunities, if not realities, for division between the child and the stepparent. If the family is going to function well, it is a lot easier to do with two adults who agree about how things should run.

Children thrive on consistency and clear understanding of the rules. They may not like the rules, but they appreciate knowing what to expect. If the parent and the stepparent do not agree about what to expect, the child will know that in a second. Some children can handle that kind of unpredictability without a problem. But for a lot of children, not knowing the rules and sensing the tension between the stepparent and the parent on this issue can be anxiety-provoking.

Parents are in a difficult spot in this area. If they disagree with their partner about how to parent their child, they feel obligated to stand up for their child and what they think is right. Most parents are very alert to the fact that their child is watching, wondering if the parent is going to give in to the stepparent's every demand at the child's expense. It can be a terrible predicament for a parent.

The one thing that can be helpful to think about is that children thrive in well-functioning families. It does not necessarily matter if the family is a first family or a stepfamily or a single-parent family. When the adults are handling life's issues and supporting their children, the children are usually well-adjusted people. If you are going to have a happy stepfamily, it is going to start with a supportive marriage. Make your marriage a priority and the children will see the security that comes from two people figuring out their differences to support them.

In addition, it is important that parents address the changes directly with their child. Confirm for them that there will be changes with the addition of a stepparent in the home. But also assure them that you will always love them and do what you believe is in their best interest.

Then you just have to figure out what that is.

If a parent and a stepparent simply cannot agree about a discipline issue, they still need to come to some kind of decision. In many households, the parent is the one with the final say. It is their child, after all. But the best solution is one that the adults can agree on.

Stepparents, while not the parent, are often still responsible for their stepchildren for some portion of time. Custodial stepparents, especially, have a lot of the responsibility of day-to-day parenting. If the stepparent is asked to take on these responsibilities, then the couple must make every effort to reconcile their disciplining differences so that the child can be clear about the expectations of the household.

THE TOLERANCE GAP

STEPPARENTS AND PARENTS are likely to feel their differences in parenting more acutely in the area of discipline than in any other area of family interaction. They have different ideas about how a child should act; they have different ideas about how parents should act. Parents and stepparents often find each other completely unreasonable on this issue.

Parents are able to see themselves in their children, and with that view, parents are more likely to be secure in their confidence of their children's future. To view bothersome habits as phases, not as deep-seated personality flaws, to focus on the child's hobbies or talents or interesting ways of looking at the world. Stepparents, especially new stepparents, cannot see themselves or their influence in a child's behavior, looks, or habits. Stepparents do not have the sense of recognition that parents have.

Parents have other advantages over stepparents when it comes to raising children. Almost all parents have a deep well to draw on when it comes to loving their child no matter what kind of attitude or behavior the child has at the moment, or over several moments.

At least as significant as that deep well is the seasoning of a parent. A parent builds a gradual tolerance for clothes left on the floor, for loud voices and jumping around, for incessant demands made with indignant entitlement. Parents come to accept that as normal for a child. And their child's particular style of being a child does not usually grate on a parent.

Stepparents do not have that deep well of love to draw on. They do not have any seasoned tolerance or acceptance of a child's behavior. Without these cushioning buffers, stepparents might be appalled by what their stepchild does. And they might be doubly appalled that the parent lets it happen.

Stepparents are much more likely to notice when the child doesn't do his chores, when he's being disrespectful, when he's lying about something, when he's manipulating his parent. Stepparents may feel like the parent is ignoring the mantra of child discipline experts: firm limits and consistency. So the stepparent may try to overcorrect for what he sees as a parent's leniency and inconsistency.

The parent is much more likely not to keep score of his child's troublesome behaviors. Which means that parents and stepparents often end up clashing over what the child does. Parents may retreat even further from bad behavior because they feel like the stepparent is overly harsh. This can get to such a sore point that many stepparents are often secretly cheering when a parent does come down firmly on unacceptable behavior.

When we know that stepparents and parents are likely to view the same behavior in very different ways, it can defuse a lot of the defensiveness on both sides of the argument. It also helps ease tensions to clearly define who will do what when it comes to discipline.

LET THE PARENT BE THE DISCIPLINARIAN

STEPPARENTS WHO CORRECT a stepchild from the beginning of their relationship will likely find themselves frustrated not only by the stepchild's response, but often by the lack of support from the parent, as well. It may be completely instinctive for the stepparent to correct a child. But it almost certainly will not feel natural for the child. When a parent senses his child's discomfort, he may get defensive for his child.

The biggest thing that the parenting team can do to create a successful discipline strategy is to have the parent take the lead. Parents need to be the ones, particularly in the early days of a stepfamily, to lay down the law and enforce the consequences.

Children have a hard time taking correction from someone they do not see as a parental figure—someone they may not know very well or like very much. And the older a child is, the more likely it is that he'll be very vocal about not accepting another adult's authority over him. Adolescents can hardly stand the parents they have already; they have no interest in picking up yet another. At least not the correction part of parenting. Most children really enjoy having another adult interested in them and their lives.

And that is where an effective stepparent concentrates his energy in the beginning. Try to show the child that you are interested in him, that you want to have a relationship with him. Look for the things that you enjoy about his personality or hobbies and work, slowly, on building a relationship with the child.

There will be times in most families when a stepparent has to be in charge. The parent has to be away from home and the stepparent and child are left together. This is the kind of situation in which it is very helpful to have clearly-defined house rules. If the adults are clear about what the rules of the house are, it is easier to be clear with the child.

And when the stepparent has to be in charge, the framework for the rules is already in place. He can more comfortably remind a child of a rule, not because it is his wishes, but because that is the way things work in the house. Some stepparents find it helpful to lay the rule at the parent's feet, as in "Oh, I can tell you'd like to stay up later, but you know your dad said that you need to be in bed at nine P.M."

Even with a framework in place, a child will have a difficult time accepting a stepparent's authority if the child senses that the adults aren't united about the framework. One common complaint of stepparents is that they have all the work of raising a child, but none of the authority. If a parent wants a child to respect the stepparent's authority, the parent should make that expectation clear to the child. One child told me that he knew he had to listen to his stepmother because his father had told him, "If it's coming out of (your stepmother's) mouth, it's just like it's coming out of my mouth." Doesn't get much clearer than that.

There are exceptions to every rule and the parent-in-command rule is no different. Stepparents do not have to tolerate being treated badly by their stepchildren. Hopefully, if a stepchild is rude or disrespectful to a stepparent, the parent will chime in right away with an admonition and a reminder about the rules of the house (which hopefully include respectful behavior). But if the parent fails to defend the stepparent or if the parent is not around, the stepparent can certainly underscore his own expectations about how to be treated.

"I don't like your sarcastic tone and I'm not going to talk to you right now."

Later, the parent and stepparent can discuss the situation, and if called for, the parent can reinforce the message of the stepparent authority. But a parent has to believe that the authority is in the child's best interest, or the parent will not be very credible.

ACKNOWLEDGE EACH OTHER'S CHALLENGES

EVEN WHEN A stepfamily is going through big changes, a lot of tension can be minimized and hurt feelings avoided if you work to understand and accept what is difficult about those changes for each person.

A child who is used to his parent's way of running things may already be unhappy with the changes forced upon him by his new stepfamily. Suddenly, his parent is changing the way he does things, changing expectations in the house. A change in a parent's expectations is always difficult. But when the child also has to deal with another adult assuming positions of authority, the child can really feel burdened.

A child might also be troubled by what he perceives as his parent's loyalty shifting toward the stepparent. It is typical that single parents give their children more of a voice in the way things run in a house. When a parent remarries, it is often difficult for the child to share his parent's love, time, and energy. But it may be as difficult to be cut out of the decision-making loop as the parent shifts to planning with the new stepparent.

Parents and stepparents alike can mention that they know there have been a lot of tough changes and that they can see how it would be maddening for the child. The child may not like the situation any better, but empathizing with him may make him feel more understood.

As I mentioned earlier, the shift of aligning to a stepparent is difficult for the parent as well. Parents who are very close to their children and share everything with them may feel that they are betraying their relationship with their child. It can feel like an impossible balancing act to try to please both the child and the partner. If parents are feeling overwhelmed by opposing demands from the child and the partner, parents may need to make some demands of their own. Parents can remind stepparents that they are willing to work on a discipline strategy, but they would appreciate some patience on the part of the stepparent. Parents can gently remind stepparents that there is a history to this family that will not disappear with a snap of the fingers.

Stepparents are the outsiders in an already formed family. But that does not mean that the stepparent has no ideas about how a family should run, how he wants his family to run. Stepparents often have some unrealistic ideas about how children behave. At the same time, stepparents often have some good ideas about how things might run more smoothly. As an outsider coming in, they can see how a family operates in a way that the people involved cannot. Stepparents often feel like their ideas are dismissed and that they are expected to just live with whatever the family has always done.

It is a rare home where parents feel like they discipline exactly as well as their ideals would dictate. If the stepparent and the parent can listen to each other's ideas without defensiveness, they can make a plan that works for everyone.

When it comes to creating a discipline plan, it helps to do some research into what you can realistically expect step/children to do at certain ages.

KNOW WHAT CHILDREN ARE LIKE

WHEN THE CHILDREN are born, the race is on and parents are usually so busy they are lucky if they get to eat three times a day. Given all we're doing, it is hard to find time for thinking, reading, and learning about how to parent our children.

We take lessons for a million things—learning to ski, to knit, to draw, to refinish furniture. We read manuals (OK, well, some of us read manuals) for TVs, VCRs, cell phones, and Palm Pilots. Figuring out a cell phone can be tricky, but it's got nothing on figuring out how to raise a child.

Raising a child is hard work. Raising a child in a stepfamily is even harder work. If you spend the time as parents and stepparents to take advantage of all the resources available to you, to read the manuals about children out there, you will have an easier go of it.

There are books, videos, classes, seminars, tapes, parenting and stepparenting support groups, and child's playtime groups all dedicated to giving you some context for your child and how to parent him.

By being around other children and listening to other parents, by reading about what typically developing children are doing at particular ages, you can get a fresh breath of perspective on your teenager's hibernation in his room.

Understanding children's development becomes even more important in stepfamilies because of the tolerance gap between parents and stepparents. If a parent really believes the child's behavior is typical and not to be worried about, but the stepparent is very concerned about patterns that are developing in the child's behavior, some outside perspective might help clarify the issue for both adults.

My husband and I sometimes call parenting summits. We go to the library, stock up on parenting books on a particular subject, and we spend a day or a weekend focusing on how we are going to address a particular issue. My husband and I are both writers and we are used to doing research. We actually really enjoy it. I know that the thought of hanging out with a bunch of parenting books might not sound like a great way to spend a weekend for a lot of people. But parenting takes enormous amounts of energy. Knowing about some different approaches always rejuvenates us; we always feel more united and ready to get back to it with renewed commitment.

EQUAL TREATMENT OF CHILDREN

CHILDREN ARE ALWAYS on the lookout for favoritism from the adults in their lives. This is even more prevalent in stepfamilies, in which not all children have the same parents. There can be his children, her children, and our children all in one household. Some children may live with you full time; some may live with you only on the weekends. Some you may see sporadically. When it comes to enforcing the rules of the house, the adults will find that the household runs with less conflict if the rules are equally applied to all children.

This may be difficult for all kinds of reasons. Adults are generally more likely to notice infractions in their stepchildren than they are in their own children. And in stepfamilies, it is common to have a wide variety of ages in the same household, further complicating the setting of suitable limits and expectations for each child.

But the payoff is worth the work. It is simply not fair to expect the child who lives in the house full-time to have several cleaning chores and a weekend child to have none. The children will recognize the discrepancy and will likely feel resentful of both each other and the adults.

There are times when a parent or stepparent may be annoyed at a particular child and feel like over-punishing. It is fine to feel that way; it would be unusual if you didn't. Just don't act that way if you want to create or maintain harmony in your home.

STAY OUT OF OTHER PEOPLE'S FIGHTS

ANOTHER WAY THAT you can promote harmony in your home is to let people fight. It may sound as logical as the ramblings of the rabbit in *Alice in Wonderland,* but it is usually true. In stepfamilies, relationships happen in triangles. A child and a stepparent are arguing about something and the parent jumps into the fray. A stepdaughter and a daughter both want to play with the same toy at the same time and an adult comes in to mediate a peace settlement.

Sometimes, the best way for people to settle their differences is to work through them. Children learn much by arguing with each other. They learn about how to get what they want, how to apologize and start again, how to negotiate, and how to be graceful in the face of someone's anger. It may not look like they are learning any of those things, but they probably are. And if a parent always comes in to smooth over conflicts between children, children do not figure out how to smooth over conflict for themselves nearly as effectively.

It can be difficult to listen to children bickering and being ugly and snide, and adults certainly ought to put limits on the fighting. They can call hitting and any other forms of physical aggression off-limits, for example. And others in the house may not want to listen to the fighting, so it makes sense to ask the children to go somewhere else. There may be specific times when a peace treaty needs to be enforced; you can declare that all arguing has to be put on hold until after dinner.

And letting people fight doesn't mean you should drop your responsibilities to train your children either. You still need to talk about how they behave, still set limits, and give suggestions about particular incidents.

But in the moment of an argument, it is usually best to let children figure out their own problems. If there is a big age difference and there is a risk of one child actually physically hurting another, obviously the parent will want to step in.

This advice works for another common triangle in stepfamilies as well. Stepparents and stepchildren sometimes find much to argue about. And a parent often jumps right into an argument that doesn't have anything to do with him. Many parents find an amazing sense of relief when they stop trying to manage the relationship between their spouse and their child. They can feel that relief because what usually happens is that the stepparent and the child start to figure out their own differences and get along better.

DISCIPLINE BETWEEN HOMES

EVERYTHING I HAVE discussed in this chapter can be applied to the other household as well. It is hard for families who have a high-conflict relationship with the other household to imagine sitting down with the other parent and, possibly, the other stepparent, and discuss these issues.

Still, the child is going between the two homes and if you're going to define the best possible circumstances, then working with the other household fits that definition. If you can agree on a basic framework of what you want the child to learn and how to teach those things, you will be more than halfway there.

When it comes to a united front, there is nothing better than knowing that all the parents involved in a child's life are supporting the same ideas of how to raise him. When you are working together, the child cannot play one household off of another because the parents are all talking to each other. The parent in the other household will certainly appreciate the deference to his role as primary disciplinarian and will likely appreciate the inclusion of his spouse as an important partner in raising this child.

It's important to acknowledge that the divorced couple may have some painful history that may include disagreements about how to raise the child. And the parent in the other household may be wary about the stepparent's involvement. But by working cooperatively with the other household, you teach your children that you can negotiate and manage your lives, even in difficult circumstances. This kind of modeling is the best training there is.

Obviously, this arrangement is out of reach for some families at some points. If you are not at this place with the other household there are a few things you can still do for yourself and for your children. You can work on the discipline in your own home. You can realize that the children can handle the differences between the homes if you do not criticize the other household. And you can keep the door open to the possibility that some-day you may have a different relationship with the other household.

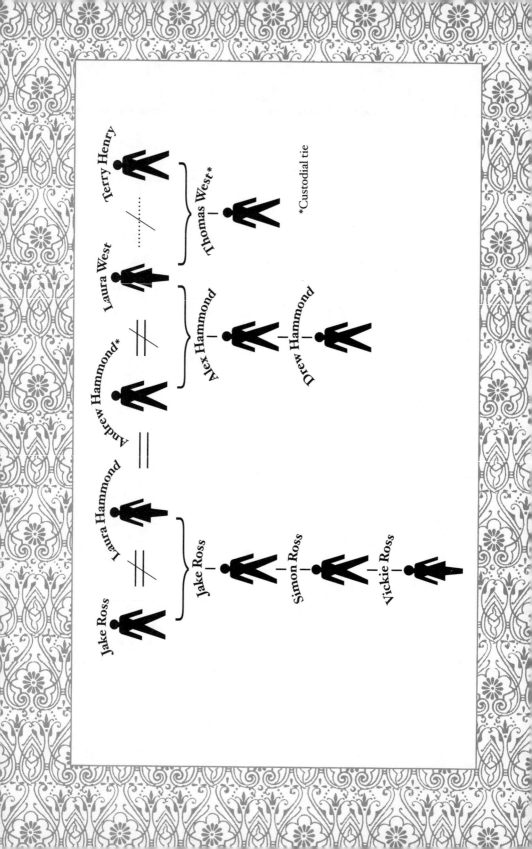

Jake Ross — Laura Hammond ≠ Andrew Hammond* = Laura West ⋯ Terry Henry

Jake Ross — Simon Ross — Vickie Ross

Alex Hammond — Drew Hammond

Thomas West*

*Custodial tie

12

THE HAMMOND/ROSS FAMILY SYSTEM OF FORT WORTH, TEXAS

❧

CHILDREN/STEPCHILDREN:

Thomas West, the twenty-five-year-old son of Laura West and Terry Henry, is Andrew Hammond's stepson. He was raised by Andrew Hammond after Andrew and his mother divorced. He lives on his own, outside the family home.

Alex Hammond, the twenty-two-year-old son of Andrew and Laura West, lives outside the family home.

Drew Hammond, the seventeen-year-old son of Andrew and Laura West, primarily lives with Andrew and stepmother Laura Hammond and sees his mother sporadically.

Jake Ross, the twenty-two-year-old son of Jake Ross, Sr. and Laura Hammond, lives outside the family home.

Simon Ross, the nineteen-year-old son of Jake Ross and Laura Hammond, lives primarily with his mother and stepfather Andrew and sees his father occasionally.

Vickie Ross, the seventeen-year-old daughter of Jake Ross and Laura Hammond, lives primarily with her mother and stepfather Andrew and sees her father occasionally.

MOMS/STEPMOMS:

Laura Hammond is mother to Jake, Simon, and Vickie Ross and stepmother to Thomas, Alex, and Drew Hammond for the past seven years.

Laura West is mother to Thomas, Alex, and Drew Hammond and has had sporadic contact with her children since divorcing Andrew.

Dad/stepdad: Andrew Hammond is father to Alex and Drew Hammond and stepfather to Thomas Hammond and Jake, Simon, and Vickie Ross. Andrew works as a photojournalist at a local TV station.

Two long-time single parents with well-established routines have much to reconcile when they try to raise their children together after getting married.

*I*N THE LIFE of a child, five years is a long, long time. When he became a single parent, Andrew Hammond spent five years seeing his three boys through myriad changes.

In that time, Drew, the four-year-old, grew from a kindergartener to a fourth-grader. Alex went from being a nine-year-old fourth grader to a high schooler. Thomas went from being a thirteen-year-old middle schooler to being old enough to live on his own.

Andrew's family got used to the routines in those five years. By the time Andrew met and fell in love with his second wife, he and his boys had some definite ways of doing things in their home.

Laura, as a single mother, had some definite patterns established as well. When she divorced her first husband in 1987, she spent seven years raising her three children the way that she thought best.

When these two single parents combined their homes to create a stepfamily, they had, between them, twelve years of habits and routines to reconcile. They knew it would be tough; they just didn't know how excruciating and seemingly endless the process would be.

"It's basically been unlike anything I imagined," Andrew said. "I knew that there would be some issues with getting the kids to mesh and behave and with Laura getting used to my kids and me getting used to her kids. But I just figured we would get through those rough times in a few months or a year and we would have them nailed down. But it went way past that.

"Things just kept coming up," he said. "There were always new issues to get used to and problems kept coming up."

A WHIRLWIND ROMANCE

ANDREW AND LAURA met in January 1995. They married, to the day, four months later. Laura still can't believe that they moved that quickly. A mutual friend, Lindy, set them up.

"She kept telling me about this friend," Laura said. "She'd say, 'He's a great guy.' And I was like 'No, thank you, I'm not interested.' That went on for about eighteen months. One night she called me and I guess I was in the right mood and I said, 'OK, give him my pager number; that seems safe.'"

Laura agreed to go to lunch with Andrew. But as she sat at her desk waiting for him to show, she wasn't so sure. She had heard that his nickname in high school had been "Rat Hammond."

"Oh, Rat Hammond," she said. "And I thought, Hmm . . . a rodent. I hope that's not a sign."

By the end of the lunch, she wasn't at all worried. She just wanted to see him again.

"It was like a whirlwind," she said. "We went out that one time and he was just the greatest guy and I don't know what happened because I was never going to get married again. People would say 'marriage' and I'd run."

With Andrew, she ran for the altar. At the time it seemed like the right thing to do. Now it seems impulsive—and out of character.

"I think back on it now and I wonder, 'What was wrong with me?' The deal was I meet this great guy, fall madly in love with him, we get married, we move in the same house, and I see how different we are. He wants to spend all the money; I don't want to spend any of it. I'm so ABC, one-two-three; he's so spontaneous. It was not 'happily ever after.' That was not it at all."

In those early days, they were both so in love and so looking forward to their lives together, that they figured that combining the two households would work out, even if there were bumps along the way.

"We allowed the kids to spend some time together to see how they would get along," Andrew said. "I wasn't trying to fool myself that this was going to work perfectly. We both knew there would be a lot of work and some issues we would have to get used to. Both of us were coming from being single parents, so we were pretty set in parenting."

When the children got along well, the adults were happy. The children weren't pleased about their parents' rushed marriage, but Andrew and

Laura knew they wouldn't live together with the children without being married and they didn't want to have a lengthy engagement period.

They began to spend a lot of time together. But four months is a short time to get to know someone. And they had other things they were running around trying to do while getting to know each other—they both work at least full time in addition to raising their children.

"I was behaving very well," Andrew said. "I wanted to impress her. I wanted her to like me. And as far as her knowing who I was, she didn't."

"The real running started after we got married. She had to learn to know me and everything that I stood for and all the negative things that I had as a protective single dad, and I had to do the same thing with her," Andrew said.

After the shock of the wedding, everyone had to adjust to much tighter living quarters when Andrew and Laura decided to move her family into Andrew's house.

"We were drawing up the floor plans and saying, 'He can sleep here, she can sleep here,'" Andrew said. "And we'd look at each other and say, 'Nawww, this isn't going to work.'"

But they did it anyway. And it has worked, to varying degrees, for the past seven years. There were times when Andrew thought there was just no way that his marriage could survive. There have been bitter fights about how to discipline the children, about one parent favoring his or her own children over the other's, about money and what they should spend it on. Andrew and Laura clashed, screamed, and cried with all the force of their strong personalities.

Laura and Andrew both had to deal with the critical eyes and comments of the other. When they were living alone, they never had to check with another adult about what to do with the kids. They ran the house their way. But with two adults in the home, they both had to get used to each other's ways and decide if they were going to do things differently themselves.

FIGURING OUT THE NEW ROUTINES

IN LAURA'S HOUSE, when her three children, Jake, Simon, and Vickie went to bed, they stayed there. Laura not only couldn't afford the latest fashions, she was cautious about what her children wore, wanting them to be dressed neatly and modestly. And when it was dinnertime, the four of them sat down to eat together. Things were different at Andrew's house.

"They're helter-skelter," she said. "They're eating here, they're eating there. They're in their room. I was confused. I said, 'What is this? Where are you going?'

"Andrew says, 'Sweetheart, let it go. As long as they eat, let it go.'"

Andrew is proud of raising his sons by himself after his first wife left. He not only raised his two sons from his marriage, but his stepson stayed after his mother left.

All three of the boys are on solid tracks and are doing great things in their lives. When he met Laura, Andrew believed that he knew a thing or two about good parenting. When Laura criticized the way he let his boys dress in the latest Nike fashions, or the dinner routine, Andrew felt annoyed. He'd been doing a perfectly fine job parenting before Laura showed up. Why did she think she knew better? There were seemingly endless details to sort out and each other's idiosyncrasies to get used to.

"When I take my dirty clothes off, I fold them and put them in the basket," she said. "He says, 'Why are you doing that?' They're dirty; they're going in the laundry. He calls me an alien. He just says it out of fun."

She knows that the past seven years have taught her to be more flexible.

"I've changed a lot," she said. "I've made changes. I didn't fall off the earth when I did it, so I guess it was all right."

Where to worship

The church was a big part of Laura and Andrew's lives when they were raising their children separately. They're both Baptists; Andrew belonged to a more traditional Baptist church and Laura belonged to a more non-denominational church. They were both very active in their churches, going several times a week and participating in activities. When they married, they knew that the church would continue to be a solid foundation that they would draw on. But neither of them wanted to switch to the other's church.

"When Andrew and I met the biggest fight we had is what church we should go to," Laura said. "My pastor said I should go to Andrew's church. I have come to learn that wherever I go, God has put me there for a reason. It has taken me several years to even get comfortable with the church. But there is a plan there. I just believe God has a plan."

Equal discipline

Andrew and Laura argued frequently about consistency when dishing out punishment with the kids. Andrew said that they were able to agree about what was a punishable offense pretty readily—for example, they agree that a failing grade is unacceptable.

"The problem came in the sentencing phase of the trial," Andrew said dryly.

The maddening thing for Laura was that Andrew would say one thing and then do another. Andrew would punish a child by confining him to the house, but then allow the child off punishment to play on team sports or other activities. Andrew thought it was obvious that those kinds of things should be an exception.

"One thing that was not included in punishment was if one of the children were participating in some sort of event that they had to be in, like a basketball game or track or football or something else," Andrew said. "That's something that they couldn't really miss out on or they would be on trouble on the team or with the group that they were with."

Andrew knows that Laura sees herself as the heavy-handed one around the house, but he doesn't feel like he's bowed out of taking tough disciplinary action when he's needed to. Andrew remembers one time in particular. Drew got in trouble, and it was fairly serious. Andrew doesn't remember now what the offense was, but he remembers having to make the call. He took Drew off the basketball team for the rest of the season. But since he got remarried, whatever he does, Andrew feels stuck between his children and his wife.

"She says I'm too lenient on them and they say that I'm too hard on them. Most of the time I'm in the middle of her perception of what I'm doing and their perception of what I'm doing," Andrew said. "It's just amazing that they can see me act so differently. It doesn't matter which way I go, somebody's going to wind up not being satisfied with the action, with the discipline."

The other difficulty came when they both believed that the other was favoring their own children. Laura said that if Andrew isn't consistent with the children, it really affects the way she parents her children. She doesn't feel that it's fair for his children to go off to one of their activities on the weekend and for her to keep her children at home.

"He puts the kids on punishment, but then the weekend comes and they're off punishment to go places. That's not punishment. If you're on punishment, you stay. I don't care where you're going for the weekend, you're on punishment," Laura said. "Then we get to the point where I'm said to be harsher than he is because I just believe that if you're on punishment, you don't talk on the phone, you don't watch TV, you go to your room. And then when the weekend comes, you really don't go anyplace. It doesn't end up being enforced and I'm walking around mad because they're not learning. They're being rewarded for something that they shouldn't be."

When Laura told Andrew that he favored his own children at her children's expense, he really took offense. Still, he talks about it in his characteristic light-hearted, half-joking sort of way.

"I didn't want to face the reality that I was treating her children differently because I didn't think I was," he said. "To this day, I still don't think I do. I say to her 'How could I, the perfect, single, three-boy raising father, treat somebody bad? I don't treat anybody bad. Go ask my friends.' And she's tearing her hair out."

Money and the other household

Andrew likes to spend money; Laura likes to save. Andrew is generous with grown up toys for the children; Laura likes to save. Andrew tries to help out his father; Laura likes to save.

His philosophy with the children is that if they're getting good grades and pulling their weight around the house with chores and not getting into trouble, he'll buy them whatever he can afford. Several of the children have their own cars; several have cell phones. With six children involved in college, sports, and other activities, expenses are sometimes out of control.

Andrew and Laura tried to sort out the money together for a while.

"We opened a joint bank account and I ruined that thing," he said. "We said, 'This ain't going to work.' So then we said, 'You just pay your bills out of your account and I'll pay out of mine.' But then I'm putting money in her account and she's not putting money in my account. I said, 'Wait a minute. You've got all the deposits going into your account and I've got all the withdrawals coming out of mine. When do you get to put money in my account?' We have, like, four checking accounts. This is Enron in the house."

And when money is tight, the same issue comes up again and again: Laura wants Andrew to call his ex for child support. For a few years, Andrew got child support for the children. But now it's been years since he's received a check. Andrew wants his ex-wife to support her own children, but he doesn't feel like the hassle of dealing with her is worth the money. Their marriage ended after Andrew discovered that she was having an affair. She doesn't see the boys very frequently and so Andrew has almost no contact with her.

"The only time I talk to her is when I call over there looking for the boys. I see her at something here or there," he said. "We don't hate each other, not openly I'm sure. We just don't talk. She has nothing to say to me. And I have something to say to her, but I'm not going to say it to her."

Still, he knows that his and Laura's lives would be more comfortable if they got some financial help from the boys' mother.

"I guess I've sort of shut myself off to being angry about it. I just want her to do what a parent should do for her child," Andrew said. "She doesn't help fund anything. No medical expenses, no trips, no activities. Only birthdays and Christmas. And all of our kids are really active. I mean really, really active."

So when Laura pushes him to call and ask for support, he knows he should.

"My wife is really on me about that: 'You need to, you need to, you need to.' 'I know, I know, I know. I'm going to have to approach my ex about it.'"

THE FINAL PUSH

THESE DAYS, ANDREW and Laura prefer to laugh at the challenges. They can't always pull off the laughter; there are still tense times. But they have managed to take two fully-formed families and combine them into one family with its own traditions and own ways of doing things. The children all get along and it's not unusual for Laura to awaken in the middle of the night and hear two or three of them milling around in the kitchen.

"When the older boys come home, it will be two in the morning and a bunch of them are in the kitchen laughing," Laura said. "You're smelling Ramen noodles and popcorn. We call them the kitchen thugs. They just rumble around like little rats. They're pretty cool. We've never had any trouble."

If Laura and Andrew hadn't been able to get past the feuding and get around to accommodating each other to some degree, it would have been very easy for them to continue functioning as two separate families under the same roof. But they see, after seven years, that they have made solid progress.

"The thing about our relationship is that we can talk about those issues together," Andrew said. "She has her perspective, and I have my perspective. We still have different perspectives. I wasn't going to change her perspectives and she wasn't changing mine. Over the years we've just had to say, 'Let's try not to fight.' I'm not going to be drawn into it like I have been in the past."

"We're better prepared. We're better in the sense that I know that those issues have already been sort of ironed out. But it's still a little bit in the back of our minds that 'he's choosing his over mine' or 'she's choosing hers over mine.' So that still exists a little bit, but we don't let it turn into some big blowup like we used to."

Even through all the tough tensions in his stepfamily, Andrew never doubted that he loved Laura.

"We wouldn't have been able to stick together if we didn't really love each other," he said. "She's sweet, she's wonderful. She's a good wife and she's a good mother. And I love her to death. She needs to hear that."

Many of the issues that get in the way of that clarity—the discipline, the money, the favoritism—will soon be out the door with the children. The youngest of the six is seventeen years old and soon they will all be off living their own lives.

Andrew and Laura are excited about things big and small. They may get to take a vacation that isn't to a family reunion. They can clean the bathroom, and it will stay clean. Maybe they'll fix up the house.

The day-to-day grind of raising teenagers will be over. There will be plenty of child stuff to sort out over the years as weddings and more grandchildren come along. But now, with such solid ground to stand on, Andrew and Laura are sure their family can handle it.

13

$\mathcal{P}$LAYING BY THE ROLES

❧

THERE IS NOTHING predestined about how we act in step-families. Each family has its own ways of interacting, its own ways of deciding who is going to play what role.

In every family, people adjust to each other and each take on a certain role. In some families, women do all the cooking and men do all the yard work. But in stepfamilies, there are common roles that people sometimes fall into without considering whether the role suits their needs or the needs of the family system.

Sometimes, a role dictates certain expectations, certain beliefs, certain assumptions. It can be useful to examine these expectations and assumptions to see if they are realistic, to see if they are fitting. To see, ultimately, if we want to continue playing by the role we have developed.

Many a stepparent has been accused of trying to take a parent's place in a child's life. Many a parent has been accused of not doing enough for her child. Many a husband or ex-husband has been accused of bowing out and letting the women deal with the conflicts.

If you find that you are often frustrated by your position in the family, or if you feel disrespected by how others in the family system behave in their roles, you can look at some of the common pitfalls of that role to see if yours needs to be adjusted. One study suggested that most family members are unclear about what role the stepparent should play in stepfamilies.

Your whole family may benefit from a frank discussion about what you each expect from your relationships and how you can all best support a well-functioning family.

When you're thinking about the different roles in your family, it is useful to remember that you can ultimately only control what you do. You may be able to see very clearly how *someone else* should change. But you can only actually change how you behave. It is almost inevitable, however, that when you change the way you interact with people, they, eventually, will change the way they interact with you.

If you don't have a clear idea of what your role should be, or if not everyone agrees on what the role entails, the situation can get difficult quickly:

- A new stepmother decides to throw herself into the role of a parent to her stepchildren. She starts picking the children up at their mother's home, calling to make arrangements, going to school conferences. She believes that she's showing her husband and stepchildren how dedicated she is, how interested she is in making the family work.
- The mother, who has for years dealt only with her ex-husband about their children and arranging the schedule, is aghast. She feels like the new wife is an overly-ambitious interloper. She may cry foul and demand that her ex-husband tell his new wife to back off. The children, too, may be startled by such a drastic change in their family's routine.
- The husband, though, finally has some help as a single parent and he's not at all inclined to tell his new wife to stop helping. Instead, he tells his ex to deal with it. The children, even if they don't overhear the argument between their parents, can feel the tension.

Now no one is happy.

Each person in this scenario is playing by his or her role. The stepmother is trying to do the right stepmother thing, the mother is being protective of her turf and her routine, the husband trying to make it all OK, and the children are stuck in the middle of it all.

Ideally, all the parents involved in a child's life should be able to sit down and decide what things everyone is comfortable doing. More often, we operate on instinct, habit, and assumptions about what we are supposed to do in our roles.

If you look at each role, you can see the motivation behind each person's actions. If you try to keep your emotions at a manageable level and try to look at it like a anthropological exercise, you will begin to see that there are not usually any clear-cut bad guys. Everyone is muddling along the best he or she can, doing what he or she believes is the right thing.

The stepmom

Everyone knows the story of the evil stepmother—casting her stepdaughter aside in favor of her biological girls, or worse, sending a woodsman out to kill the stepdaughter because she's the fairest in the land. It is a hard rap to overcome.

So let me just dispose of the whole business right away. There are some stepmothers who differentiate unfairly between their children and their stepchildren. There are some stepmothers who don't treat their stepchildren very well. There are some stepmothers who go out of their way to be nasty to their stepchild's mother.

But that's simply because stepmothers happen to be a part of the human race. The fact is that stepmothers, like mothers, are mostly good to their stepchildren, mostly work very hard to do the right thing, mostly strive to be respectful of their stepchild's mother, mostly work hard to make their new family work.

Studies have shown that stepmothers have the most difficult position in a stepfamily system. These women come to a new marriage, some of them for the first time, some of them without children of their own, and they try to make a new family. In every family, the woman is usually the one most concerned with the details of running a house. It is not automatically different in a stepfamily. Stepmoms, as the women, often end up being the ones to organize the family's schedule, arrange vacations, do the clothes shopping, and tend to the cuts and scrapes. As anyone with a child knows, there is plenty of work to be done in a house with a child. It is almost inevitable that a stepmom ends up doing some of it.

The difficulties come on several fronts. Often, stepmothers end up feeling taken for granted by the husband and the child for the work they do. They feel like they are given a lot of the work of raising a child without any corresponding affection and acceptance.

When the mother adds in her own unhappiness about the stepmother's involvement with the child, the stepmother often feels completely misunderstood and unappreciated.

Husbands, friends, and relatives, even the stepmother herself may expect that the stepmother should jump right in, love the child, and treat the child as her own. The fact that this almost never happens can cause a huge amount of guilt, resentment, and hostility from all of these quarters.

The reality is that sometimes stepparents and stepchildren don't even like each other and are miles away from love. But everyone still has to live together, so try to find some ways to make it through.

Stepmothering dos and don'ts

Go slowly. As a new stepmother, it seems the right thing to do to become involved in your stepchildren's lives. But try to remember that there is a family already in place and no matter how much you think they are doing wrong, it is their way of doing things. Trying to come in and change the routines between the households might freak the child and the mother out. If you try to push a relationship on a child too quickly, some children recoil. The rejection, whether from a small, cute toddler or a brash, indignant teen, is real and it hurts. Let the relationship develop over time.

Respect the role of the mother. If you are able to, assure the mother of your stepchild that you know that you are not going to try to be the child's mother and that you do not want to replace her. If this is not true, you need to reexamine your goals. Even if you believe that the mother is emotionally unbalanced, irresponsible, absent, or doing damage to the child, you must acknowledge the fact that this child's got one mother—and she is it. Children love their moms. Never undermine that love. If you want to volunteer at your stepchild's school, be sure you aren't stepping on the mother's toes. If you want take your stepdaughter to get her ears pierced, check with mom first.

Support your husband. There are all kinds of ways to be involved in your stepchild's life behind the scenes. Supporting your husband without taking over all of his responsibilities is a workable balance. If you believe that your husband needs to make some adjustments with the other household, talk to him about it. Try to be encouraging and supportive. Remember, he was doing this (long) before you got here, so try to be respectful of the work he has done, even if you see room for improvement.

Tell you stepchild what you want. Your stepchild is trying to figure you out, too. You may not know where your relationship with the child will go, but it doesn't hurt to tell her that you want to have a relationship and that you are interested in getting to know her.

Pay attention to what you need. If you find yourself terribly discouraged, spend some time taking care of yourself. Make sure you are not putting all of your energy into relationships with little or no payoff. I am not suggesting that you isolate yourself from the family, but there is a healthy way to disengage from the struggles instead of letting them consume you. If you are concentrating on things that make you happy, you will have more energy for the things that are tough. Take a class, pick up a hobby, start a book club or a dining-out club. Do something fun for yourself and do not feel guilty about it.

Don't take over for your husband. Many stepmothers start by taking on too much of the load of caring for the child. Do you know the doctor's office number, but the child's dad doesn't? How about the child's shoe size? Do you know the child's teachers better than her dad? One of the roles we fall into without realizing it is the traditional roles of men and women in a household, a first family household. Things are changing, but the current reality remains that women tend to most of the nitty-gritty details of running a house. So stepmothers, because they are women, fall into the traditional role of running the house which includes, of course, taking care of the children. The problem is that most stepmoms begin to feel resentful about caring for their husband's child, especially when their husband complains about how she does it and the stepchild's mom wishes she would just knock it off. Far better to play a limited supporting role and let the father find out when his child's science fair project is due.

Don't expect your stepchild to be perfect. One area that stepmothers commonly feel frustrated about is the discipline or the habits of their stepchildren and the seeming lack of concern about these issues from the father. Sometimes, stepmothers who have no experience with children have definite—if unrealistic—ideas about what these children should look like and how they should behave. To make sure your expectations are realistic, check out some child development books or take a parenting class.

Don't ignore any grief you may have. This is especially true for stepmoms who were never married before and don't have children of their own. As much as stepmothers love their husbands, it may still be difficult to accept that their family will never be the first family, that they'll always have to share their family with their husband's and stepchild's history. Every one of life's most poignant moments is somehow connected to this history. When a stepmother and a father have their first baby together, it is not the first for him. If a stepmother has no children of her own, she may be grieving that. When the family has Thanksgiving dinner, it is automatically compared to how the first family did things. It is important, especially for the children, that this history is not outlawed in stepfamilies. But the stepmother might have to recognize that, even while being respectful of that history, it certainly is a loss not to have a family where the only traditions and memories are the ones created in their own home.

Be clear about what you want. Don't expect that your husband will know what you need and attend to it. Half the time, it is difficult enough for most people to figure out what they need themselves. But particularly in a stepfamily, it is important that you are clear about what you want and that you are clear with your husband about what you are asking for. You cannot just expect that he will know what is bothering you and fix it. You can't even know for sure that he will do what you ask. So, for example, your husband likes to tell his child stories about their first family (and every child loves to hear these stories). You don't have any interest in hearing about the first family's good times. You can ask your husband, out of the child's hearing range, to try to be sensitive to the fact that these stories make you uncomfortable.

THE MOM

SOME MOMS END up feeling pretty bruised by the whole stepfamily dynamic. When women marry and have children, they almost never imagine that the day will come when they have to pack up their child's bag to send her off to another household on a regular basis.

When they do divorce, they might imagine that they will have to divide their time with their husband, and that may be difficult in itself. But most women don't get far enough along in that thought to imagine that there will also likely be another woman who will be, in some way, a part of their child's life.

When another woman begins to do things that look a lot like mothering for their child, a lot of moms have no tolerance for it. Mothers choose the fathers of their children. Now, another adult is becoming a part of the child's life and the mother had no say in picking this person. If the stepmother's values or habits don't seem to correspond well to the mother's it can be dreadful to have to send their child to the other household.

Mothers are often amazed at the things that their ex-husband allows his new wife to do for their child. It is maddening to mothers that the father does not do more to support his own child. Often, mothers blame the stepmother for forcing herself into the child's life.

When a child likes the stepmom, it is often threatening to mothers. Even if women rationally know that it is a good thing that a stepmom and a child get along, there is often a part of a mother that wants her child to be devoted to only her.

There are plenty of mothers who handle the presence of another woman in their children's lives not only with acceptance, but with grace. It may be that you can't do that at this point, but somewhere down the line, you may feel differently about your child's stepmother. In the meantime, it will help your child to work on being civil.

Mothering dos and don'ts

Recognize the power of traditional male/female roles. It may not be right, but the reality is that women still rule the home. Most mothers, if they think back to when their husbands lived with them, will realize very quickly that their husbands were not the ones to do the majority of the chores that involved the children. When men remarry, it is very common for them to fall into the same role with their new wives. It is frustrating for mothers that the fathers of their children do not do more of the day-to-day work of rearing children. But if they didn't do it with you, they are not likely to just wake up one day and take on all the work of parenting if they can leave it to someone else. I am not saying that this is conscious or even that men don't do a great deal of the work for their children. But it is common for stepmothers to try to help. Try to give the stepmom in your life the benefit of the doubt that she's not trying to take your place.

Include the stepmother in parenting discussions. Every family has different ideas about how this works. In some families, particularly those with very active mothers and fathers, the stepparent really does take a back seat and the parents do their thing. Often, though, if a stepmother becomes a key player in a child's life, it is only considerate for the parents to include her in decisions that greatly affect her life as well. Try to remember that while you are used to dealing with only the father of your child, the other household has turned into a "dad and stepmom" household. If you constantly leave out the stepmom, that sends a pretty clear message—not only to the stepmom, but to your child.

Give your child permission to love her stepmom. One of the most difficult positions a child can be in is to really like, even love her stepmom, but know that her mother disapproves. Children can benefit from having more than two loving adults in their lives. Your child's stepmother may not be perfect, she may seem overly stringent and even nasty to your child. Your child may complain to you about her stepmom. It may be that she doesn't like her. It may also be the case that she senses your disapproval and wants to assure you that she is on your side. Whatever the case, this child has a stepmom now and she's going to be a part of your child's life. A mother can do a lot to help her child with this new relationship. A child should never have to feel guilty about loving another person. Your child loving another adult does not take away any of the love she has for you. Children's hearts can expand to love many adults, even imperfect adults. Allow for it. Make sure your child knows that you can handle it. If you can't, it may help to reexamine why this is so threatening to you.

Expect changes. The marriage of an ex does not just mean changes for a mother's child. It is almost certain that mothers will notice changes in the relationship with her ex when a stepmother becomes involved. Maybe you used to talk frequently and hash things out with friendly conversations several times a week. Maybe you met over coffee. You might have felt you had a great parenting relationship with your ex. And then the stepmother came in and screwed it all up. Or maybe you fight constantly with your ex and the new stepmother will help ease some of the tension. Whatever the case, you can expect that your parenting relationship will change.

Do not try to maintain your ex's allegiance. You and your ex are divorced. For whatever reason, the two of you were not able to sustain a marriage. It may be tempting to flaunt your longer history in a stepmother's face, it may be tempting to feel like you know him better than she ever will. It may be intriguing to hear your ex tell you about his frustrations with his new wife. But to what end? If you want to poison your ex's new marriage, this is a good way to do it. Be clear, even if your ex is not, that his allegiance should be to his child and his wife—not to his past. Do not call on former intimacies, do not fondly reminisce about old times, do not pull out inside jokes between the two of you. These kinds of things are a complete affront to the relationship between a husband and a wife. The stepmother and her husband are trying to build their own life together. If you can allow them the space and time to do that without becoming defensive about your relationship with your ex, it would be a gift, not only to their marriage, but to your kid.

Do not minimize the child's time with his or her father. Mothers sometimes love their children so much that they believe that their relationship with their children is more important than the children's relationship with their father. But children adjust better to stepfamily life with unfettered access to both parents. It might be more practical at some point to have a primary home, but the key is that the child needs to feel free to see both parents. Children need both of their parents. This can be difficult if a mother feels like she has to push for the father's involvement. But if men and women are going to be equal parenting partners, not only are fathers going to have to step up and do more, but mothers are going to have to make it easier for them to do that. If mothers want their child's father to act like a fully-invested parent, they have to treat the father like a fully-invested parent.

The dad

DADS HAVE DIFFICULT dynamics to deal with in stepfamilies as well. Overall, men tend to be less emotionally troubled than women in stepfamilies, but there are several challenges that fathers face.

The biggest area that men struggle with is how much involvement they will have in their child's life. This area is changing rapidly and it is becoming more common for men to have half-time or even full-time custody of their children. Courts around the country are changing from a system where it was assumed that the mother's home would be the primary residence to a system that sees the value in children spending equal time with both of their parents.

Many men want to be involved parents, but they do not have a good role model for what that means. When a mother makes it difficult for a father to be involved, some men do not know how to negotiate for a more equitable arrangement.

There are a growing number of men's support groups that help men not only with the legal and practical details of child custody, but also with the emotional tangle that sometimes comes with custody disputes. It can be distressing to feel dismissed as a parent simply because you are a man.

In addition to the potential for disputes between the two homes, dads often have to face conflict in their new stepfamily. Their wives may push for a change in the schedule, either for more or less time with the children. And when the children are with the father and the stepmom, the father may feel as if he's performing a tightrope act—treading carefully to avoid upsetting the fragile balance of peace between his child and his wife.

Fathering dos and don'ts

Be clear about your expectations. It helps to know what you think your wife's role is when it comes to your children. Do you consider her another parent, a friend to the child, an adult role model? Fathers can help a stepmother clarify which child-related tasks he expects from her, and which he doesn't want help with. It also will help your child and your ex-wife to hear how you envision your new wife's role.

Step up to the work. Do not abdicate your child-raising responsibilities. Do not expect that your wife will just take care of things. And do not leave the work for your child's mother either. It may be that when you were married, your child's mother got the soccer schedule, called the school for the events calendar, arranged parent/teacher conferences, and kept you apprised of the next piano recital. But you are not married to your child's mother anymore and now those are your responsibilities. For things that make more sense for one parent to handle, such as dentist and doctor appointments, do not assume that your child's mother will take care of them. If you want to be considered a fully-invested parent, you need to act like one.

Support your wife. Your wife may have some trouble adjusting to her role as stepmother to your child. What you do has a major impact on her adjustment. Work with her to decide on what child care her role will include. Be clear with your child about your expectation of respect for the stepmom. Back her up in front of the child, even if you don't agree with her at the moment. You can come back later and talk about how you would like to handle such situations.

The best way to support your wife is to support your kid; if you are an involved, active, and thoughtful parent, you ease the burden of the stepmother's role.

Be mindful of the stepmother's contribution. Your wife signed on to a life with you and your children. But that does not mean that you should take the work that she does for your child for granted. Be sure to let her know that you appreciate her commitment to your child. When she is doing things that you do not like with your child, it might be hard to remember that she is likely doing what she thinks is best. Try to respect her ideas and work together to find a parenting mix that works for both of you.

Do not expect a stepmother to be a mother. Stepmoms are just not going to have the kind of motherly love for a child that a mother will. In the beginning, the best a father can ask for is a mutually respectful atmosphere and an attempt to get along. It may happen that the stepmother and the child will grow to love each other. But it may not. Stepmothers need to be relieved of the duty to love your child. Your wife fell in love with you, not your child. Accept that and work within that reality.

THE STEPFATHER

WHEN IT COMES to relations between the two homes, the stepfather often emerges relatively unscathed. There seems to be very little of the conflict between stepfathers and fathers that is so common between mothers and stepmothers. Men just don't seem to have the same sense of turf protection when it comes to another man getting close to their child. A lot of times, fathers and stepfathers are friendly, even friends. Even when that is not the case, men are more likely to be reserved in their comments and actions. Stepdads may believe that their stepchild's dad should be doing something differently, but stepfathers are also less likely to push for the change either directly or through their wives.

The biggest conflicts that stepfathers usually face are with their wives. There are often conflicts about discipline, about how much influence and what rank the stepfather should have in the household. Often, stepfathers believe that their wives are too lenient on the children, and stepfathers are often accused of being too harsh and of having unrealistic expectations of the stepchild.

Stepfathering dos and don'ts

Go slowly. Give your stepchild and your wife a chance to adjust to your presence in their lives before you make any major demands about the way things are run. You may be anxious to show your commitment to the family, but try not to overwhelm people who are used to living in a single-parent household.

Respect the role of the father. Your stepchild loves her father; respect the child's right to love and have a relationship with him. Stepfathers can have meaningful and strong relationships with their stepchildren, but they should never undermine a child's love for her father.

Support your wife. You may not like everything that she does with her child, but your wife has been running things (long) before you got there, so respect the work she has done, even if you see room for improvement. If she is having a difficult time, try to empathize with her. She does not need you to fix everything for her, but she does need you to listen to her.

Plan discipline before acting. Do not come in with a heavy hand and expect to be warmly welcomed. Discipline is a big issue for stepdads, but it is important that stepdads have a realistic idea about what to expect from children. Read some books, do some Web surfing, and talk to other dads. You can rely on your own instincts, but only to a point. If you have never had children and are suddenly living with one, even typical child behavior can be jarring. So find out what to expect. This is too important to just wing it.

Do not avoid the problem. If you feel that things are very difficult and you're unhappy with the way your household is running, do not just sit on those feelings. Whatever the situation, ignoring it is not likely to make it easier or change it. In fact, some problems grow worse as they fester without resolution. Keep the communication open. If you do not feel that your wife or stepchild is hearing what you have to say, keep trying. Sometimes, we all need help talking to each other. Try not to wait until you are so pissed off that you don't know where to start.

THE MOTHER/STEPMOTHER DIVIDE

IN A LOT of stepfamilies, the most acrimonious relationship is that between the mother and the stepmother. The hatred that these women feel for each other is sometimes so strong it stretches believability. We have all heard of the evil stepmother. But do you know about the PBFH? If you have been on any of the angst-filled message boards for stepmoms, you will know that the PBFH is the psycho-bitch-from-hell, or in other words, your stepchild's mother.

These are the stepmothers who are so overwhelmed, so burdened, and so bitter about their lives that they resort to venting in some really hideous and dangerous ways.

It seems—at least if you ask some stepmothers—that an inordinate number of mothers are, well, not looking out for their children's best interest. These stepmothers say they are dealing with mothers who agree to schedules and then change them at a moment's notice, who threaten and bully the stepmother or father and often take them to court over the slightest disagreement. These mothers often are drunks, drug users, women of questionable morals, or living with men who have similar issues.

They leave their children without explanation, often returning to demand time and affection from their hurt children. They make promises to their child and don't make good. These are the mothers who speak badly about the father, and most certainly about the new wife. These women, from the stepmother's perspective, are bent on making life as miserable as possible for their children and the child's other home.

From the mother's perspective, the stepmother is trying to take over the role of mother in her child's life. The stepmother is controlling, manipulative, and turning the mother's child against her. The stepmother is teaching her child things that go against a mother's values. The stepmother is impossible to please, setting the child up for failure. She is harsh and nasty to the child. She physically reprimands the child to the point of child abuse. Furthermore, the stepmother has destroyed the relationship between the two homes and thinks she knows more about raising children than the child's own mother.

The gulf can seem irreconcilable. Even in situations in which there are not these kinds of extreme views, the relationship between the women in stepfamily systems is usually difficult. But in milder cases, and even in extreme cases, there are things you can do to mend the bridges and to try to come to some kind of practical, workable way of raising the child together. You don't have to love each other—hell, you don't even have to like each other. But you are mixed up in each other's lives, and more importantly, in your step/child's life. So you might as well try to make your interactions as painless as possible.

If I had to pick just one thing that I hope people can take away from this book, it would be in the area of how women in stepfamilies relate to each other. You already know my bias—women are the ones who truly run the household. What I mean by that is that women are the ones who pay more attention to relationships, to nurturing, to fostering an environment in which people can grow and get along. Women can also do the opposite. I don't want to say that this is all women's work. I implore the men to be involved and to create as much harmony as they can. But what I found over and over again in my research is that the men in stepfamilies are basically happy as long as their wife and children are happy. Men want everyone to be happy and usually will do whatever they can to make the peace.

What this means is that women have the opportunity to create the peace in their households and between their households. Women have the power to make or break their stepfamily. It is a power we should recognize and not waste.

But so many of us have spent so much time fighting each other that we do waste our energy. Instead of recognizing the value of another woman in our lives, we hate her, we resent her, or we simply tolerate her.

I consider myself a feminist, but I certainly don't walk around talking about the sisterhood and how we all have to get along because we are women. But I do think that on a very practical level, women have the power to work together, not only for the good of the child, which is the ultimate goal, but also for our own happiness and peace of mind.

When the other woman in your life drives you crazy, when she takes up too much space in your brain, it is time to get real with yourself and with her about what is going on.

A huge part of the problem between moms and stepmoms is that they do not talk to each other. Maybe this works for some people. What I found is that the less contact that there was between the mom and the stepmom, the more the two loathed each other. It is easier to hate someone you don't have to confront, someone you don't really even know very well, someone who has a lot of control over important areas of your life without your input.

But when you make the mom or stepmom into a monster, you also can build a pretty elaborate web of resentment, disdain, frustration, and misunderstanding. With clear communication and effort on both women's parts, a lot of those webs can be cleared away.

It sounds like a fairy tale, I know. And maybe for some of us, it is.

But I have seen amazing turnabouts. There are many, many cases of women who spent years at each other's throats, disrupting their families and making life miserable for their husbands, their children, and themselves. And then something happens. Whether it is just time, or whether one of the women reads a book that opens a new door for them, or one of the women makes a friendly comment and the goodwill builds. Whatever happens, these women are somehow able to see each other in a different way. And years of pressure can start to deflate.

Either of the women involved in this relationship has the power to change what she does to make the situation better. Chances are, your child's mother or stepmom is as unhappy about the conflict as you are. There are some concrete things you can do to start the process. These can be difficult if you are in a highly bitter relationship. But they can also be amazingly effective.

Bridging the divide

Say something good about the other household. It may be that you need to really stretch here, but you can find something good to say. If you can't come near the relationship with the child, say something more abstract. "I heard you were going to Venezuela—that sounds like fun. I always think traveling is the best experience."

Apologize for some small infraction. It helps to start small. Especially if you know that something pisses her off, go out of your way to apologize and acknowledge your fault. "Oh, we're fifteen minutes late, I'm sorry about that. I know it's important to you that we be on time."

Be kind to her children. This only works with children that are not your step/children, for example, your husband's ex-wife's child by her current husband. I'm going to assume here that you will all be good to your own step/child. Any mother can hardly resist someone genuinely interested in her child. If you know something about the child, show some interest, or give the child some sincere compliment. It could be as simple as "Nice shirt."

I know these things seem small and possibly insignificant. But our lives are made up of thousands of small, insignificant moments. When we put all the moments together, they create our relationships. If we are moving right along, we can try some bigger things.

Let her know you want your relationship to be different. You could ask her out for coffee, you could write her a note. Several stepmothers and mothers I know have given their child's step/mother the book *Stepwives: Ten Steps to Help Ex-wives and Stepmothers End the Struggle and Put the Children First*. The book is dedicated to improving the relationship between mothers and stepmothers, whom the authors call "stepwives." That's a pretty clear call for peace.

Own your own garbage and expect the fallout. There is probably not one of us who hasn't done something we regret in our relationship with our child's step/mom. When you lower your guard enough to admit your faults, you are really opening yourself up for criticism from this woman who you know despises some of the things you have done. Often, people who are apologizing and being vulnerable are met with graceful forgiveness, or at least cautious silence. But that is not always the case. I have known cases of one woman apologizing for her part and hearing, in turn, about even more of what she had done wrong. Sometimes, there can be an unleashing of tormented thoughts and pent-up feelings. It can feel really uncomfortable, but if you don't get defensive, it is still possible to save the conversation and move on.

Have a plan for practical, respectful interaction. Stress the fact that you're not looking to be best buddies. But also have some idea of what you do want. What are the issues that infuriate you? How would you like to see them resolved? Where are you willing to compromise?

Do not fall back on old patterns of interaction, even when she does. It is very difficult to change a pattern of behavior with another person. When she starts doing the same old thing, it may be tempting to respond in the same old way. Try to stop yourself and do something different. If she starts accusing you, don't defend yourself. Simply acknowledge her upset. "Wow, this is a sore point for you. Can you tell me what you would like to see happen?"

Do not expect change to happen overnight. There will be times when you or she or both of you fall back into sniping and complaining about each other. Cut her and yourself some slack. Especially if you have been at each other's throats for some time, it will take a while to undo your old habits.

Do not let problems fester; handle them. Don't expect her to read your mind. She can't. If something is bothering you, you either have to tell her about it and hope that she will accommodate you, or you have to blame yourself for not taking care of the problem. It is not fair to be angry with someone for something they are doing unless you have explained that it bothers you. If they still don't stop the annoying behavior, then you can get angry.

Do not expect perfect harmony. You will likely still get angry at her. Getting angry at people you have relationships with is part of the deal. It is not the end of the world. You can still work with people who make you angry. And just because some things they do make you angry doesn't mean that everything they do is wrong.

Do not shut the door to friendship. When women become real with each other, when they have a relationship that requires work and commitment, as all relationships do, it is more difficult to outright hate someone. And it is a lot easier to cut someone some slack when you know why they are doing what they are doing, even if you still don't like it. Sometimes, moms and stepmoms find out that they actually like each other. They not only form an alliance and work together for the sake of the children, but they become friends. This is a pretty rare circumstance and certainly not for everyone. But if it happens to you, consider yourself fortunate.

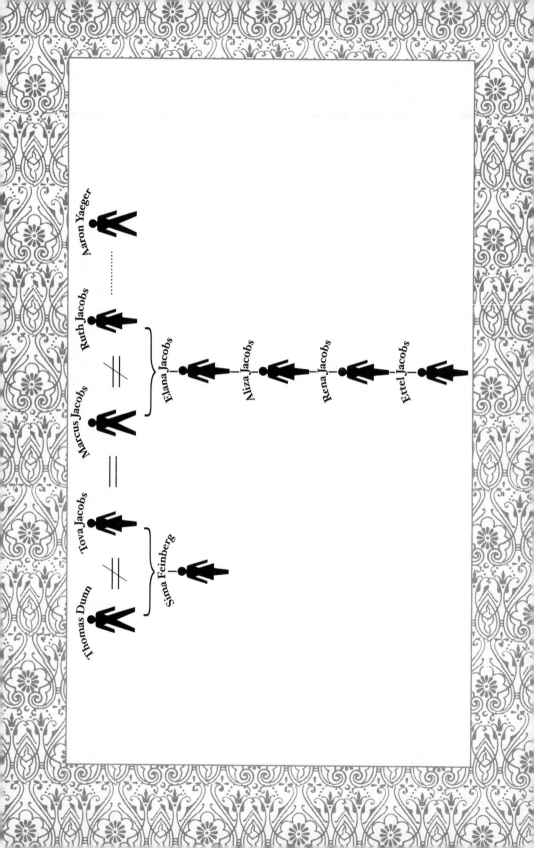

14

THE JACOBS FAMILY SYSTEM OF NEW JERSEY

⚜

CHILDREN/STEPCHILDREN:

Elana Jacobs, the seventeen-year-old daughter of Marcus and Ruth, lives half time at both parents' homes.

Aliza Jacobs, the fifteen-year-old daughter of Marcus and Ruth, lives half time at both parents' homes.

Rena Jacobs, the thirteen-year-old daughter of Marcus and Ruth, lives half time at both parents' homes.

Ettel Jacobs, the eleven-year-old daughter of Marcus and Ruth, lives half time at both parents' homes.

Sima Feinberg, the sixteen-year-old daughter of Tova and Thomas, lives primarily with her mother, and sees her father rarely.

MOMS/STEPMOMS:

Ruth Jacobs, mother to Elana, Aliza, Rena, and Ettel, divorced Marcus, and is engaged to be married to Aaron.

Tova Jacobs, mother to Sima, stepmother to Elana, Aliza, Rena, and Ettel, is married to Marcus.

DADS/STEPDADS:

Marcus Jacobs, father of Elana, Aliza, Rena, and Ettel, and stepfather to Sima, is married to Tova.

Thomas Dunn is the father of Sima.

Aaron Yaeger is the soon-to-be stepfather to Elana, Aliza, Rena, and Ettel.

> This family has handled their transition into a stepfamily virtually unscathed. There are adjustment issues, as there are in all families, but the adults have led the way for the children to handle them adeptly.

*Y*OU HAVE TO be high-spirited if you're going to keep up with this family. With five girls ranging in age from eleven to seventeen, the family is on the move, conversationally, at every moment.

It's common for two or three lively exchanges to be happening at any given moment around the dinner table. The girls are all strong-willed, opinionated, and sharp. As they talk about subjects ranging from SAT exams to family parties, someone is always questioning, occasionally criticizing another's comments ("Are you joking or are you stupid?"), ready with a comeback or a howl ("Don't yell at me, it was just a question"). Hanging out with these girls and their parents is a boisterous good time.

Around the dinner table or not, the conversations of the girls are a mix of English and Hebrew. They're constantly testing out a newly discovered Hebrew word or phrase, checking on a principle of the religion that they study even more intently than mathematics or science. They will easily spend half an hour trying to figure out how one of the stories in the Torah ends. If two of the girls can't figure it out, they'll call in reinforcements in the form of their older sisters. The girls aren't stodgy or arrogant—they're just as likely to tackle who the cute boys are at school and what movie they last saw as they are to discuss the proliferation of drugs in public versus private high schools or Israeli politics.

These girls, solid, smart, and sensible, have spent the past three years of their lives adjusting to the divorce of their parents, the remarriage of their parents, and the shifts in homes and family structures that are inherent in creating a stepfamily.

This family, both in their mother's and their father's homes, are surrounded by books, ideas, and debates. All of the parents in the girls' immediate lives are highly educated and heavily engaged in their children's lives and in the world around them. They have created homes full of vigorous discussion about the way the world works, their personal history, the culture they live in, and the subjects the girls are studying in school.

In the past few years, each family member has had some difficult realizations, and some painful times. But the people in this family are impressive in their ability to make their new families work, to be respectful to each other, and to put the greater good before their own desires. In such a cooperative environment, all the girls are able to identify ways that they're happier now, in their stepfamilies, than they were in their first families.

IDEALS MEET REALITY

MARCUS AND RUTH met at work when they were in their early twenties. Marcus had been raised in a strict Orthodox home and Ruth had been raised in a non-religious home. When they met, Marcus was living in the Orthodox community and Ruth was living a wholly secular life. Their conversations at work were interesting and fun and their attraction to each other grew. But they knew that this issue of religion, of lifestyle, was a serious obstacle to any long-term commitment.

Even when their dating became more serious, Marcus wouldn't tell his parents about Ruth. It was a dilemma, because Orthodox Jews can only marry other Orthodox Jews. Not only that, but if someone were to convert to Judaism, the conversion was supposed to be purely motivated by the desire to follow the life — not to marry someone.

But it was the only way they were going to be together, and Ruth found the religion very comforting and clarifying in her life. She decided to convert. Converting to this branch of Judaism is a long process. Converts must learn Hebrew, and must learn to live the lifestyle, keeping kosher and living by the rules of the religion. There is a conversion ritual, and only then is it acceptable to marry into the religion.

Ruth decided to make the commitment. Since the process was to be a long one, Marcus went to Israel for nine months while Ruth moved in with two Orthodox women and got to work. Ruth loved Marcus, but she loved the idea of the religion as well. For her, the man and the religion were so intertwined that she thinks she fell in love with both at the same time.

They eventually did marry and had four girls. But the marriage was difficult. When they were young they talked and talked about their lives and their beliefs. But somewhere along the line in their marriage, they stopped talking about things that mattered. The relationship became crushed under the weight of criticism and frustrations that weren't resolved. They reached the point where they couldn't find their way back to that place of supportive or loving conversation. They grew resentful of each other, untrusting, and the fighting became almost constant. Eventually, Ruth asked for a divorce.

NEW RELATIONSHIPS

WHEN HE MOVED out, Marcus didn't imagine that he would remarry. But within six months, he had met Tova and their relationship progressed quickly. Tova says that she knew after two months of dating Marcus that they were perfect for each other. And she ought to have known; she had spent enough time since her own divorce systematically searching for a husband. She used Jewish dating services online and screened people out, looking for a someone who shared her beliefs, who suited her personality, whose children were an asset, and who was a good provider. Marcus fit the list.

Tova has one daughter, Sima. Initially, Tova was a little overwhelmed by Marcus's four girls. But soon, the families began going to synagogue together, spending time at Marcus's home. They married about six months after they met. They bought a house together where Marcus's girls live half the time; Tova's daughter is there full-time.

Ruth, meanwhile, went on with her life as well. When Marcus left, things didn't shift as dramatically in her life. Especially that first year, the transition to divorced life was eased by several factors. For one thing, she had spent several years grieving over her marriage as it was ending. By the time Marcus actually left, she mostly just felt relief. When Marcus moved into a small apartment, they agreed that he should take only two of the girls at a time, once a week. So Ruth didn't feel that her house was suddenly quiet, or that her girls were gone.

And Ruth is not a sentimental person. She's sees great value in the girls having their father in their lives, so she's never felt any pangs of sadness when the girls go off to the other household. She feels that it's good for them, a broadening of their lives. Her attitude is probably a significant factor in why the girls themselves see the situation so similarly.

Ruth eventually started dating again and, in a twist on history, Ruth fell in love with a man who isn't an Orthodox Jew. Aaron is in the process of learning Hebrew, studying to become an Orthodox Jew, and the two intend to marry once Aaron has completed the process. Aaron is a force in the girls' lives, and they appreciate his stories of his travels, and his life. The girls all expect the relationship to become a marriage, so it is one more piece of their stepfamily that works well for them.

. . .

It didn't just happen

In this family, more than most, their religion is inseparable from their personalities. It's not that they come across as disproportionately pious, but they, as a family, have a way of incorporating their beliefs into action, into reality. They are very clear about how they believe things should be and they work hard to act accordingly.

The degree to which their religion or their personality has to do with this is impossible to sort out. But there was very minimal backstabbing during the usually tumultuous first years of forming a stepfamily, very few side digs, and little sarcasm, even when, given the situation, those things would have been understandable, even expected. This family has come through the stepfamily development to a comfortable place amazingly unscathed.

One thing that I found in all the families that have managed the challenges of stepfamily life well is that they had some kind of support network to draw on. This family system was set up particularly well to make use of support from several places.

I found this family because Tova is a member of the Stepfamily Association of America, the biggest and most respected stepfamily organization in the country. Her name was on a list of families that I contacted asking if they would be interested in participating in this book.

So, at a minimum, Tova had some knowledge and understanding of what to expect in her stepfamily life. She had some context for the things that she was experiencing in those early days of combining households. She'd also read a few books on the subject, although she didn't find them very applicable to the life she wanted to create.

It wasn't the stepfamily-specific support, though, that helped this family the most. The majority of support came from their way of living, which thrives on deliberate and rational ways of making things right in their lives. Again, whether this is mostly personality or mostly the strength of their religion is hard to distinguish.

The adults in this family used their education, their backgrounds, and their skills in communicating to find the resources to make their family work without unnecessary bitterness and resentment.

This is not to say that everyone always behaved absolutely admirably, or that people didn't ever feel bitter or resentful or angry. But the adults were able to separate what they felt from what they did. And what they did, for the most part, was to act in the best interests of their children, and ultimately, in the best interests of the entire family system.

It's clear that this way of managing in the world has been passed on from the parents to their children. Sima doesn't have a lot of contact with her father, for logistical and other reasons. But the other four girls benefit from two households that are flexible and easy to move between. Not only do they benefit from having both of their parents committed to them, but there's another, lifelong advantage that can't be overestimated. These girls have learned how to deal with difficult situations and make them work peacefully. It is a boundless gift.

COMMITTED AND COMFORTABLE

BOTH FAMILIES LIVE in New Jersey towns about twenty minutes across the George Washington Bridge from Manhattan. Marcus and Tova's upscale neighborhood is bustling with shops and restaurants, a small town in the country's largest metropolis. Both neighborhoods cater to the local Jewish populations; even the Chinese restaurants and doughnut shops are kosher.

Ruth's home, the first family's original home, sits on the corner of a quiet residential street. Marcus and Tova's house is open and roomy, a brick Tudor on a street with big trees and children biking by.

Elana and Aliza and Sima go to high school at the private Orthodox Jewish school. Rena and Ettel go to the private Orthodox Jewish grade school. Ruth has worked for years as a computer analyst. Tova designs Web sites and Marcus works as an engineer.

As their children get older, the family sees them growing into responsible, interesting people. They like what they see and they know that they have done their best to make it happen.

RUTH JACOBS

RUTH GREW UP in Manhattan, the daughter of parents with a highly unconventional way of raising their children. Their goal for their daughter was to raise her to be an independent thinker and so they spent a lot of time talking to her about their values and the ways of the world. But her parents, she said, didn't believe in rules and regulations. Her mother, especially, was idealistic and she believed in doing things because they were the right things to do. They didn't nag her about homework, didn't set bedtimes, and didn't flinch about her smoking pot. If Ruth decided that she wasn't going to school, her parents said that was her choice. But even without the boundaries, Ruth didn't cause problems; she was basically a well-behaved child.

When she met Marcus, the differences in their upbringings were stark. Ruth was completely attracted to him; she was attracted to the structure and sense of his life.

"I remember the first thing he said that really impressed me and it was about him and about Orthodox Judaism at the same time," Ruth said. "I just didn't get what Orthodox Judaism was all about. Why are you doing all these things? Why are you eating this and not eating that? Why are you doing this and not doing that? What's the whole point? Could you sum up for me what's going on?

"He said, 'God created the world and He created man and it's a good start, but it's not perfect. It's up to man to take that last step and make it perfect. Men have the ability to do good and the ability to do evil, men have free choice. And the idea is to do good and complete the work.' And I heard that and I thought, 'Wow, that is a goal that is big enough to devote a life to.' You can incorporate it into your everyday life. It's a philosophy you can take with you every day, and every time you do something, you say to yourself, 'Is this improving the world or not?'"

So she was able to look at the Orthodox rules in a different way—the rules were important to show that she was devoted to the underlying beliefs. Ruth had seen a lot of divorce in her family. Her parents had divorced, and divorced again. Her grandparents had divorced. She thought that by marrying Marcus, she wouldn't have to deal with that issue.

"One of the reasons he was attractive, or maybe one of the reasons Orthodox Judaism was attractive, is that I thought this wasn't going to happen. There's no way. The thing about Marcus and the thing about Orthodox Judaism is it's so geared toward family and traditional values, it just seemed really, really safe," Ruth said. "And it's true. He never would have initiated a divorce. If I had wanted to stay married to him, I could have had that."

Ruth still has a difficult time pinpointing what went wrong in their marriage. She knows that they fought all the time for the last couple years—the house was always full of tension and Marcus felt criticized by everything she said.

She knew that when they divorced, it was likely that he would remarry. But she said, whatever their difficulties in living together, she believes that their core values are the same and she feels good about the way they're raising the girls. She knows that sending them to Marcus's house is a good thing, so she can relax and enjoy the time that she has to herself. She never seriously considered trying to have the girls more time than she does—as is common in a lot of families.

"He's the father and I'm the mother. He really has equal right to them as I have. They love him, they enjoy spending time with him. It wouldn't be doing anyone any good if I tried to sever that connection, if I tried to say, 'You can only see them every other weekend,'" Ruth said. "I think it's a good thing. He's such an involved father."

ELANA JACOBS

ELANA IS A soft-spoken, thoughtful, calmly mature seventeen-year-old. She is analytical and rational, wistful and contemplative.

She said that her parents' divorce has its practical downsides, but over-all, it's brought lots of good things to her life. It's a hassle, for example, to switch back and forth between her parents homes every few days.

"I always leave something," she said. "If I lose a textbook, maybe it's in one house, maybe it's in the other. It's easier for things to get lost. And I don't really get used to the house when I come because I'm always think-ing 'Today I'm here, tomorrow I'm there, the next day I'm here.' That's why it will be nice when I get to college because I'll be in one place for a while."

Still, the practical difficulties are just one part of the stepfamily life.

"It also has twice as many good parts," Elana said. "I have friends who live by me on both sides. There are two different neighborhoods and if I want to go someplace, I can go to either one of them."

Elana worries sometimes about her father. He is a worrier, she said, and sometimes she gets pulled into worrying, too. For example, she said, he was a lot more upset about the divorce than she was. He was worried that she would be upset, worried about what would happen. Elana was sad and upset about the divorce for a while. But she said that after she dwelled on the upset for a while, she relaxed and figured it would be fine, and it has been.

"I don't wish that they had never gotten divorced," Elana said. "I don't think that my life is any worse than it would be without the divorce. It might be better.

"I have more experience with the world, with different people. I got my computer because of it. When my dad moved out he took the other one. Tova and Sima are from Woodstock. Tova had a totally different childhood. And Aaron has lived all over the country."

She welcomed Tova and Sima to her family. She was happy to get to experience being in her own father's wedding—she found it an interesting twist on family relations. And she really likes having Sima as a stepsister. Still, Elana worries about her sometimes, too. Elana knows that there are times when it is hard for Sima to find a place amongst the four very close sisters she didn't meet until she was a teenager.

"She doesn't say it, but you can just tell," Elana said. "She doesn't feel like she belongs a lot of the time. My sisters and I all grew up together. I feel bad about it."

Elana feels closer to Sima than her other friends, but not as close as she does to, say, her sister Aliza. Elana imagines that the relationships will just get stronger.

"By the time we all get out and have our own families, we'll be all the same," Elana said. "I don't think I'll be any closer to Aliza or Sima, or Rena or Ettel."

SIMA FEINBERG

SIMA'S LIFE CHANGED drastically when her mom remarried about three years ago. At thirteen, she moved from the town she was living in, the easy access to her father, the friends she knew, the school she attended, and the home she lived in.

She moved into a brand-new home with her new family—not only a new stepfather, but four stepsisters as well.

She's happy about most of the changes. But moving away from her dad has been terribly difficult for her. She said that it's the hardest thing in an otherwise good life. She used to see him about half of the time, then every other weekend. Now she sees him once or twice a year. They talk on the phone, but the logistics of seeing each other are difficult. He lives a few hours away and the bus system is complicated enough that she'd have to miss school to visit him.

"I miss my dad. A lot," Sima said. "There's really no way of getting there. He can't drive here and no one here can drive me there. I don't think about it every day, because that would be . . . I wouldn't be able to enjoy my day," she said. "There isn't really anything that hard about living here because

I'm very happy. That's the hardest part—I miss my dad. I'd rather see my dad more often."

There are a lot of perks about her new family. She's happy for her mother, and she considers Marcus a parent-like figure whom she respects and likes. But the best part is the four sisters she gained from the stepfamily.

"It's a lot better than being alone. I love having sisters. It's never boring. I've always wanted a sibling. People always used to say, 'Oh, you're so lucky, you're an only child,' Sima said. "I say, 'It's so boring. You go home and there are people there. I go home and it's like, "'Oh. Hi, Mom.'"

"So now I don't have to go home and be totally disconnected from my friends, I have someone here."

It's hard for her when the other girls are at their mother's home. She said the house is so quiet, it's almost unrecognizable as the same place. Sometimes, though, it's tough to be a part of a sisterhood in which she's the only one who hasn't grown up with the group. Sometimes she feels like she's still the outsider in her own home.

"Sometimes it's hard. I say they're my sisters, because to me 'step' anything or 'half' anything is stupid. But then they'll say, 'This is my stepsister.' It's different for them because they've always had sisters. I've never had sisters. They've had sisters their whole lives, I've been alone. I've always wanted a sibling."

Mostly she feels close to her sisters. She said that children who are entering a stepfamily should try to look for the good things, try to be optimistic.

"Don't think like, 'Oh my God, this is going to be horrible, I don't like this person, I don't know this person, these people aren't my family.' Think, 'Oh, cool, new people.'

"Basically, except for the living-with-them part, my sisters are like my friends, they just know a little bit more. I love it."

ALIZA JACOBS

ALIZA WASN'T SHOCKED by her parents' divorce, but she was somewhat sad. And it was hard in the beginning, getting used to the two different ways the households run.

Now, a couple years into it, the routine is familiar and comfortable. Her mom doesn't allow candy, but TV is OK. Her dad's house there's no TV until after 8 P.M., but she can have candy.

"I know on Friday when I come to my mom's house, I can go on the computer, I can go watch TV, I can go do what I want to do. At some point in the night, I will have to take a shower," Aliza said. "At my dad's house there will be a list of chores I have to do. I just adapt because now I'm used to it."

One of Aliza's biggest concerns when her parents divorced was that her mother would stop being religious. She knows that her mother converted, at least in part, to marry her father and Aliza wondered how committed her mom would be with her dad gone.

"I know she believes in God, but she doesn't like all the rules and regulations," Aliza said.

Aliza trusts that her parents needed to divorce for a good reason, whether that was personality clashes or clashes over parenting styles. She can't really see anything difficult about living in a stepfamily. Part of the reason, she believes, is that she sees her dad half of the time—so she has solid relationships with both of her parents. There are hardships, but she doesn't see them as particularly linked to the stepfamily situation. On the other hand, Aliza sees a lot of benefits.

"I know people who go to my mom's synagogue and people who go to my dad's synagogue, so I know a lot of different kinds of things because of that diversity," Aliza said.

She said that she gets to have different experiences at each home.

"With my dad, we talk about politics and stuff like that, intellectual stuff," she said. "My mom doesn't talk about stuff like that. She talks about movies, normal stuff. Not stuff you have to read about and watch CNN all day to know what they're talking about. If my mom were to sit at one of my dad's meals, she'd be bored. If my dad were to sit at one of my mom's meals, he'd be bored."

TOVA JACOBS

FOR SOMEONE WHO has committed herself to raising her daughter with a new husband and four new stepdaughters, Tova seems unperturbed. And she is.

Building a new home with Marcus and his girls hasn't been effortless, but Tova said that she and Marcus are so well suited that whatever difficulties there are, they've been able to sort them out together. She said that her husband's support is one of the main reasons that the transitions of the past couple years have been relatively seamless.

"He and I are so made for each other, it's scary sometimes," Tova said.

"We have the same communication style. We have the same values and goals in life. Marcus has expectations of his girls and he lets them know 'Tova does have parental authority and you do have to listen to her.' They're all good kids. They're all doing well."

Tova does worry some about her daughter. Sima used to see her dad about half time before she and her mother moved away from her father. With the first move, she still got to see him every other weekend pretty consistently. But now, Sima's parents live hours apart and Sima very rarely sees her father. Tova says she knows that the girl misses her father, but that there are a couple reasons that they don't see each other much anymore. First, the transportation is difficult and Sima's dad doesn't have a car to make the trip. The bus system in New York would take her there, but Tova said that scheduling around the Sabbath is always a challenge.

The other reason they don't see each other is more difficult to explain to her daughter. Tova said that Sima's dad has a lot of medical and other problems. She said that he's had tuberculosis, severe varicose veins, and depression. She said he got a medical discharge from the army after serving in the Korean War. She said he's been diagnosed with obsessive-compulsive disorder and receives social security payments for his disability.

"Her father is pretty destitute," Tova said. "He can't drive here, he can't afford to pay for her bus fare, even one way. He's also feeling like, the last time that he spoke to her, that he didn't want her to see him because he didn't want her to see him so down-and-out. I feel sorry for him but my pity is tempered by the fact that I feel like he put himself in this situation. Sima sees him and she gets very scared for him."

Sima's father resents that Tova moved the girl away from him; he is unhappy that he doesn't get to see his daughter as much as he did. Tova understands, but mostly, she feels that his life is difficult and depressing. She doesn't harbor any resentment toward him, but she gets exasperated with his long list of troubles. Sometimes, she doesn't even want to call him because he just goes on for hours.

"I just find it burdensome. He's a lonely person," she said.

Marcus Jacobs

Marcus is still sad that his marriage of fifteen years didn't work out. He wouldn't have gotten divorced, he had thought it more likely to get killed in a plane crash, or eaten by a shark. Divorce wasn't even a thought.

But his marriage fell apart and he had to readjust his plan for the rest of his life. Now, three years later, he thinks that everything has worked out for the best. His life with Tova is active and fun and what they want it to be. He's happy that he and Ruth went through mediation and have worked hard since then to raise the children together. He's trying to take the lessons of his first marriage into his second.

"I still think about these things, I think about how to avoid a similar situation with Tova, I just want to make sure the same sort of situation doesn't happen," Marcus said. "There are so many things that are different. Tova was brought up in the same sort of family structure that I was brought up in. There were certain expectations in terms of children, in terms of spouses."

So while they still argue sometimes, their household runs fairly smoothly. The girls have some concerns, as any adolescent does. But mostly, all four of the girls are fabulously successful, stable, and involved in many activities.

The hardest thing for Marcus about raising his daughters in two homes is that he feels that there's a large part of their lives that he really can't access. He tries to be careful about making the girls uncomfortable.

"I love my children, they're my children. I like to know what's going on in their lives. I like to know if everything's OK, if there are problems, if there's this, if there's that. What they did," Marcus said. "I can't really ask them that. I can't say, 'Do you like what's going on at your mother's house?' I can't do that. First they sense this—their antennae are up all the time. And second of all, it's really none of my business. Ruth has a right to raise her kids the way she wants at her house. In my house, I have a right to raise my kids the way I want. But I can't tell Ruth to raise the kids the way I want."

It's more important to him that the girls feel good about both of their parents, that they see cooperation, and never feel as though one parent is pitted against the other. And he sees the successes that his daughters are having as evidence that what the parents are doing is working.

15

CHILDREN IN THE MIDDLE

∝❦∝

A STEPFAMILY WITHOUT any children is not a stepfamily, it is a divorce.

It is hard to divorce and remarry. But when you remarry with children, or when you marry someone with children, the stakes are that much higher. You have other lives to consider, to shape, to work into the plan.

All parents—step- or otherwise—want what is best for the child and best for the family as a whole. In first families, figuring out what is best for our children is difficult. In stepfamilies, multiple homes and multiple adults with a vested interest in the child compound the difficulties.

But all these layers can be a very good thing, not only for the child, but also for all the adults. Stepfamilies that are working well provide a lot of benefits to children. They encounter more personalities, more ways of living, they may go on more vacations, and they have more knowledge of the world. Children in stepfamilies often have many influences, both from additional family members and additional life experiences.

There are benefits for the adults in well-functioning stepfamilies as well. Adults may get to have some time off, a break from their child, which can be a healthy thing for both the child and the adults. The adults can use their time to focus on their own relationship, one of the keys to maintaining a strong marriage and family. And when stepfamilies work well, parents also sometimes get an interesting perspective on their child from the other household. You may see or hear a part of his personality that you don't have any experience with. Stepfamilies can broaden each person's experience in living and raising a child, if you allow it.

Parents who divorce often worry about the effect of the divorce on their children. But children whose parents divorce don't necessarily have trouble. It is not the divorce itself that causes the predictions for children to have more of the problems we fear: higher rates of anxiety, depression, anger, and just being less well-adjusted. Children can develop these issues in any kind of family arrangement that is functioning in high-conflict mode. It is the conflict, the screaming or cool silence, the tension and animosity that make life miserable for children. These things make life miserable for all of us. This kind of life is not what any of us would choose if we could see a better way.

When parents divorce and work harmoniously together, making the child's needs a high priority and being respectful toward each other's households, children in these homes often thrive. And so do the adults.

There are no hard-and-fast rules about how to treat children. Each family has to sort out what they think is important and acceptable in the treatment of children in their home. But it helps to be thoughtful about it. Stepfamilies can be very complicated and addressing those complications head-on often takes away a lot of their power to harm your relationships, either with your children or with the other adults in your life.

Some families find it useful to consider the following ideas when it comes to thinking about what the children in a stepfamily need.

CHILDREN HAVE A HISTORY

REMEMBER THAT CHILDREN'S history is as important to them as yours is to you. They may have fond memories of their lives in their first families. It is almost a cliché that children in stepfamilies at some point imagine or ask if everyone in their family could live together in the same house. Small children in happy stepfamilies don't see the reasons for living in two separate homes.

Obviously, the adults do. But you can still honor your children's fantasies; you can allow them their memories and help them to feel good about the good things in their lives, both past and present. When you feel defensive or competitive with that history and cut the child off, the child will start to get the clear message that there is something wrong with those memories.

It is often difficult for stepparents, particularly, to share their lives with this history. But that is not the child's fault. If stepparents are uncomfortable with the child talking about their past, the stepparents have to come up with some comfortable ways of dealing with the past. The more you allow for discussions of memories or fantasies, the more the child will be able to process what has happened in his life. And the closer you become to him at the same time.

But if the thought of listening to one more story about the first family is making your stomach turn, try to make it easier for yourself without squashing the child's need to talk about his life. Maybe you could ask him to draw a picture about the way things used to be, or his fantasy of what a house with everyone living together would be like.

"Mama, are you getting divorced again?"

Children's history also influences the way they look at the future. Adults usually cannot approach their second marriages with the same assured confidence that they approached their first marriages; and neither can their children.

If children are young enough when their parents divorce, they may grow up with the stepfamily as their "typical" family. But as children get older, they start to realize that if the first marriage did not work, it is entirely possible that the second won't either. This realization can have all kinds of ramifications for stepfamilies because the child has to learn to trust that the new family isn't going to disintegrate.

A child who remembers his parents arguing before they divorced may be overly sensitive to arguments. A child whose parents divorced shortly after having him may be very anxious around the birth of a new baby in the stepfamily, using childhood logic to determine that adults have a baby and then get divorced.

Children may consciously or unconsciously distance themselves from step relationships. If the marriage does fall apart and the child's relationship along with it, the protective guard they've put up will ease the pain of the loss. But it also prevents children from getting close to people.

A lot of these issues will only heal with the assurances that a solid marriage and time can provide. In the meantime, you can try to recognize these fears and let your children know how typical they are.

When history hurts

Sometimes people think that because children are so young when something happens, it doesn't affect their lives. That is not usually true. People often mistakenly think that if a parent dies, it will be easier to raise that child because there was a clean break, a clear thing to grieve. That is not usually true, either.

If life in the first family was dysfunctional, if the children were abused or neglected or just not cared for very well, it may be even more difficult to respect the children's fond memories of their former lives. You may think the child is creating a memory of fantasies, and he may be. But it's a rare family that has no good in it. Almost everyone can remember some good times. It is simply not your place to squash the good memories for a kid.

The idea that you need to respect your children's memories and feelings about their old life, about their other parent, may hold even more credibility when the history is painful. The child is now not only hurt, but defensive for his other parent.

Children and parents have a tie that cannot ever be completely severed. They can be out of touch for years, they could have parted bitterly, they could have dismissed each other completely. But there is still that kid-parent connection that withstands all of these assaults. Consider children who are adopted and spend years searching for their birth parents. It is a human instinct that cannot be denied.

When you accept the fact that your step/child's history is as real and meaningful to them as yours is to you, you can be respectful of that history in ways you had not thought of before.

WHEN YOU CRITICIZE THE PARENT, YOU CRITICIZE THE KID

ONE CONCRETE THING you can do to respect your step/child's history is to never criticize the other parent. Most of us would subscribe to this commonly given advice, at least in the abstract. Sometimes, it is a lot harder to know what criticism looks like in everyday life.

Especially if there's a lot of nasty conflict between the two homes, there will be things that the other parent does that are distasteful, disrespectful, and sometimes, oh, so wrong. But you need to be very careful about how you address your anger and disappointment with whatever the other parent does. Most children are unable to differentiate criticism lodged at their parent from criticism lodged at them. So even when something is clearly upsetting, you need to refrain from pulling your children into any ranting or venting about the other parent. It is just too painful for them to hear. Far better for the child to hear some words of support or encouragement from you that don't involve the other parent.

"Oh, honey, I'm sorry you didn't get to go to the zoo today. I know you were looking forward to it." In keeping your statements away from the other parent, you focus your attention where it belongs — on your step/child.

"MY MOM MAKES THE BEST COOKIES . . . "

CHILDREN WHO LIVE in two different homes are bound to make comparisons. Have you ever compared vacation spots? And you only stayed there for a week or two. Children who go back and forth between homes have legitimate lives in each of the two homes. If you lived somewhere else every other weekend, you would certainly consider it a huge part of your life. So do children. The fact that some of them constantly compare the two homes is just natural. It may drive some people crazy to constantly be told about how great the other household is. But a lot of the comparisons might just be regular child conversation, and they might just feel comfortable enough in your home to talk to you about the ways things are done differently.

There may be other reasons for the discussion about the other house. Some children may feel guilty if they are enjoying themselves at one house, and they almost need to remind themselves that the other household is a big part of their lives. It is a reassurance for them that, if they point out that "Mom's cookies are the best" then they are not being disloyal to Mom. Even if they love your cookies.

As usual, I vote for direct communication on this front. If a child seems to be needling you with references to the other household, let them know that those kinds of comparisons make you uncomfortable. But try not to shut down communication about the other household. Children should not have to feel like the other part of their lives is taboo in your home.

THEY GROW UP SO FAST,
BUT THEY ARE STILL CHILDREN

IN MANY STEPFAMILIES, the adults feel that their children have a better understanding of the world because of the complexities in their lives.

Some adults talk frankly to their children about every subject, including relations between the adults.

Some adults don't talk to their children at all about the relations between the adults. Usually, a child can handle whichever style a parent uses, as long as it is consistent. If a parent talks to a child about everything else, but never mentions anything about relations with the other home, the omission will be obvious. If a parent doesn't talk to a child about anything ever, the child will be shocked and likely overwhelmed to suddenly hear the inside scoop on the parent's feeling about the other household.

There are two points to remember when talking to children about stepfamily dynamics. One is that children will usually ask if they want to know more, assuming that you have created a receptive environment. Don't go on and on about something as their eyes glaze over.

The second point is related. Children sometimes seem as though they can understand a lot more than they actually can. Children just do not have the breadth of experience and context for the way things work in the world that most adults do. So if your child hears you say that you want your ex to drop off the face of the planet, it may seem like a minor infraction in a moment of frustration to you. But it may seem horribly nasty to your child and he may fear that you really want to harm his other parent. Don't assume children can absorb information on an adult level.

COMFORT IN THE HOME

IMAGINE IF YOU had to pack your stuff and leave home every other weekend, or every other week, or for a few months every summer. This is what you ask your children to do. And you owe it to them to make those transitions as easy as possible. You want your step/children to feel comfortable in your home and there is plenty you can do to assure that they are.

Talk to your step/children. See if there is something that they need and be specific. Children will usually tell you what they need if you are clear about the choices. One thing that might help is to come up with some kind of a checklist, like the one used when children go to camp. Ask if they need toiletries, clothing, shoes, coats. If you expect your child to lug those things back and forth between the two homes, then be clear about that. If money is not an obstacle, it will help the child to be able to come to your house without worrying about whether he'll have clean underwear. If the adults show some real interest in making a child's space comfortable, the child will usually respond in turn.

There will always be some things that have to be carried back and forth between the homes. Some things are just too prized for children to leave behind. It might be their new toy, their favorite stuffed animal, their trusty slippers. My niece has a special bag that she carries her clock in, back and forth between her mom and dad's houses.

Some families have rules about things they buy having to stay at their home. I understand the frustration of buying something for a child and having it disappear into the black hole that is the other household. But I also know that for a lot of children, not being able to have their stuff with them at their house (wherever that may be at the moment) is a very frustrating experience. Adults and children need to sort this out together.

It helps children to feel some of themselves in each of their homes. Ask for their input on the grocery list, what chores they want, where the family is going on vacation. Include them in important family discussions, even if it means waiting until the weekend to have the discussion.

And you can let the children have free access to their other homes while they're with you. Some adults are highly annoyed that their step/child wants to call the other household. But again, you should try to explore why you're feeling annoyed about this. If you're feeling competitive with the other home for time or love, or if you're hurt because the child doesn't call you when he's in the other household, then that's something, as adults, you might just have to suck up. A child should never be told that he can't call his parent. Imagine telling a visiting friend she can't call her husband while she's visiting you. Imagine what her reaction might be. The other household is at least as important to the child—let him have access whenever he needs or wants it.

WHO DO YOU LOVE MORE?

THERE ARE ALL kinds of ways that children can get caught in the middle in a stepfamily. They can get caught between divorced parents, between a parent and a stepparent, between a stepsibling and a parent.

Parents should do their best to always assure a child that she is our number one love. It's very common for a child to ask his mother if she loves him or her new husband better. Please, please don't take this opportunity to explain to your child the different kinds of loves in the world.

Just let him have it—just give him the "prize." Your adult partner should be able to figure out the nuances of different kinds of love. But children can't and they just need to be assured that they're still number one.

Children can also feel threatened by other children, especially if their dad is living with a stepsibling more than with them—children can wonder if their dad will love the stepsib more. Take the time to reassure children of their place in your heart.

In another twist, I used to frequently tell my stepson that he was my favorite boy on the planet. When I got pregnant, I figured I'd better come up with a new strategy. And so he became my favorite ten-year-old boy on the planet. And my girl is my favorite three-year-old girl on the planet. Kids need their place, so let them have it.

A time for all

Sometimes, we're so busy trying to make our stepfamilies work as a whole that we forget to nurture the individual relationships in the family. Each unit in the family needs to have time to nourish and build their individual relationships, as well as the family relationship.

The married couple, if they want their children to be happy, will spend time strengthening their own relationship. Children need to have time with their parents alone, and time with their stepparents alone. When each of these units is working well together, they create strength in the family relationship.

Children won't feel penalized by living in a stepfamily and will begin to feel lucky if they see their parents and other family members working together for the common good.

16

THE LENNON/JOHNSON/ URBANSKI FAMILY SYSTEM OF MINNEAPOLIS, MINNESOTA

❧

CHILDREN/STEPCHILDREN:

Luke Urbanski, the thirty-one-year-old son of Allison and Jim, lives outside the family home.

Annette Douglas, the twenty-eight-year-old daughter of Allison and Jim, lives outside the family home and is married.

Nick Lennon, the twenty-four-year-old son of Betty and Tom, lives outside the family home.

Jason Lennon, the twenty-two-year-old son of Betty and Tom, lives outside the family home.

MOMS/STEPMOMS:

Allison Lennon is mother to Luke and Annette, and stepmother to Nick and Jason.

Betty Johnson is mother to Nick and Jason.

Kate Urbanski is stepmother to Luke and Annette.

DADS/STEPDADS:

Tom Lennon is father to Nick and Jason, and stepfather to Luke and Annette.

Jim Urbanski is father to Luke and Annette.

Jim Johnson is stepfather to Nick and Jason.

One half of the family system worked well in shielding the kids from a painful divorce and the subsequent forming of a stepfamily. The other side of the family system didn't work well for the children or the adults. The hardships between Tom, Betty, and Allison in raising Nick and Jason continue to be a palpable force in most of their lives, but particularly for Jason and Tom, who haven't spoken in more than two years.

$\mathcal{T}$OM AND ALLISON Lennon's home, in an upscale suburb of Minneapolis, could be a showcase for a designer-home magazine. Their hardwood floors gleam, the classic furniture sits stately in the spacious living room, the mantle is decorated with matching candles in perfect symmetry.

Their kitchen recently underwent a major overhaul. Today, it is a model of an efficient workspace, complete with center island and elegant touches, such as lighting that gives the room a warm glow. The deep red walls are decorated with sketches of chickens; a poinsettia sits on the beautiful oak table. Tom and Allison sit at the table in the bright bay window looking out on to the deck they built over the same summer.

The kitchen says a lot about Tom and Allison. They knew what they wanted and were determined to have it. They also knew that it wouldn't be an easy process, but that in the end, it would be worth the work. They went through so much to get the kitchen just the way they want it. They had to strip their old kitchen down to the beams, they hauled out the old appliances, they broke through the outside wall to create the bay and expand the walls. They ripped down five load-bearing walls. The work was grueling and the place was a mess. The mess is cleared away now. All that's left is the beauty and sense of calm and order.

Their marriage has followed a similar track of wreckage and repair. Tom and Allison are happy together—they are each other's best friend. But the beginning of their relationship was one of painful choices, difficult maneuverings. It was spawned by secrets and broken promises. They were both married with children when they started to see other. When they decided to divorce and start anew, both spouses were surprised, disappointed, and angry. Tom's children were very young; Allison's were just starting adolescence. The divorces took a heavy emotional toll on both families. There was a lot of work to get their marriage to the point where it is today. They both feel solid and supported by their relationship.

But it is a marriage that, statistically, never should have made it. Besides what Allison calls their "sordid history," Tom had been married twice before. He is a Vietnam veteran, and had struggled with alcoholism. Add to those issues the challenges of raising Tom's two boys and the situation could have easily knocked down another marriage.

A lot of things helped along the way. In this stepfamily system, Tom and Allison's home was the center household. Both had their children coming and going from the house to households of their ex-spouses. On Allison's side with her ex-husband, relations with the other household were amazingly respectful, calm, and almost always focused on what was best for the children. On Tom's side with his ex-wife, there were bitter fights and feelings, accusations of negligent or indulgent parenting, and major conflicts with the two boys. Today, one of Tom's sons refuses to have any contact with him.

The day-to-day hardships of raising children between two homes are behind Tom and Allison now. They now have time to concentrate on their own relationship and their own interests. It took a long time to get the sense of calm and order in their stepfamily, but today, they've made it. Neither would say that their happiness has been without some substantial costs, but they are happy together and they are grateful for the sense of calm and order in their relationship.

Allison and Jim's marriage

Allison was dissatisfied with her life and she made a New Year's resolution to get out of an unhappy marriage. A short time later, she began working for a man she had met during a Marriage Encounters class. She and Jim had been in the support group for about two years. Tom, the man from the class, hired her for a temporary position and the two became closer. After she quit working for him, they began to talk frequently and the attraction was strong. Allison said that her first husband, Jim Urbanski, has always been a good man, but that she was missing an emotional connection that she couldn't even identify herself at that point in life.

When the Urbanskis divorced, their son, Luke, was ten years old and their daughter, Annette, was seven. The couple decided to minimize the impact of the divorce by leaving the children in the family home. Instead, the adults would be the ones to go back and forth between two homes. Allison and Jim rented a single apartment and they rotated their time between the family home and the apartment. It was a difficult arrangement, but they made it work for many months.

From these cooperative beginnings, they formed the foundation for what would be a truly joint custody arrangement with their kids. Both parents were actively involved in their children's lives. Over the years, there were many different arrangements with the children, but whatever the schedule, the goals were always the same—that the children have solid relationships with both of their parents.

TOM AND BETTY'S MARRIAGE

TOM HAD ALREADY emotionally left his marriage even before his second son was born. Betty knew their marriage was in trouble; Tom told her while she was pregnant that he was unhappy. But she had no idea how much trouble the marriage was in until Tom told her that he was seeing a woman who was from another couple in Marriage Encounters class.

When Tom left to marry Allison, the sting was painful for Betty. On top of the pain of rejection, Betty felt like the majority of the parenting of their two boys fell to her. The boys were three and five years old when Tom and Betty divorced. They were high-energy boys who were difficult to raise from an early age, acting out with troublesome behavior. In the first few years after the divorce, Tom wouldn't take both of them at the same time.

Betty had a hard time sending her boys off to their father's new home, and his new life with the woman he had chosen over her. She spent years hating what he had done, and hating him.

And the boys' behavior grew more and more extreme. Today, Nick and Jason are adults and have stabilized somewhat from the time when they were getting into trouble with the police, with their school, and with their parents. Betty has a close relationship with both of her sons. Tom is close to Nick, the older son. But Jason hasn't talked to his father in two years. Tom considers this the most painful aspect of his life.

Both Tom and Betty regret that their relationship and the relationship with the boys didn't work better between the two homes. Tom said Betty held the boys back from him, as if she was so angry about the way their marriage ended that she could never let the boys go freely between the two homes. Betty said that if Tom had worked as hard at his relationship with their boys as he did on his relationship with his stepchildren, things would have been a lot different.

Three homes, one family system

ALL THE CHILDREN are grown up now. The youngest of the four children between these households is now a twenty-two-year-old man. One of the children is married and the parents are all settling into their relationships with their adult children. Soon after the original divorce, each of the adults in the original two marriages remarried, bringing stepparents in on both sides of the children's lives. The stepparents on both sides were very involved with their stepchildren. Neither stepparent brought children of his or her own to the marriage.

In this one system, this family had all the things that can work so well in stepfamily life and all the things that can be so painful and difficult. There are great accomplishments here, and great disappointments as well.

Luke Urbanski

AT THIRTY-ONE YEARS old, Luke Urbanski still doesn't know exactly why his parents got divorced. He's asked his mother about it a number of times, but he's only gotten vague answers. He's pretty sure the divorce was his mother's idea—he remembers conversations before the divorce between his parents and it sounded like his dad didn't want the marriage to end. Luke says that at this point, the reasons for the divorce don't really matter.

"We talked about it at lunch one day when I was in college," he says. "I was trying to figure out whose idea it was because they didn't tell me any reasons for it. And I was kind of pointing the finger at her. At some point, there's no point in sitting and wondering about it. She said they stopped loving each other, my mom saw a problem and my dad didn't see any problem. I was just like, 'whatever.' That's all there was to it, I guess. I don't really care. I don't think about it anymore, at all. That was like ten years ago that I talked to her. Ever since then I just realized that there are some things there's nothing you can do about. There's no point in trying to figure it out, because there's nothing to figure out."

But he remembers pretty vividly what life was like before he was eleven, before his parents divorced. They had dinner together, went to games together, they talked together as a family.

"I thought it was great, but apparently my parents didn't think so. I just liked having a mom and a dad to talk to at the same time," he says. "After the divorce, someone was always missing."

Soon after the divorce, Luke met his soon-to-be stepparents. He remembers liking Tom immediately.

"I thought he was really cool," Luke says. "He was into fighting and karate and things like that. I was twelve and I thought that stuff was cool. He would say, 'Let's look at buying Ninja stars and let's make this weapon out of wood.' And we'd do it. My dad wasn't in to that, so it was cool."

Today, they play pool or build things together and Luke feels lucky to have Tom as an extra parent.

His relationship with his stepmother doesn't have the same kind of warmth. She's fine, they get along OK, he said. But he doesn't have a strong connection with her. He said that his dad is happily married and that's the most important thing.

Overall, he says he wouldn't go back and wish his parents had stayed married. He says there are more advantages to a stepfamily than disadvantages.

"For one thing, it makes you realize that when you do get married, make the right choice from the beginning and stick with it so you don't end up getting divorced," Luke says. "My parents' long second marriages just go to show that it's a matter of picking somebody and sticking with it and working on the problems as they come up instead of saying the answer is to split up. I've been shown examples of what works and also seen a situation where it doesn't work."

ANNETTE DOUGLAS

THE ONLY DISADVANTAGE that Annette Douglas can see in her stepfamily is that with so many people she loves in two households, seeing them all enough can be a logistical feat.

She has no complaints. For years, her friends have envied what they saw as the ideal stepfamily. Annette can see why they think so. When her parents divorced, Annette was about seven years old and she remembers it being a sad time for her. But she soon saw her parents building relationships with the people who were to become her stepparents. Her parents were, in their typical way, careful about introducing these new people into her life, and she never felt defensive about having new partners for her parents. She could see that her parents were happy, and that made her happy, too.

As she grew up and spent half her time at each of her parents' homes, she trusted her parents—all four of them—to do the right thing for her. For example, the adults always lived no more than ten minutes from each other. They went to her sports games and talked to each other afterward. They always listened to her when she had ideas about the schedule.

Looking back as an adult, Annette said these kinds of specific things helped her family work so well together.

"My parents were really flexible; they really, really made an effort to put me and my brother ahead of themselves," Annette says. "They never spoke about each other in any negative way. Both my stepparents put a lot of effort into being sensitive about our relationships. My family was just really engaged. All four parents involved really did a great job, in my eyes."

Annette wishes that all of the children in her family could have had the same experience. She considers her stepbrothers, Nick and Jason, a part of her family. She cares about them and what happens in their lives. She sees Nick at family gatherings these days, but she hasn't seen Jason in almost two years. The boys were four and six years younger than she and as she got older and left the house, she wasn't around for the traumatic events that led to Jason's distancing himself from their family.

"The people in this family are important to me," Annette says. "I feel very sad when I think about Jason."

Still, for the most part, things continue to work well for her. When she visits home now, she stays with her mother and Tom, but has ample time with her dad and Kate. She said it can get complicated at times, trying to fit everyone in, but that even as an adult, she still appreciates the respectful way that her parents share her time.

Annette expects that someday she and her husband, Roger, will have children. And she sees only more love and flexibility and kindness for a grandchild. Annette will be happy to have the support.

ALLISON LENNON

THE TWO HALVES of Allison's lives were so different.

On the one hand, she and her ex-husband worked so well together, and their children seemed to do well. She got along with her ex-husband and really likes his wife, her children's stepmom.

But the other side of her family—her stepfamily—was infuriating. Tom's boys were rowdy, mouthy, always in trouble. Jason, especially, was a thorn in her side.

"He is the one who has not succeeded in any way, shape, or form," Allison said. "He's a great tragedy."

Jason has been in her life since he was two years old and Allison doesn't remember a time without trouble. If ever children were playing together and someone got hurt, Allison could almost count on Jason being at fault. She said that the parents tried professional therapy, tried to figure out how to help him, but Jason floundered through his childhood. As he grew older, Jason's problems became more serious and Allison started to dread his visits.

One night, all four parents went to the police station after the cops picked Jason up for stealing from his employer and buying pot with the proceeds. Allison was livid and found the whole incident completely distasteful. Jason was scheduled to go to Tom and Allison's house for the weekend, but Allison made it clear that she didn't want the kid in her home.

"It was not my finest hour," she says. "I'm sure there's a place for me in stepmother hell for that one."

After that night, Tom and Allison decided that the next time Jason was over they would sit down with him and really have it all out. But Jason never came over after that. Allison believes that he knew he'd have to face the discussion of what happened and he just didn't want to deal with it.

Tom and Jason kept in touch for a while after that, going out for dinner together, meeting away from the house and away from Allison. Until, Allison said, the time that Jason used their credit card number to ring up two thousand dollars worth of hotel rooms, pizzas, and the like.

"That was a turning point for Tom," Allison says. "He would always say 'He never did anything to us.' But he couldn't say that anymore. Tom filed a police report against Jason."

It was the last time either of them heard from him, although they get reports of his whereabouts from Nick, his older brother. Allison says she's sad about the whole situation, especially for Tom.

Her relationship with Nick is much better, after some tenuous teenage years. Allison says he is smart and she's happy that he's in college. Nick comes over to the house and helps with family projects. Allison says that they don't have a warm, close relationship, but that she cares about him and they get along pretty well.

Allison's first family

On the other side of the stepfamily, Allison's relationship with her children's other household has been comparatively smooth and easy to manage. Allison really likes Kate; she said she's been a good stepmother to her children.

Allison is grateful that she and her ex-husband have been so cooperative and able to raise the children well together. Still, she knows that leaving her first husband for another man wasn't easy for the kids, at least for her son.

It's been almost ten years since they've talked about the divorce. And before that conversation, he never said much about it. But one day, Allison met Luke at a coffee shop and he told his mother what he really thought.

"He said I put my happiness ahead of everybody else's. He had never addressed it that directly before. He really just kind of let it all out," Allison said. "I'm sitting in this coffee shop, sobbing. I'm just sobbing. I knew he was hurt. I knew this, he just never said it. And even though it hurt, I knew that it was good that he finally found the words to say it. He's grown a lot."

They've only talked directly about the divorce and the circumstances around it a handful of times. Usually, their conversations are more general. Luke comes over and spends time at his mom and Tom's house. He and Tom are fairly close and they all see each other frequently. They have dinner together and Luke helps on house projects such as building the back deck.

Allison considers her daughter, Annette, the success story of the family. The two are very close, just as they have been since Annette was a precocious, easy-to-raise, affectionate little girl.

"She is very emotionally and psychologically aware and empathetic," Allison says. "She's just a great kid and I feel so blessed to have a kid like her."

BETTY JOHNSON

IT WAS THE end of the yoga class and the instructor was starting on the final exercise. "Lie still on the floor, create your circle of thought. Invite someone who you're in conflict with into your circle." Betty lay there and lay there, trying to think of someone who she was having conflict with. Her circle remained empty.

Later, she thought about the exercise and remembered her ex-husband. "Hmm . . ." she thought to herself. "I wonder when I stopped hating him."

There wasn't any particular moment that it just stopped. Time passed after he left her for another woman and she managed to get on with her life. And then he sent her a letter, apologizing for hurting her. That helped. Besides, now she is so in love with her husband, and they're so happy together, that in some ways, she's grateful that things worked out as they did.

But those early days were bitter times. She, for one, had meant what she had said about "until death do us part." She was supposed to be have been a stay-at-home-mom, raising her boys. Instead, she worked and tried to raise them the best she could without very much help from Tom. Instead of help, she got criticism for the way she parented. Betty really did hate him.

"I always wished he'd get hit by a Mack truck because it would be so much easier to parent alone," she said.

Now, she has been happily married for thirteen years and both boys are grown up. She doesn't wish a truck would hit Tom anymore. She doesn't really wish anything about him anymore. He just doesn't have any power over her emotions.

"He's not an influence anymore," she said. "He's not anything anymore."

But when the boys were growing up, she was very angry with him. Just seeing him when they exchanged the children made her blood boil. And Betty felt that Tom was always critical of how she raised the boys, even though Tom didn't have any better luck controlling their behavior when they were at his house.

Betty wishes that they could have parented better together for the boys' sake. She feels that the boys got shortchanged because she and Tom got divorced and couldn't figure out their differences well enough to work together.

She also feels that Tom spent a lot of his energy doing things for his stepchildren, things he didn't do for his own children.

"The boys and I could never say Annette's name without saying 'perfect Annette' because we were always hearing how wonderful she was," Betty said. "Tom and Allison did the field trips, took Annette's team to the away-basketball games, all that stuff. The boys didn't get that."

She knows that Jason isn't talking to his father; she believes that the biggest roadblock to the relationship is Tom's wife, Allison. Both of Betty's boys really struggled with Allison, but especially Jason.

"There were grounds; he was rotten to them. He's done some really nasty things," Betty said. "But who's the adult here?"

Betty said that she's always been able to separate the behavior from the kid. When she looks at her husband, Jason's stepfather, she sees that he, too, was able to forgive Jason and welcome him back. But not Allison. Betty said that Allison has never been able to see any good in Jason. There were times when Allison made her feelings perfectly clear. Betty will never forget when the cops picked up Jason. Betty and Jim, Tom and Allison went down to the police station to figure out what to do. Betty was supposed to be leaving town and Jason was scheduled to stay at his father and Allison's house.

"She said, 'I don't want that piece of shit in my home,'" Betty said.

And to make matters worse, Tom just stood there. He didn't stand up for his son. Betty was crushed. Even though he was in trouble, he was still their son and his father had just let someone completely degrade him. After that incident, Betty decided that she just wasn't going to waste her time dealing with the other household. She stopped talking to Tom about the boys and everyone was on their own. So, although Jason comes home to her house for holidays and she talks to him regularly, she doesn't call Tom and tell him about the visits. As far as Tom knows, Jason is lost. But Betty figures that these days, that's for the two of them to work out themselves.

Still, Betty would like to see Jason have a relationship with his father. She believes in family ties and she thinks it's important for Jason to repair the relationship. She knows that Tom has tried to make amends, but for now, Jason's not interested.

So she enjoys her time with her boys and tries not to worry about things she can't change. She's grateful that both of her boys are close to her and becoming ever closer to Jim, their stepdad. She never gave up on them and now she feels that she's reaping the rewards.

"It's history," she said. "Life is good. They are nice kids."

Tom Lennon

Tom glows when he talks about his stepchildren. He remembers taking Luke out shooting with a .22, building skateboard ramps, showing him tae kwan do and the punching bags. He remembers Annette giggling with her friends in the basement, and all the talking they did while he drove her to and from her many sports events.

The whole time the kids were growing up, Tom and Allison would sit with them after dinner and talk. He said it was these simple times that grew his relationships with his stepchildren.

He wishes that his own sons had been around more for those kinds of moments. When Tom left his wife, he didn't get to see his boys as much as he wanted. He said that as far as he was concerned, the boys could have stayed with him all the time. But that never happened. The boys were only allowed over when it was their scheduled time.

Tom says his oldest son, Nick, went through some troubles as a teen, but that he's pulled himself up and is doing well. Tom says Nick is resilient, strong both internally and externally. They have a warm, close relationship today.

But Tom is still waiting on his youngest son. He says that no matter how much he loves the other three kids, no matter how much fun they have together, there's always an empty spot where Jason should be.

"That's a huge amount of pain in my life," Tom said.

JIM URBANSKI

IN EVERY STEPFAMILY, there's ample opportunity to take the low road—to blame, and criticize, to badmouth and complain.

Jim Urbanski just didn't see the usefulness of it.

When his first wife told him she was cheating on him and that she wanted to end their marriage, the news took him completely by surprise. He had enjoyed their marriage and although it wasn't without problems, he felt that their marriage was pretty typical. He liked his family the way it was. But he realized rather quickly that his family was about to change dramatically.

So he started figuring out how to best go about such big changes. The day after Allison told him the news, he found a therapist. He wanted to try to work with Allison in couple's counseling, but that didn't work out. He did go to Allison's counselor with her for one session. In that session, Allison's counselor said that, knowing Allison's situation, there wasn't any point in continuing couple's counseling.

"With that, I accepted it, that's where we were going. I just shifted gears to say, 'Well, this isn't what I want, but I'm powerless, I can see this isn't going to change.' I was told this wasn't going to change. Allison said it wasn't going to change and the counselor just really confirmed it. So I

decided it would be minimally painful for myself and the children to pro-
ceed cooperatively."

It wasn't easy. But Jim tried to look at it as a practical matter. He got
help through his counselor, he read some books. Over the years, he joined
a men's group and he and his second wife have been active in a stepfamily couple's group. He said that his resourcefulness has made all the difference in creating harmony in his life. Not only for him, but also for his
children and his second marriage.

"The guiding principle for me for the last seventeen years was that the
adults are more mature and have resources and networks," he said. "The
adults will have to work through this and they're equipped to work
through it (whether they do or not). But the children aren't. And so I had
this theme right from the beginning that anything we could do to help the
kids get through it, we should do."

One of the things Jim and Allison did early on is to arrange the schedule to accommodate the children—not the adults. In the initial months of
their separation, the children stayed in the family home and the adults
rotated in and out. Jim and Allison rented an apartment together and
shared both spaces on alternating weeks. Jim made sure he had duplicates
of everything possible at both the house and the apartment. The adults
had rules—If you use something up replace it, keep the place clean. Jim
was angry about what his exwife had done to their lives, but the anger
didn't make him unable to be cordial and polite to her, to work with her
toward the best situation. And the apartment seemed like the best situation at the time. He had no interest in fighting. He worked not to give
in to petty animosities, even when he was angry and resentful.

"I didn't take it out on her or the kids. I very much chose to avoid that.
I had anger and resentment, but I wasn't seething," he said.

The shared apartment and family home lasted many months, and then
Jim bought a small house two blocks away from the original family home.
Through the years, Jim and Allison arranged a variety of schedules
between the two homes, but both parents, and both of their spouses, were
actively involved in both the children's lives.

The two couples recently hosted Annette's wedding together. It was the
first big event they hosted for their adult children. But as Luke and Annette
were growing up, the two couples often chatted together, cordially conversing after basketball games or at other family events for the children.

Jim and Kate have been married for more than seventeen years. After
his divorce from Allison, Jim knew he wanted to marry again. He didn't

particularly like being single. He calls it his personal "triumph of hope over experience."

But when he met Kate, he had good reason to be hopeful. Bringing Kate into his and his children's lives felt easy, natural. He was mindful of the fact that the relationships all needed a particular kind of attention, so he and Kate talked explicitly about how things would be from the beginning. She had a parenting role in the household, but all the adults involved understood that the two children had a mother and father both very involved and working together. Jim said that he believes Kate's success in her role as a stepmother came in large part because of who she is and because the relationships developed gradually.

Looking back over the past two decades and watching his adult children now, Jim's happy with how things turned out. He feels that he did the right thing for the children, and that's the most important thing for him. But he also made things easier for himself, his wife and, in turn, for the other household. Jim said none of it would have gone as well without all the help he's had over the years.

"It turned out as good it could," Jim said. "It wasn't like I was so wise and smart and did all these right things."

Looking back over the years, Jim said that there was help from many places. The dynamics of stepfamilies are so complicated, he said, that there's really no way to see all the angles without some help. He had a men's support group, a couple's support group, friends, readings, and a psychologist. He's very happy in his life, in his marriage and in his relationships with his kids. It's not that he doesn't know that stepfamilies can be tough work. But he's done the work. And now, stepfamily life is sweet.

17

𝒲HERE ARE THEY NOW?

ᴏ𝒲ᴏ

𝒠ACH PORTRAIT OF the families involved in this project describes just one moment in time. In some cases, I've spoken to families extensively for more than a year. In others, I visited the family only briefly and spoken to them occasionally. But in every case, I've merely provided a snapshot of what was happening in their lives at that particular time. Since the original reporting of the book, there have been many changes in the families, some of them significant.

Some of the families were in the middle of dramatic changes when they allowed me to come in and watch and ask questions. Others noticed small changes as they thought more about their stepfamilies and started talking about what works and what doesn't.

Most people involved in the book thought it was a good experience, but a couple people were disappointed with the results of their participation. Following is a brief update about what has happened in the families, according to the families, since we started on this path together.

. . .

THE MADSEN/SHORT FAMILY SYSTEM
OF MINNESOTA

HELEN AND TODD feel that things have definitely improved in their relationship. Helen continues to push for clear boundaries between Todd and his ex-wife, Wendy. Helen feels that her husband is finally listening to her and respecting her feelings.

Helen said that she and Todd recently went to her stepdaughter Jamie's play and they sat in the front row, where Helen chose to sit.

"Wendy said hello, but she wasn't all chatty. For the first time, I didn't feel smothered. I thought, 'Oh, this is what concerts are supposed to be like. I can handle this,'" Helen said. "I definitely feel like a new door has been opened. It's a new path. I'm not going to be stepped on anymore. It's taken me a long time, but I will stand up for what I believe is right for me and my family. I'm done being the doormat. It feels really good."

But it doesn't feel better for everyone. Wendy talked about the same play with a completely different perspective. She said that she was working backstage and wouldn't be sitting in the audience, but that she saved the perfect seats for Todd, Helen, and the rest of their family. But then Helen didn't want to sit there, she wanted to sit on the other side of the theater, where they couldn't see Jaime's key scene very well. Wendy said the whole thing is frustrating.

"It's just getting worse," she said.

THE DIAZ/JORVIG/KERTZ FAMILY SYSTEM
OF DALLAS, TEXAS

EVERYONE IN THIS family system is happier than they were with each other when we first started talking a year and a half ago. Interestingly enough, one of the couples—Valerie and Tony—decided not to participate in the book any more because they were afraid that some of their comments would wreak havoc with the other household. We spent time together in Dallas and they talked to me some on the phone, but after several months, decided that they didn't want to talk about the situation anymore. The adults in the other household, Matt and Pamela, believe that things are slowly getting better. When Fern didn't click with her teacher at school, Matt and Valerie worked together amicably to solve the problem and get Fern into a new classroom.

One day, after Fern's soccer game, Matt and Pamela went out to eat at a local Chinese restaurant. Next thing they knew, in walked Fern and her mom. And then something happened that certainly would not have happened even a year ago.

"We all wound up sitting down at the table together," Matt said. "We talked, mostly about Fern, not about much else. Pamela was kind of stressed about it at first, but it was OK. It wound up being surprisingly pleasant; it was not horrible and awkward and quiet. Fern was pretty excited about it."

Not everything is wonderful, of course. When Fern had school teacher conferences and Matt ended up having to work late, Fern, Valerie, and Pamela had to be at conferences together. The tension was just too much.

"I won't do it again," Pamela said. "It was just too uncomfortable."

But on the home front, Pamela has had other major successes. Her mother, who has been resistant to her relationship with Matt and Fern from the beginning, seems to be learning to accept that these are important relationships to Pamela. Pamela told her mother that her comments about the relationships have been hurtful. Recently, Pamela's mother came to town and spent three solid days working with Fern and Pamela painting Fern's new bedroom.

"We've all come a long way," Pamela said.

THE WILKOWSKI/FAYE/RAY FAMILY SYSTEM OF NORTHERN WASHINGTON STATE

SO MUCH HAS changed in this family since I first started talking to them and so much has remained the same. There is still a lot of high drama in this system, and relations have turned sour between the two main households. There have been serious breakdowns of communication between the Michelle and Chris and Maria. Maria no longer sees the children at all—they don't come to Chris and Maria's house. Two of the girls again accused Maria of child abuse and so now Chris comes and spends the day with his kids three Saturdays a month. There are no overnights. One of the girls is going to court to answer to a harassment charge that Maria has pushed for. The charge stems from an incident a year ago when the girl called Maria at work and allegedly threatened her stepmother. Maria said that there have been several opportunities for the girl to make amends and get the charges dropped, but the girl hasn't wanted to.

Michelle got evicted from the farmhouse. At the same time, Chris's father died and his house was empty. Chris and Maria are renting the house to Michelle at the cost of upkeep until the youngest daughter is eighteen—another five years.

Ed said that he's still with Michelle, but only by the barest of threads. He says he maybe sees her once a week. He's still not sure why.

THE HORN/SEIDL/WINTER FAMILY SYSTEM OF MINNEAPOLIS, MINNESOTA

PARTS OF THIS family eagerly embraced the whole process of participating in this book. Other parts of the family were far less enthusiastic.

For Cynthia, Miranda, and Rob especially, the telling of their stories and the sharing of their stories with each other has opened the way for them to become even more intimately connected.

They sat together and read their section of the book around the table Christmas morning. The talked about each other's sections and talked about things that had never been so explicitly discussed.

"It's a profound, liberating perspective," Miranda said. "Just being able to talk about it and name stuff out in the open has deepened and improved conversations since then."

But for Lisa, the project didn't improve things. She and I sat for a couple of hours in an initial interview, and we talked several times on the phone. When I wrote her section, I asked her to read it and she made some small comments. She didn't seem upset by the section, but she didn't say much about it, either. About two weeks later, she called me, angry. She hadn't heard from her daughter, and she said that the book was making her family worse, not better. She thought that the whole premise of the book was flawed. She said that she didn't think that she should be having these kinds of intimate conversations in public with her daughter. Then she declined to read any other section from her family system—including the ones from her two children. She has chosen not to participate in the project any further.

· · ·

THE MORGAN/MERDAD FAMILY SYSTEM
OF MESA, ARIZONA

THE OLDEST CHILD in this family, Hannah, went off to college. Since Hannah and her stepdad were the ones who had a lot of the conflict in this family, things around the house settled considerably after she left. She returned recently to live with her mother and stepfather and to work.

Stephanie, Hannah's mom, said something happened while her daughter was away at college.

"Things have gotten so much better," Stephanie said.

One day, Stephanie said, Hannah actually called Randy, her stepdad, at work to see if she could bring him some fish and chips. Stephanie sees this as a huge step.

"She is different; she is more accepting," Stephanie said.

And so the house has become more peaceful, even with all of them under the same roof again.

"We've been having a lot more family dinners and there's been a lot of conversing with Randy included," Stephanie said. "It's been amazing."

THE HAMMOND/ROSS FAMILY SYSTEM
OF FORTH WORTH, TEXAS

LAURA AND ANDREW feel that they've almost reached the finish line. Since the beginning of this book project, they've seen another of their kids through high school graduation and they're about to scoot the last two up the aisle for their diplomas.

So three of the kids still live at home, but the time is coming soon when Laura and Andrew won't have the responsibility of raising children. And that decrease in pressure has paid off in their relationship.

"Thing are going well here," Laura said. "A lot of things have changed over the years. A lot of problems we were having, we don't have anymore."

THE JACOBS FAMILY SYSTEM OF NEW JERSEY

RELATIONS BETWEEN THE home and in the homes of the girls continue to run smoothly. Ruth and Aaron are close to being married and the girls are growing up. Elana, the oldest, is graduating from high school and leaves in the fall to spend a year in Israel. Sima still doesn't see her dad, and it's still hard for her. Otherwise, the families are getting along and working well together to plan things like Ettel's upcoming Bat Mitzvah.

THE LENNON/JOHNSON/URBANSKI FAMILY SYSTEM OF MINNEAPOLIS, MINNESOTA

WITH ALL THE kids grown-up adults, there haven't been any major changes in this family system since they began participating in the book. The one thing that a few of the parents interviewed said was they realized that even though things ran smoothly, they never talked explicitly about what it was like to live in a stepfamily with their children. Or that they never talked explicitly about some of the hard things during the break-up of the first families and the formation of stepfamilies. So the adults plan to take on some of those conversations.

RESOURCES

GENERAL RESOURCES

Stepfamily Association of America (SAA): A wealth of information and support for families dealing with stepfamily issues. This is the place to start. Web site: www.saafamilies.org

Your Stepfamily: The official magazine of the SAA, free to members of the SAA, is also online at www.yourstepfamily.com

Therapists List: It is key for people in stepfamilies who are seeking professional help to find a professional with experience in stepfamily issues. If a therapist treats your family like a first family, the therapy won't be very helpful and could be very frustrating. The Stepfamily Association of America has a state-by-state list of therapists trained in stepfamily issues. Web site: www.saafamilies.org/programs/affildir.htm#mn

The Family Medallion: This organization sells a line of products, such as the three-intertwined-rings medallion, for couples to use in including their children in the marriage ceremony. The medallion is meant to acknowledge the importance of children when a parent remarries. Web site: www.familymedallion.com/index.html

Two Again Ministries: In Mesa, AZ, a Christian-based organization that helps educate and support stepfamilies. The group also works with churches. The Web site (www.twoagain.org) includes a list of Christian resources.

BOOKS

Becoming a Stepfamily: Patterns of Development in Remarried Families by Patricia Papernow (Analytic Press, 1998). An excellent resource for families. Gives a realistic big-picture perspective of the issues facing stepfamilies.

Mom's House, Dad's House: The Complete Guide for Parents Who Are Separated, Divorced or Remarried by Isolina Ricci (Fireside, 1997). Concrete, practical help, including how to make a parenting plan.

The Enlightened Stepmother: Revolutionizing the Role by Perdita Kirkness Norwood (Avon Books, 1999). Everyone in a stepfamily, not just stepmothers, can learn a lot about how stepfamilies run from this book.

Stepwives: Ten Steps to Help Ex-wives and Stepmothers End the Struggle and Put the Kids First by Lynne Oxhorn-Ringwood, Louise Oxhorn, and Marjorie Vego Krausz (Simon and Schuster, 2002). This book focuses on how to overcome the conflict between the two households.

The Complete Idiot's Guide to Stepparenting by Ericka Lutz (Alpha Books, 1998). Funny and full of graphics, this book has a lot of information in a *USA Today*–type format.

BEST OF THE WEB

Stepfamily Association of America: A wealth of information and support for families dealing with stepfamily issues. This is the place to look for the most complete, most useful resources. Web site: www. saafamilies.org

Stepfamily information: Peter Gerlach is dedicated to improving stepfamily relations with this educational, research-based interactive site. Web site: www.stepfamilyinfo.org

Stepfamily Network, Inc.: This is a nonprofit organization based in California working to help support and educate people in stepfamilies. Web site: www.stepfamily.net

StepTogether: A support site for stepmothers, this site has several message boards, but also has many good resources and links to other sites. Web site: www.steptogether.org

CHILDREN'S BOOKS

Help! A Girl's Guide to Divorce and Stepfamilies by Nancy Holyoke and Scott Nash (Pleasant Company Publications, 1999). For girls in grades four through eight, the resource draws on letters sent to the *American Girl* magazine. The question and answer format includes quizzes and information for girls, to help them understand their changing family.

GENERAL PARENTING

Raising an Emotionally Intelligent Child by John M. Gottman, Joan Declaire, and Daniel P. Goleman (Fireside, 1998). Gottman researched patterns of interactions between parents and their children and describes successful and unsuccessful parenting methods. He gives a point-by-point plan to better connect with your child and to develop emotional intelligence.

How to Talk So Kids Will Listen and Listen So Kids Will Talk by Adele Faber and Elaine Mazlish (Avon Books, 1999). This book makes so much sense. Any of the books by these authors are really great for parents.

Children: The Challenge by Rudolf Dreikurs, M.D. (Hawthorne/Dutton, 1964). Dreikurs outlines his ideas for how parents can help their children learn and avoid common traps, such as power struggles.

The Explosive Child: A New Approach for Understanding and Parenting Easily Frustrated, Chronically Inflexible Children by Ross W. Greene, Ph.D. (HarperCollins, 2001). Greene is a pediatric psychologist who helps parents understand and develop strategies for working with these difficult-to-raise children.

Becoming The Parent You Want to Be: A Sourcebook of Strategies for the First Five Years by Laura Davis and Janis Keyser (Broadway Books,

1997). This is just what it says; the authors help parents to be thoughtful about their approaches with their children.

Get Out of My Life, but First Could You Drive Me & Cheryl to the Mall: A Parent's Guide to the New Teenager, Revised and Updated by Anthony E. Wolf, (Farrar, Straus and Giroux, 2002). This is a survival guide for parents of adolescents.

$\mathcal{A}$CKNOWLEDGMENTS

I WANT TO THANK all the families who bravely told their stories. You generously gave your time, experience, and insight so that others could have an easier path. I know that many people will recognize their dilemmas in your voices.

There were many people along the way who helped me find families interested in participating in the book, who answered my questions, who read sections of the book and gave me valuable and encouraging feedback. I want to thank Margorie Engel and Claudia Dougherty at the Stepfamily Association of America, Dr. Patricia Papernow, Roger Coleman at the Family Medallion, Maureen McCarthy, Ann Orchard, and Mark Boswell.

I want to thank my editors at Marlowe & Company, Sue McCloskey and Matthew Lore, for supporting the project.

You don't finish a book without your friends hearing all about it every step of the way. I am fortunate to have kind friends who listen well and share their wisdom with me. I want to thank Sarah Clark, H. J. Cummins, Jill DeSanto, Kyia Downing, Ruth Hornstein, Nancy Kenney, Lynette Lamb, Maura Lerner, Amy Robinson, Robbie Weisel and Ellen Ziegler for their unending support. My own stepmoms group—Stephanie Effertz,

Mary Kissinger, Lynda Michielutti, and Trudy Paulson—has been a supportive lifeline.

My brother, Daniel O'Connor, pushed for this book. It's really because of his insistence that I wrote the book even though I knew I'd be having a baby in the middle of it. "Just settle yourself into the realization that it's going to be insane," he said. He was right, but now it's done. Thanks Dan.

My children, Samuel and Irene, deserve a lot of thanks for trooping along during the trips across the country to interview families. I love you guys. I want to thank Nate, my stepson, who continued to teach me stepfamily lessons throughout the writing of the book. I love you and I hope this book makes sense to you, if not now, someday.

I have an amazing extended family and I want to thank my siblings, aunts, and in-laws who all pitched in with childcare and other support to help me get this book done. But it wouldn't have happened without JoAn O'Connor. As my mom, she's my most reliable fan. She has supported me in whatever I try to accomplish and that in itself is critical. She read early versions of the book and gave me the kind of praise that every writer should be so lucky to have in the middle of a project. But more specifically, she's also the one who traveled around the country with me, caring for my two small children while I went out to interview families. Thanks Mom, you're grandma extraordinaire.

And finally, to my husband, Joseph Hart. I thank you, of course, for all the dinners and solo bedtime routines with the kids, for my time away, and the hundred other practical things you did so I could be free to write. But mostly, I want to thank you for always telling me the book is going to be great. Your unfaltering faith in the project, in me, is invaluable.